Lars Brownworth is an author, speaker, broadcaster, and teacher based in Maryland, USA. He has written for the *Wall Street Journal* and been profiled in the *New York Times,* who likened him to some of history's great popularizers. His books include *Lost to the West: The Forgotten Byzantine Empire that Rescued Western Civilization*, and *The Normans: From Raiders to Kings.*

THE SEA WOLVES

A History of the Vikings

LARS BROWNWORTH

First published in the United Kingdom in 2014
by Crux Publishing Ltd.

ISBN: 978-1-909979-12-3

Copyright © Lars Brownworth, 2014

Also available as an ebook:
eISBN: 978-1-909979-11-6

Requests for permission to reproduce material from this work
should be sent to
hello@cruxpublishing.co.uk

For Thomas, just beginning his own adventures

CONTENTS

THE EXPLORERS

THE TRADERS

THE HOMELANDS

A WHO'S WHO OF THE VIKING WORLD

Ælla *(mid 9th century) King of Northumbria who according to legend executed Ragnar Lothbrok. He was killed in 867 by Ivar the Boneless and the Great Heathen Army, supposedly as revenge for Ragnar's death.*

Athelred the Unready *(c. 968 - 1016) King of England during the last great wave of Viking attacks.*

Aethelwulf *(c. 795 - 858) King of Wessex and father of Alfred the Great.*

Athelstan *(c. 894 - 939) First Anglo-Saxon monarch accepted as 'King of the English'.*

Alcuin of York *(c. 735 - 804) English scholar who was one of the leading intellectuals of Charlemagne's court.*

Alfred the Great *(c. 849 - 899) King of Wessex who defeated the Great Heathen Army. Laid the foundations of the medieval kingdom of England.*

Aud the Deep Minded *(c. 834 - 900) Norwegian wife of the king of Dublin, Olaf the White, later settled in Iceland.*

Basil the Bulgar-Slayer *(958 - 1025) Byzantine Emperor who founded the Varangian Guard.*

Bjarni Herjólfsson *(10th century) Norwegian explorer who first sighted mainland America.*

Bjorn Ironside *(9th century) Son of Ragnar Lothbrok; In 860 he led a semi-legendary raid into the Mediterranean with his brother Hastein.*

Brian Bóruma *(c. 941 - 1014) High King of Ireland who tried to unite the island under his rule. Killed at the battle of Clontarf.*

Brodir of Man *(11th century) Danish Viking mercenary who according to legend killed Brian Bóruma at the battle of Clontarf.*

Cnut the Great *(c. 985 - 1035) Viking king of England, Denmark, and parts of Norway. He was the son of Svein Forkbeard and conquered England from Athelred the Unready and his son Edmund Ironside.*

Columba *(c. 521 - 597) Irish missionary credited with spreading Christianity in Scotland. The monastery he founded on the island of Iona in western Scotland became an early Viking target.*

Cuthbert *(c. 634 - 687) Patron saint of northern England, his remains were kept at the monastery of Lindisfarne, target of the first major Viking raid.*

Charlemagne *(c. 747 - 814) Frankish king and first monarch of the reborn Western Roman Empire.*

Charles the Bald *(823 - 877) Frankish emperor, son of Louis the Pious. He confronted Ragnar at the first siege of Paris and bribed him to leave.*

Charles the Fat *(839 - 888) Frankish emperor, great-grandson of Charlemagne. He was the last member of Charlemagne's dynasty to rule over a united empire. He relieved a siege of Paris in 886 by bribing the Vikings to leave.*

Charles the Simple *(879 - 929) Frankish king, cousin of Charles the Fat. He attempted to stop Viking raids by allowing them to settle in Normandy.*

Edmund Ironside *(c. 989 - 1016) King of England and son of Athelred the Unready. He agreed to divide England with the Viking king Cnut.*

Erik Bloodaxe *(c. 885 - c. 955) Viking king of Norway and York, son of Harald Fairhair.*

Erik the Red *(c. 950 - c. 1003) Norwegian Viking who colonized Greenland. Father of Leif Erikson and Freydis.*

Freydis *(10th century) Daughter of Erik the Red; early colonizer of Vinland.*

Garthar *(9th century) Swedish merchant who was the first Viking to deliberately sail to Iceland. He spent a single winter on the island.*

Godfred *(late 8th century) Danish Viking warlord responsible for constructing the first sections of the Danevirke.*

Godwin *(c. 1001 - 1053) Earl of Wessex, powerful advisor to Edward the Confessor and father of Tostig and Harold Godwinson.*

Gorm the Old *(d. 958) First Viking king of Denmark, father of Harald Bluetooth.*

Guthrum *(d. 890) Leader of the Great Heathen Army during its invasion of Wessex.*

Håkon the Good *(c. 920 - 961) Third king of Norway, youngest son of Harald Fairhair and brother of Erik Bloodaxe.*

Halfdan *(d. 877) Son of Ragnar Lothbrok and one of the leaders of the Great Heathen Army. Briefly controlled London 871-2.*

Harald Bluetooth *(c. 935 - 986) Viking king of Denmark and parts of Norway; Son of Gorm the Old, responsible for the Christian conversion of Denmark.*

Harald Fairhair *(c. 850 - 932)* First king of Norway, father of Erik Bloodaxe and Håkon the Good.

Harald Greycloak *(d. 970)* Son of Erik Bloodaxe, king of Norway. Assassinated by Harald Bluetooth.

Harald Hårdrada *(c. 1015 - 1066)* King of Norway and half-brother of Saint Olaf. Served in the Varangian Guard, conquered Norway, and died at the battle of Stamford Bridge.

Harald Klak *(c. 785 - c. 852)* Danish Viking warlord that the Frankish emperor Louis the Pious attempted to use to Christianize Denmark.

Harold Godwinson *(c. 1022 - 1066)* Last Anglo-Saxon king of England. Killed at the Battle of Hastings by William the Conqueror.

Hastein *(9th century)* Possibly a son of Ragnar Lothbrok. Led a semi-legendary raid into the Mediterranean with his brother Bjorn Ironside.

Helgi *(d. 912)* Swedish Viking who succeeded Rurik and moved the Rus capital from Novgorod to Kiev. Also known by the Slavic name Oleg.

Horik *(d. 854)* Son of the Danish warlord Godfred, exiled Ragnar Lothbrok after the latter's raid on Paris.

Ingólfur Arnarson *(9th century)* First permanent settler of Iceland. Settled and named Reykjavík.

Ingvar of Kiev *(d. 945)* Swedish Viking who succeeded Helgi in Kiev. Led the Rus on an attack on Constantinople.

Ivar the Boneless *(9th century)* Most famous son of Ragnar Lothbrok. Led the Great Heathen Army in a successful attack on England.

Leif Erikson *(c. 970 - c. 1020) Son of Erik the Red, first European to land in North America.*

Louis the Pious *(778 - 840) Frankish emperor, son of Charlemagne who unsuccessfully attempted to deal with Viking attacks on continental Europe.*

Máel Sechnaill *(948 - 1022) ex High King of Ireland who reclaimed the title after Brian Bóruma's death at the battle of Clontarf.*

Naddodd *(9th century) Viking explorer who is credited with discovering Iceland.*

Odin *Chief of the Viking gods, known as the 'All-father'.*

Olaf Haraldsson *(995 - 1030) Norway's patron saint. Viking king who attempted to Christianize Norway and was killed at the battle of Stiklestad. Half-brother of Harald Hardråda.*

Olaf Sitricsson *(c. 927 - 981) Viking king of York and Dublin, son of Sitric One-Eyed.*

Olaf the White *(c. 820 - 871) Viking king of Dublin; co-ruled with Ivar the Boneless.*

Olaf Tryggvason *(c. 960 - 1000) Viking king of Norway, attempted to forcibly Christianize Norway and died at the battle of the Svold.*

Olga of Kiev *(c. 890 - 969) Regent of Kiev, wife of Ingvar of Kiev. Her acceptance of Christianity set the stage for the conversion of the Rus.*

Ragnar Lothbrok *(9th century) Legendary Danish Viking. Led a successful raid on Paris in 845. Father of Ivar the Boneless, Hastien, Halfdan, Ubba, and Bjorn Ironside.*

Raven Flóki *(9th century) Norwegian Viking who named Iceland and started its colonization.*

Rollo *(9th century) Norwegian Viking who settled in France and founded Normandy.*

Rurik the Rus *(d. 879) Swedish Viking who settled in Novgorod and founded the first Viking state in Russia.*

Sigfred *(9th century) Viking warlord who led an unsuccessful siege of Paris in 885.*

Sitric One-Eyed *(late 9th century) Viking king of Dublin and York, grandson of Ivar the Boneless. Attempted to create a Hiberno-English kingdom.*

Sitric Silkbeard *(c. 970 - 1042) Viking king of Dublin. Last major Viking figure of Ireland. Started a revolt against the High King Brian Bóruma but withdrew before the battle of Clontarf.*

Snorri Sturluson *(1179 - 1241) Icelandic poet who composed the Heimskringla, a history of the Norse Kings.*

Sven Estridsson *(c. 1019 - 1074) Viking king of Denmark. Fought a fifteen year war with his neighbor Harald Hardråda.*

Svein Forkbeard *(c. 960 - 1014) Viking king of Denmark, son of Harald Bluetooth. Conquered England in 1013.*

Sviatoslav of Kiev *(c. 942 - 972) Ruler of Kiev, succeeded Ingvar. He was ambushed trying to cross the Dneiper River and his skull was made into a drinking cup.*

Thor *Most popular of the Viking gods, especially with farmers and sailors.*

Thorfinn Karlsefni *(11th century) Viking explorer who attempted a permanent settlement in Vinland.*

Thorgils the Devil *(9th century) Viking sea-king who founded Dublin.*

Thorvald Erikson *(9th century) Viking explorer, brother of Leif Erikson. Was the first European to be killed in the Americas.*

Tostig Godwinson *(d. 1066) Brother of king Harold Godwinson, invited Harald Hardråda to attack England in 1066.*

Ubba *(9th century) Son of Ragnar Lothbrok, one of the leaders of the Great Heathen Army.*

Vladimir of Kiev *(c. 958 - 1015) Ruler of Kiev, converted the Rus to Christianity and provided the first Viking recruits to the Varangian Guard.*

PLACES

Armagh *Spiritual center of Ireland; burial place of St. Patrick*

Brattahlíð *Erik the Red's farm in Greenland*

Constantinople *Capital of the Byzantine Empire*

Denmark *Southernmost Viking kingdom*

Dneiper River *Major Rus water route to Constantinople*

Dorestad *Important trading center of Charlemagne's empire; present day Wijk bij Duurstede in the Netherlands*

Dublin *Most important city settled by the Vikings in Ireland*

Essex *One of the minor kingdoms of early Anglo-Saxon England. Controlled the land around London*

East Anglia *One of the major kingdoms of early Anglo-Saxon England. Located in the southeast of the island*

Eastern Settlement *First and largest colony started by Erik the Red in Greenland*

Frisia *Coastal region along the southeastern shores of the North Sea; present day Netherlands and Germany*

Greenland *Largest island on earth, settled by the Vikings in the 10th century*

Hebrides *Archipelago off the northwest coast of Scotland*

Hedeby *Most important trading center in the Danish peninsula; near present day Schleswig*

Iceland *Volcanic island in the North Atlantic just below the Arctic Circle; settled by the Vikings in the 9th century*

Iona *Monastery on an island off the west coast of Scotland, founded by St. Columba*

Kent *One of the minor kingdoms of early Anglo-Saxon England. Controlled the land around Canterbury*

Kiev *Most important Rus city in the east; capital of first centralized state in Russia*

Landnámabók *Medieval Icelandic book detailing the settlement of Iceland.*

Lindisfarne *Burial place of Cuthbert, patron saint of northern England; site of the first major Viking raid in 793*

Mercia *One of the major kingdoms of early Anglo-Saxon England. Located in the center of the island*

Miklagård *Viking name for Constantinople*

Northumbria *Northernmost of the seven kingdoms of early Anglo-Saxon England*

Norway *Westernmost Viking kingdom of the Scandinavian peninsula*

Novgorod *First major city of the medieval Rus state.*

Orkney Islands *Archipelago in northern Scotland southwest of the Shetlands*

Reykjavik *Capital of Iceland*

Shetlands *Archipelago located roughly sixty miles north of the Scotland*

Staraya Ladoga *First outpost settled by the Rus*

Sussex *One of the minor kingdoms of early Anglo-Saxon England. Located on the Channel coast*

Sweden *Easternmost Viking kingdom of the Scandinavian peninsula*

Vinland *Viking name for the North American continent; most likely Newfoundland*

Wessex *One of the major kingdoms of early Anglo-Saxon England. Located in the southwest of the island*

Western Settlement *Second Viking colony in Greenland; located northwest of the Eastern Settlement*

York *Major city of Northumbria, center of Viking power in England*

Volga River *Major Rus water route to the Caspian Sea and Islamic markets*

OTHER

Althing *Assembly of all free Viking men, usually summoned to vote on important decisions*

Battle of Clontarf *Most famous battle in Irish history, fought between the Irish High King Brian Bóruma and an alliance of Irish and Viking rebels*

Battle of Stiklestad *Fought between the exiled king Olaf Haraldsson and his former subjects*

Danegeld *Literally "Danish-money"; bribes paid by English and Frankish kings to convince Vikings to leave their lands*

Danelaw *Area of northern England originally held by Guthrum and settled by the Vikings*

Danevirke *Massive earthen wall extending along the neck of the Jutland peninsula to protect Denmark from Charlemagne's empire*

Dubgaill *'Black Foreigners'; Irish name for Danish Vikings*

Findgaill *'White Foreigners'; Irish name for Norwegian Vikings*

Gallgoidel *'Foreign Irish'; Irish name for those with mixed Viking-Irish blood*

Gothi *Icelandic elder respected for his reputation, knowledge of the law, and generosity*

Greek Fire *Byzantine secret incendiary weapon*

Hagia Sophia *Main cathedral of Byzantium and the Orthodox world*

Heimskringla *History of the Norse kings written by the Icelandic poet Snorri Sturluson*

Jarl *Viking noble*

Khazars *Powerful barbarian tribe controlling the Volga River access to the Caspian Sea*

Land-Waster *Harald Hardråda's battle flag*

Longphort *Viking shore fortress which allowed them to winter in enemy territory*

Ragnarok *Mythical Last Battle where the gods would be overwhelmed by the ice giants*

Raven Banner *Woven in a single day by the daughters of Ragnar Lothbrok, it carried the favor of Odin*

Skræling *Viking name for the Natives populations of the North American continent*

Treaty of St. Clair-sur-Epte *Agreement between King Charles the Simple and Rollo which created Normandy*

Varangian Guard *Viking bodyguard of the emperors of Constantinople*

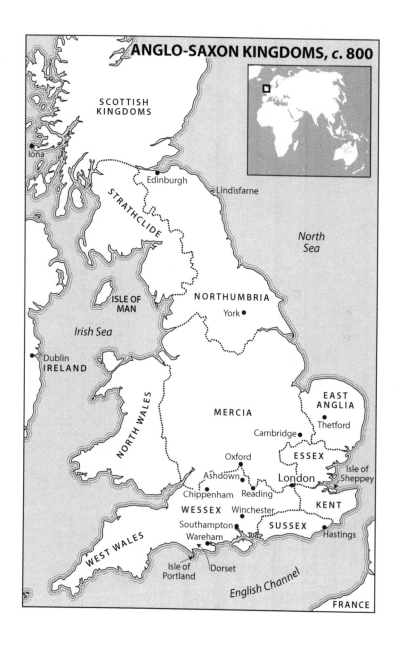

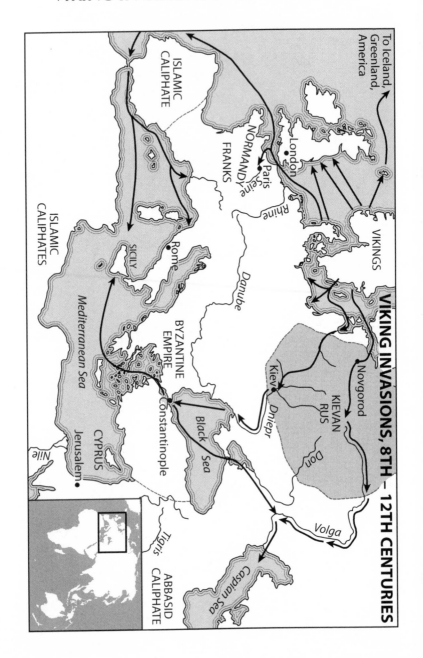

VIKING INVASIONS, 8TH – 12TH CENTURIES

KIEVAN RUS IN 11ᵀᴴ CENTURY

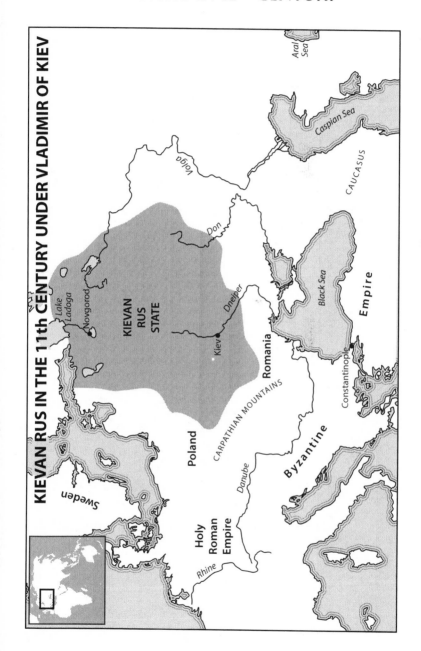

NORMANDY & ENGLAND C. AD 1066

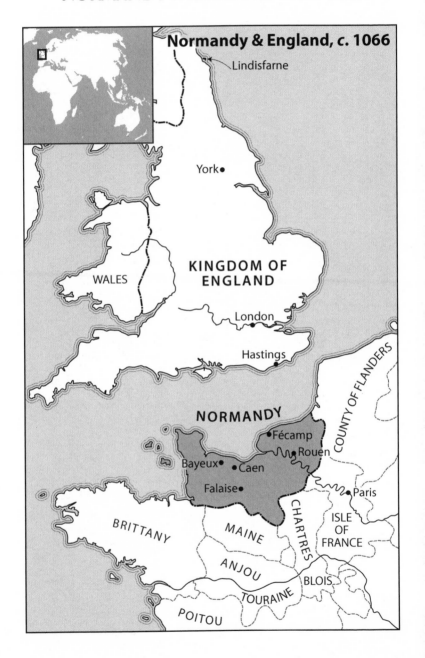

Normandy & England, c. 1066

Lindisfarne

York

KINGDOM OF
ENGLAND

WALES

London

Hastings

COUNTY OF FLANDERS

NORMANDY

Fécamp

Rouen

Bayeux • Caen

Falaise

Paris

BRITTANY

MAINE

CHARTRES

ISLE
OF
FRANCE

ANJOU

BLOIS

TOURAINE

POITOU

THE WESTERN VOYAGES OF THE VIKINGS

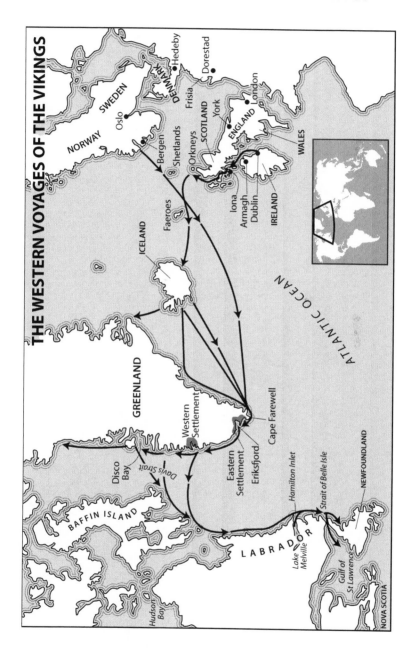

Introduction

THE HAMMER OF THE NORTH

"Wake early if you want another man's life or land. No land for the lazy wolf. No battle's won in bed."

– Edda of Sæmund the Wise, a collection of the sayings of Odin

J ust off the west coast of present-day Scotland, lies the small island of Iona, a grassy promontory with white sandy beaches, rising up out of the North Sea. Today it is a place of quiet contemplation, relatively undisturbed by the tour groups or visiting school children wandering among its enchanted ruins. Even for those who know, it is easy to forget that twelve centuries ago, these idyllic shores were the scenes of unimaginable violence.

The monastery of Iona is the symbolic heart of Scottish Christianity, one of the oldest and most important religious centers in Western Europe. It was founded by the Irish monk Columba in the sixth century and became the focal point for the spread of the faith throughout Scotland.

In the early centuries, the monks came to seek seclusion among the 'desert' of the Atlantic Ocean, and built simple beehive-shaped stone huts where they could concentrate on their prayers and vows of poverty and obedience. Over time, however, the small community became a major pilgrimage site, and a great medieval center of learning. It developed into a training school for monks with special rooms for the copying of manuscripts called *scriptoriums* that produced works of art famous throughout Europe. Chief among these was the 'Book of Kells', an illuminated collection of the four gospels that was described by its Irish contemporaries as "*the most precious object in the western world*".

In addition to its religious treasures, Iona also boasted an unrivaled collection of royal tombs. Most of the early Scottish kings, including the two made famous by Shakespeare – Macbeth and his victim Duncan – were interred in the monastery's crypt.

For centuries, the island was an oasis of peace, protected by the faith of its inhabitants and the vast ocean surrounding it. In 794, however, a ripple of fear penetrated the tranquility. Rumors reached the monks of terrible raids to the east, sister monasteries devastated by strange northern pagans. Early the next year, while the monks were celebrating a holy day, ships with prows carved to resemble serpents and dragons slipped onto the beach below the main abbey.

Leaping onto the white sand of a shoreline, which would later bear the name 'Martyr's Bay' in memory of the slain, the raiders headed for the buildings, cutting down the monks they found along the way. Smashing open the doors, they killed anyone who tried to resist, drenching the stone floors of the chapel with blood. Anything that looked valuable was seized, including rich vestments which were ripped off of the bodies of the dead or dying.

As the surviving monks fled in all directions, the attackers set fire to the great abbey and then raced down to the beach with their considerable loot. Seemingly in the blink of an eye they were gone. Left behind were bloody corpses, burning buildings, and a shattered community.

Virtually the only thing left intact was the high cross of St. Martin's, one of a dozen or so large carved monoliths that had dotted the landscape. In the side facing away from the devastated church was carved the biblical figure of Abraham with his sword raised high – as if in warning of the terrible events that had just unfolded.

The raids on the British Isles were only the beginning of a great hammer blow that fell on an unprepared Europe. The broken bodies and the blackened shells of buildings in places like Iona would be all too common in the centuries to come.

The suddenness of the violence left many occupants of Europe disoriented and anxious. The shock and despair can still be felt in the words of Alcuin, an Anglo-Saxon monk writing from Charlemagne's imperial capital of Aachen after one of the first raids.

> *"...never before in Britain has such a terror appeared as this we have now suffered at the hands of the heathen."*

The fact that the word 'Viking' still conjures up that image of blond-haired barbarians leaping off of dragon ships to plunder a monastery – is a testament to the trauma inflicted on Western Christendom during the three hundred years of the Viking Age. It is burned into our collective memory.

There is, even now, something alien about those northern warriors. The origin of the word *'viking'* itself is unknown. Contemporary ninth century records call the raiders 'Northmen', 'Danes', 'Norse', or 'Heathen'. The Anglo-Saxons, frequent targets of their attacks, did have a word *'wicing'* which meant 'sea-raider', but it first appears only in the eleventh century. A better explanation comes from the Vikings themselves. In Old Norse *vic* meant inlet or bay and the Vic district near the Oslo Fjord was a main source of iron used in sword production. The word 'Viking' probably started off as a reference to men from the Vic district and gradually came to include all Scandinavian raiders.

Endless speculation has centered on the question of *why* the Vikings suddenly erupted from their lands in the eighth century. Theories have ranged from overpopulation and political pressure to climate change and technological innovations.[1] What is clear, however, is that there was a cyclical nature to the great waves of northern Europeans leaving their homes. The first recorded migration of Scandinavian people actually predates the 'Viking Age' by nearly five centuries. As the Western Roman Empire tottered toward its final collapse, the Goths, a people originating from what is now southern Sweden invaded the empire, eventually settling in southern France and Spain.

But the Goths wouldn't have recognized themselves as 'Scandinavian' or 'Viking' any more than the raiders of the eighth century would have. Although they had a common language, the Vikings were never a single people, and most of those who lived in Scandinavia during the Viking age never left home. The raiders were a somewhat suspect minority with multiple reasons for adventuring. Single explanations, therefore, are bound to be incomplete. Further complicating matters is the fact that the Viking story has largely been told by others – histories compiled by their victims, references in the annals of the older, more civilized nations to the south and east, and the tantalizing glimpses that archeology gives us.

---

1   Historically this has been the most popular explanation. As Will Durant rather poetically put it "The fertility of the women... outran the fertility of the soil."

The Vikings vanished partly because their artists worked in wood. Summers were spent felling trees, which were turned into the feasting halls, ships, and later stave churches that made up their civilization. Of these, only the last remain more or less intact, and they represent the twilight of the Viking world.

The Vikings themselves wrote very little down. Their runic alphabet was more suited to magical spells and marker stones than epics or histories. By the time the great Icelandic bard, Snorri Sturluson, composed his *Heimskringla – The Lives of the Norse Kings* – more than four centuries had passed since the Viking Age had ended.

But those stories reflect a much older oral tradition, and they allow us to hear the spirit, if not the exact words, of the tales that Viking poets told to pass the long northern nights. They illustrate the Viking mindset in the same way that the *Iliad* illuminates that of the ancient Greeks: a true warrior went out, gained riches, built great halls and handsomely rewarded his loyal followers. Glory – and kingships – could only be won on the battlefield.

Fired by this mindset, young Viking men sailed out to the glittering lands to the south and east of Scandinavia to win everlasting fame. A measure of their success can be found in the anxious prayers that soon echoed from European churches. The abbey of St. Vaast on the northern coast of France included in its daily chants the phrase *"Deliver us, God, from the savage race of Northmen which lays waste our realms."*[2] It was a sentiment that many would soon share, from Constantinople in the east to the Americas in the west.

---

2   The version of this prayer that is usually quoted, "O Lord, deliver us from the fury of the Norsemen" was never actually used during the ninth century.

Prologue:

THE VIKING DAWN

"A sword age, a wind age, a wolf age. No longer is there mercy among men."

Völuspá Doomsday Prophecy from Snorri Sturluson's Prose Edda

The Holy Island of Lindisfarne is an unlikely place to begin the story of an epoch of violence and blood. If anything, it seems today like a place outside of time, an inconspicuous and unimpressive bit of land sticking out of the North Sea. Covered by sparse vegetation, its rocky soil slopes gently towards the tidal coasts, unencumbered by much protection from either the northern climate or the pounding of the waves.

As early as the sixth century, the island had become home to a small enclave of monks who were looking for a spiritual haven, a place where they could retreat from the world and its distractions. Within a century, a priory had been built on the island's southern promontory, and its suitability for quiet prayer had attracted a monk named Cuthbert, Northumbria's future patron saint. Renowned in life for his personal warmth and holiness, Cuthbert spent twenty-three years on the island, and his tomb – thanks to numerous miracles attributed to him after his death – became a popular place for pilgrimage among England's Anglo-Saxon population.

No other monastery better symbolized the new confidence of the late eighth century. Thanks to a series of strong rulers in both Britain and the continent, a measure of security had returned to Western Europe that hadn't been seen since the *Pax Romana*. The crumbling relics of a more prosperous time lay on all sides, but farmers, craftsmen, and monks had settled in to the sure, steady rhythms of early medieval life.

Politically, England was divided among seven kingdoms, four major and three minor ones. The most powerful of the major kingdoms was Mercia, which controlled nearly the entire central portion of the island from the Welsh border to the North Sea. The other major kingdoms were Northumbria, stretching from Edinburgh to the Humber River in the north east; East Anglia, a swampy area along England's east coast; and Wessex, which covered all of southwestern England, including Cornwall. The three petty kingdoms were Sussex on the Channel coast, Essex which controlled London, and Kent, the area around Canterbury.

Although all of England had been prospering in the eighth century, the northern regions in particular experienced a cultural flowering that was impressive enough to be remembered by historians as the 'Northumbrian Renaissance' six centuries before the more famous Italian one. Painting, metalwork, sculpture, and architecture all flourished, and it was during this time that the great Anglo-Saxon illuminated manuscripts were produced – among them the Lindisfarne Gospels, the Book of Kells, and the Book of Durrow.[3]

---

3   These three illuminated manuscripts – and the Lindisfarne Gospel in particular – are widely considered among the greatest achievements of British medieval art.

Throughout England, religious houses opened up schools that produced academics of such quality that when Charlemagne decided to sponsor his own school – the Palatine Academy – he staffed it with English scholars.[4]

Monasteries like those at Jarrow, Lindisfarne, and Iona, on the northern coasts of England and Scotland, were the main beneficiaries of this artistic flowering. Gospel books with lavish covers and gilded pages appeared along with reliquaries[5] studded with precious stones, bishop's crosiers – their symbol of office – made of delicate ivory, and vestments inlaid with gold and silver. The eighth century, which had overseen this renaissance, seemed poised to end on a note of increased prosperity and harmony. In 787 the Anglo-Saxon Chronicle reported that the farmers of England worked their fields in *supreme tranquility*. The contentment was such that one chronicler was carried away enough to write that *even the burden-bearing frame of the oxen placed their necks under the yoke in dearest love.* The shadow of things to come, however, was revealed that autumn when a look-out spotted three unidentified ships off the coast of the Isle of Portland in southern Wessex.

Whenever ships were spotted – whether hostile or friendly – it was the duty of the coastguard to inform the king's reeve, the chief magistrate of a district or town. The isle of Portland's reeve, a man named Beaduheard, must have assumed the strangers were merchants and probably rode down to the beach to direct them to a manor where they would be able obtain the necessary permissions to conduct business. However we don't know what he actually planned

---

4　The Palatine Academy eventually became the University of Paris.

5　Reliquaries are containers for holy relics

because before he had a chance to open his mouth, they loosed a volley of arrows, killing him and his men instantly.

Poor Beaduheard had the misfortune of making Europe's first recorded contact with the Vikings, and his family didn't even have the satisfaction of punishing his killers. By the time the king's men arrived the Vikings would have been long gone, sailing further along the coast or back home with whatever they had managed to snatch off the corpses. There was nothing to be done but bury the bodies and hope the strangers didn't return.

News of the attack spread quickly, and nervous local populations began to take defensive measures in case the raiders reappeared. On both sides of the English Channel farmers were recruited to serve in peasant 'levies', assemblies of local shock troops who could be called into service quickly. Some religious houses took similar precautions. In 792 the monasteries of Kent were required to contribute to raising coastal defenses against 'pagan seamen'. The Vikings, however, were not simple pirates and soon revealed the English preparations to be hopelessly inadequate. Their previous raids had merely been probing attacks, intelligence gathering to test both the prize and the defenses. In 793 they struck in force.

Their target was not – as might be expected – one of the rich trading centers such as could be found at Dorset or Southampton. These were well-guarded and in proximity to large populations which could rally to their defense. Instead, the cunning Vikings chose the monastery of Lindisfarne – isolated, prosperous, and guarded only by the prayers of unsuspecting monks.

Over the past century, English monasteries had grown fantastically wealthy, a fact which spread to the Viking homelands either through word of mouth or through trading activity. Monasteries were natural sites for the sale of imported goods – wines for communion, high quality textiles for church vestments, and precious metals for plate and reliquaries. In addition to the fortunes accumulated through gifts by pious donors, they also acted as proto-banks since local magnates frequently used major churches as safe deposits for their own portable wealth. Raiding a monastery was the Viking equivalent of winning the lottery.

Best of all, as far as the Vikings were concerned, these rich targets were virtually unguarded. All over Europe religious houses had been built in exposed coastal areas in the belief that the sea would protect their flank – an opinion that was now proved terribly wrong. The shock of that discovery can still be felt in the writings of the time. "*It was not thought possible* " wrote one cleric after the first attack, "*that such an inroad from the sea could be made.*"

Lindisfarne was wealthy even by monastic standards, and its selection as the Vikings' first target was no accident. It had been personally endowed by the Northumbrian king, and possessed a peerless collection of relics, including the sainted remains of the English monk Cuthbert and the equally famous Irish missionary Columba who had brought Christianity to Scotland. The lucrative pilgrim trade which had grown from the fame of these two alone had made the monastery fabulously rich. Various Viking groups had been active in the area for some time and, on June 8, 793, one of these groups, from what is today Norway, carried out a brutally efficient attack.

An anonymous Northumbrian monk recorded the event.

"The pagans from the northern regions came with a naval force to Britain like stinging hornets and spread on all sides like fearful wolves, robbed, tore and slaughtered..."

No one was spared. Monks who tried to resist were hacked apart or dragged down to the beach and drowned. Reliquaries were pulled into pieces and their contents dumped on the ground. Rich tapestries adorning chapel walls were torn down, altars were smashed, and everywhere the corpses of the slain lay 'like dung in the streets'.

The disaster sent a shockwave through Europe. If the heart of English Christianity could fall, then surely no one was safe. Anxious monks trying to make sense of the calamity claimed that there had been divine warning signs before the attack: sheets of lightning had been spotted in the skies several weeks before, supposedly accompanied by fiery dragons wheeling menacingly above the priory.

The disaster was widely attributed to the moral laxity of the English church. A few weeks after the raid a letter was circulated quoting Jeremiah 1:14 – *"Then the Lord said unto me, Out of the north an evil shall break forth upon all the inhabitants of the land"* – and calls for reform were made. The scholar Alcuin, writing to the Bishop of Lindisfarne with eerie clarity, identified both the cause and the proper response. *"Either this is the beginning of a greater tribulation, or else the sins of the inhabitants have called it upon themselves. Truly it has not happened by chance... You who are left, stand mindfully, fight bravely, defend the camp of God..."*

No amount of soul searching, however, stemmed the tide. The next year, the monasteries of Jarrow on the east coast and the Isle of Skye on the west were hit, and in 795

Iona Abbey was looted. Almost the entire community – monks, nuns, peasants, and animals – were dragged down to the seashore and slaughtered. It was a grim portent of the carnage to come. Alcuin, writing from the safety of Charlemagne's capital, captured the anguish: "*What assurance is there for the churches of Britain if St. Cuthbert, with so great a number of saints, defends not his own?*"

THE RAIDERS

Chapter 1

THE VIKINGS AT HOME

"One's home is best, small though it may be..."
-Edda of Sæmund the Wise

The most frightening thing about the Vikings was that almost nothing about them was known. In the eighth century, their homelands were at the fringe of the known world, a cold and inhospitable place that the civilizing hand of the Roman Empire had never touched. Scandinavia – the land divided today into the modern countries of Norway, Sweden, and Denmark – is a place of extremes. It stretches 1,243 miles from Jutland in the south to Knivskjellodden in the Arctic Circle, a distance accounting for half the length of Europe. It contains one of the continent's most mountainous countries, Norway, as well as one of its flattest, Denmark, whose highest point rises only five hundred and sixty one feet above sea level.

Of the three countries – none of which existed at the start of the Viking Age – Denmark, covering the Jutland peninsula and more than five hundred small islands, has the most favorable climate. Warmed by the Gulf Stream and the North Atlantic current, the country is a patchwork of rocky beaches, green fields, and forests of oak and elm. Since it shares its western coast with modern Germany, west was a natural direction for its young men to explore. Vikings from Denmark fanned out across the Low Countries and France, eventually crossing the Channel into Britain, and from there conducting raids as far as Spain and even Italy.[6] Although England was first attacked by raiders from what is now Norway, so many Danes infested their waterways that the Anglo-Saxon sources took to referring to all Vikings as 'Danes' regardless of where they came from.

The main Scandinavian peninsula – covered today by the modern countries of Norway and Sweden – has a much less hospitable climate than Denmark. Of the two regions, what is now Sweden has the better farmland. Its shores look east towards Russia, and most of its Vikings travelled in that direction, although largely to trade instead of raid. Their exploits are arguably the least well known, but some of the most lasting since they founded the first Russian state in Kiev.

The most rugged of the Viking lands is Norway, almost a third of which is above the Arctic Circle. The long western coast is protected from the icy battering of the Atlantic by a barrier of rocky islands and dramatic fjords which provide the 'northern way' – a navigable coastal route to the Arctic Circle – that gave Norway its name.[7] Unsurprisingly, when they ventured into the North Sea, the Norwegian Vikings pushed west, sometimes raiding and sometimes colonizing. This group founded settlements in Greenland and reached the New World around AD 1000.

In the Viking Age, both Sweden and Norway were thinly settled and largely unable to sustain large populations.

---

6   The modern Netherlands and Belgium

7   Roughly 150,000 islands lie off the Norwegian coast.

Norway's available farmland was broken up by long narrow fjords, which led into the mountainous interior, while vast, impenetrable forests, bogs, and lakes closed off much of southern and western Sweden. A surprising amount of game was available in the summers – including reindeer, elk, wolves, bears, wolverines, and foxes – but the long winters punished those who failed to plan ahead. Perhaps because of this scarcity, hospitality was highly valued, and failure as a host could start bloodfeuds lasting generations.

To pass the time they invented a number of games including *Knattleik*, a ball game similar to hockey, which attracted both large crowds and frequent injuries. Several less violent board games did exist, but the Vikings primarily valued physical fitness.[8] Their most popular activities were usually tests of strength – wrestling, sword fighting, and trying to dunk each other; endurance – climbing fjords, skiing, skating and distance swimming; or agility – throwing spears with both hands at the same time, or leaping from oar to oar outside the railing of a ship while it was being rowed.

Winners of these contests were not shy in broadcasting the fact. A Norwegian king named Øystein boasted to his brother (and co-ruler) Sigurd "*I was so good at skating that I didn't know anyone who could vie with me; but you weren't better than a cow.*"

When not fighting themselves, the Scandinavians would occasionally pit animals against each other. The most popular of these blood sports involved horses. Two stallions would be led in sight and smell of a fenced-off mare, and allowed to fight, often resulting in the death of the weaker one. Indiscriminate killing was frowned upon, but mercy

---

8   Hnefatafl was a chess-like 'hunting' game, and Kvatrutafl resembled
     backgammon.

was not a quality that befitted a warrior. One Icelandic man was apparently mocked as a 'child-lover' because he refused to participate in the sport of tossing captured babies into the air and catching them on the point of a spear.[9]

These pursuits sound brutal to our ears, but in other ways the Vikings were surprisingly modern. Unlike the usual stereotype of a rude barbarian, they were very conscious of their appearance and had excellent hygiene.[10] They carefully groomed themselves and generally bathed at least once a day with a lye-rich soap that both bleached their hair and cut down on lice. Highly prized tweezers, razors, combs, and even ear cleaners have all been found in Viking excavations.

Thanks to the absence of sugar in European diets, cavities were virtually unknown, and although half of their children died before age ten, those who survived could expect to live into their fifties, a very respectable age for the time. The average height for males was five foot eight, and females five foot three, not towering, but certainly taller than the peoples to the south with whom they came in contact.

Women, although by no means equal, probably had greater rights in Viking culture than anywhere in Western Christendom. Many girls married as young as twelve, but when the husband was away, the wife ran every aspect

---

9   He was Olvir Barnarkarl, the brother-in-law of the man who discovered Iceland. His story is told in the medieval Icelandic Landnámabók.

10 At least by the standards of the time. The Arab writer Ibn Fadlan describes the Swedes in Russia as 'the filthiest race that God ever created', and gives lurid details of their behavior - not wiping after going to the bathroom, having sex in public, and washing with the same water they blew their noses in.

of the home and made all important decisions.[11] If she remained married for twenty years – and either partner could dissolve the union at will – she had a legal right to half of the wealth her husband had accumulated.[12] Unlike in the rest of Europe, she could inherit property, divorce her husband, and reclaim her dowery when the marriage ended. Several touching rune stones have been found raised in women's honor – from the Danish king Gorm the Old who praised his wife as '*the ornament of Denmark*' to an anonymous carving proclaiming that there was '*no better housewife than Hassmyra*'.[13]

Children were encouraged to help their parents with the running of the household. Girls were taught the arts of brewing and dairy production, while boys were instructed how to hunt while skiing, and to work with wood or metal. The games they played were designed to prepare them for adulthood. A favorite exercise of boys was jumping while carrying weight and swimming while armed; a fully-grown Viking was expected to be able to swim for several miles.

---

11   Polygamous marriages were relatively common among the rich. Marriages in general were usually arranged by the parents. The Vikings took the custom of asking permission seriously. According to the twelfth century Book of Icelanders, if a man tried to marry a woman against her parents' wishes he could be legally killed by them.

12   If the husband failed to give a good reason for the divorce he could be killed by his wife's family. Crossdressing, for example, was considered a good enough reason. Both breeches on a woman and a low cut blouse on a man were grounds for divorce.

13   Perhaps the best example of the autonomy that women could achieve is provided by the Arab historian Hasan-ibn-Dihya, who wrote about a Muslim embassy to Viking Dublin. They happened to arrive when the chieftain Thorgils the Devil was away, so his wife Odda received the ambassadors and performed 'all the duties of a king'.

Order in society was kept through harsh punishments. Men caught committing adultery were hung or trampled by a horse, arsonists were burned at the stake, and, according to the Danish historian Saxo Grammaticus, those who killed their brothers were hung by their heels next to a live wolf. Rebels who flouted the community's – or later the king's – decisions were tied to horses and torn apart, or bound to an enraged bull.

Surprisingly for such violent times, the Vikings also believed that a cultured man should be musical. A popular saga told of the Norwegian king Godmund who employed a musician that played with such vigor that even the knives and dishes started to dance. Indeed, no Viking court was complete without its poets, musicians, and dancers. The thirteenth century *Orkneyinga Saga* tells of Rognvald Kali Kolsson, a political mover who counted the king of Norway among his friends, who listed harp playing among the skills he was most proud of.

Viking celebrations were probably rowdier than elsewhere in Europe. Feasts could last for quite a while – the Danish king Sven Estridsson held one for eight days – and always involved drinking. The appropriate form at these celebrations was to imbibe without inhibition, and contests were frequent, usually battles of wit where both sides tried not to show any effects of the alcohol. This was made more difficult since it was considered a grave breach of hospitality to refuse an offered horn of ale or mead unless you were old or sick.[14]

---

14 This could at times lead to trouble since a host could essentially force his guests to drink against their will. Egil's Saga has a story in which the titular hero attends a feast where his devious host keeps passing the horn. When he realized he couldn't take any more, Egil seized his host, pushed him up against a pillar, and nearly suffocated him in a gush of vomit.

Feasting and hospitality were important because for nearly six months a year the Vikings had to endure freezing, snowy winters on land and foul storms at sea. The imposing landscape and harsh conditions produced a population that was brutally capable and independent. They valued courage and despised weakness. The custom, at least among those Swedes who went east, was for a father to place a sword in his new-born son's crib and say '*I shall not leave you property to inherit. You have nothing but what you can acquire for yourself with this sword.*' This attitude, that life, glory and wealth must be seized, characterized the Norse throughout the Viking Age. When asked what faith he subscribed to, one tenth century Viking responded "*I believe in my own strength.*"

Although they had gods, the Vikings had no word for 'religion'.[15] There was no 'official' way to worship, no universal doctrine, and no central church. Instead they had a set of general beliefs with extensive local variations.[16] They saw the universe as one of concentric circles. There were nine worlds, most of them invisible, in three distinct realms. The outer one – Utgard – was populated by giants and monsters who circled like wolves in the darkness, held back only by the watchful eyes of the gods. The middle circle was Midgard – literally 'middle yard' – where humans and gods lived. The former shared the land with dwarves and dark elves, who were capable of producing magical gifts but guarded their hoards jealously. Across the *Bifrost,* a rainbow bridge that no human could cross, the two tribes

---

15   The closest they came was sithr, which meant 'custom'.

16   They also appear to have had a few 'godless' men who rejected all gods and believed that death was the final end. This can't have been too common, however, since virtually all Viking burials included goods for use in the afterlife.

of gods – Aesir and Vanir – lived in fabled Asgard, the Hall of the Slain, where the dead heroes feasted, waiting for the last great battle. The highest honor a warrior could receive was to be chosen as one of that number. The brave who fell in battle were scooped up by the Valkyries, shield maidens of Odin whose job it was to fill his feasting hall of Valhalla before the end of days.

The innermost circle was Niflheim, the world of the dead. There, in a colorless twilight watched over by the goddess Hel, were the souls of the men, women, and children who had died. This grim place was not a punishment for the wicked, rather it was the fate of most humans. The exceptions were the brave who went to live with the Aesir, and the outcasts – those guilty of adultery, murder, and oath-breaking – who were doomed to become evil spirits haunting their barrows.[17]

Connecting the three main worlds was an immense ash tree called Yggdrasil. At its roots sat the Norns, three spirits ('prophesy', 'being', and 'necessity') spinning out the fates of gods, giants, and men. Their task was to guard the tree from the Nidhogg, a great dragon who feasted on the corpses of the wicked and chewed on the roots of the tree.

Of the thirteen major gods of Valhalla, Odin and Thor were the most important, but there was no agreement as to who was more powerful. The upper classes, especially those in Denmark and southern Sweden, tended to worship Odin, while farmers preferred Thor.[18]

---

17 The Laxdæla Saga tells of Thorolf Clubfoot, a violent and unsociable farmer who came back to life to haunt his family one winter as a cross between a zombie and a vampire. His son, who eventually exhumed the body during the day to burn it, described his father as "incorrupt but terrible to look at, more like a troll than a man; black as pitch and as swollen as an ox."

18 The Danish Skloldung dynasty claimed Odin as an ancestor.

Odin the 'All-father', was the god of poetry, madness, battle, and magic, who could grant men courage or deprive them of their wits. By hanging himself from a sacred tree for nine days he had learned the secret runes, which allowed him to see the future, and more than the rest of the gods he pursued wisdom. He had sacrificed an eye for a drink out of the well of knowledge, and had two pet ravens – Huginn and Muninn – who circled the globe each day, returning to whisper their discovered secrets into Odin's ear.[19] He was a formidable god in battle – his magical spear, Gungnir, never missed its target, and his eight-legged horse Sleipnir could speed across air, water, or land equally well – but he usually depended on his wisdom to win battles.[20]

Thor by contrast, was a slowwitted god who depended on brute force to overwhelm his enemies. A red-haired deity with frightening eyes, he wielded the mighty hammer Mjolnir which could level mountains or resurrect the dead. He served as mankind's protector, constantly fighting the ice giants who threatened to overwhelm Midgard. Where Thor walked – or flew in a chariot pulled by two magical goats – storms followed, and his battles could be seen in the flashes of lightning in the mountains

Although he was always popular – particularly with those who ventured out onto the open ocean – Thor's popularity grew at the end of the Viking Age, probably because he was seen as the most able defender against encroaching Christianity.

---

19 Huginn means 'thought', and Muninn 'memory'.

20 Odin was not above stooping to low cunning to win a contest. One famous example is his battle of wit and lore against the ice giant Vafthrudnir. When he discovered that the giant's knowledge of the various worlds matched his own, Odin cheated by asking what words he had whispered to his dead son before lighting the funeral pyre - a question to which only Odin could possibly know the answer.

Viking beliefs about the future were not overly cheerful. In the long, icy dark of a northern winter, it must have been easy to believe that all warmth would eventually fail. The wolves could only be held at bay for so long. Even the Viking gods were not immortal. Ragnarok – the last battle – was coming when all of them – gods, heroes, Norns – and the great tree Yggdrasil were doomed. The shadowy dragon Nidhogg would rise from his feast of corpses, unleashing a winter lasting three years. Brother would fight brother, and plunge the world into chaos. The monstrous wolves chasing the sun and moon would catch them and snuff them out. The fire demons and ice giants would breach the walls of Asgard and the dead in Hel would break free, overwhelming the gods and heroes assembled to fight them. There was a glimmer of hope, however. Two children each from Odin and Thor would survive the 'axe, wind, and wolf age' and form a new earth.

There may have been no escape from the icy cataclysm to come, but that didn't stop the Vikings from appealing to the gods for their aid – especially at sea. The Viking world, after all, was one of water as much as land. When game was scarce, gifts from the sea – seal, whale, and walrus meat – sustained them. Travel along Norway's dramatic fjords, Sweden's coasts, and Denmark's islands, could only be made by sea. In many ways the ocean knit the Scandinavian world together, and as a result the Vikings viewed their world through the prism of the ocean. They called the spine of mountains that split their great peninsula 'Kjølen' – *the Keel* – as if Scandinavia itself were an upturned boat. Babies were laid in cradles shaped like ships, children played with toy boats, and adults designed houses like ships – at times *from* discarded bits of ships. Women wore clasps and brooches in their shape, and some men even rode with stirrups fashioned with dragon-headed prows. Even in death they refused to be parted from their ships. Great men and women merited fully fitted, ornamental vessels, complete with slaughtered animals, weapons, wealth, and slaves – voluntary or not – all interred beneath a great mound.[21] Lesser warriors were laid in simple ships, functional vehicles to carry them into eternity. Those too poor to afford the real thing were buried in pits, covered in stones arranged in the shape of a boat.

Thanks to this emphasis on the sea, the Vikings were well aware of the world to their south. Scandinavia had vast natural resources, including pelts, high quality amber and enormous iron deposits, and by the ninth century the northerners had been carrying out a brisk trade with the lands to their south and east for centuries.

The word 'Scandinavia' was in fact coined by the Roman geographer Pliny the Elder in the first century A.D. He mistook the southernmost tip of Sweden for an island and called it 'Scania' after a tribe that lived there. His contemporary Tacitus, writing at the end of the century, described its inhabitants with the word *Suiones* – from which we get 'Swedes' – as 'well-armed, acquisitive, skilled in sailing curious ships with a prow at each end...'

In those first centuries of contact with the Romans, the 'strange ships' came to trade not rob. Their wares, especially the fine horses and black fox skins, were highly valued in Roman markets. The reverse was also true. Roman goods, most often weapons, glass, and jewelry, filtered up through

---

21   The famous image of a Viking funeral - a blazing ship sailing to Valhalla - comes from the pen of an Arab writer who witnessed the funerary rites of one of the Swedish Vikings on the Volga River. Although they both were practiced, burial seems to have been preferred to cremation.

Germanic intermediaries and are sometimes still found in early Scandinavian grave mounds. This trade also brought with it knowledge of the Latin and Greek alphabet which – slightly adapted for carving on hard surfaces – formed the basis of the first Runic script.[22]

When they did interact directly, the Romans learned to respect northern prowess. Writing from Constantinople in the sixth century, the historian Jordanes described the Scandinavians as 'ferocious' opponents who were of 'extraordinary' stature. In part this was attributed to their harsh climate which, he informed his readers, was one of perpetual darkness during the winter, and unbroken light during the summer.[23] This made it necessary for the inhabitants to live off birds eggs and the flesh of animals since wheat could not grow in the extreme north. The frozen landscape was a mass of shifting tribes, uncivilized by a single guiding hand like that of the Roman Emperor. Jordanes mentions more than thirty different 'nations' within what is now modern Norway and Sweden, and tells how one in particular – the Goths – entered the Roman Empire.

This first "Viking" invasion came by land and took several centuries. The Goths migrated from southern Sweden to the Black Sea, crossing into Roman territory in the third century. They secured a great victory in 378, killing the emperor Valens in the Balkans at Adrianople, and within a hundred

---

22 The Viking alphabet has twenty-four symbols (literally 'mysteries') roughly based on the Greek and Latin cursive scripts. These are designed to be carved into hard surfaces, not written fluidly and are therefore not suited to literature. Most epic poems were memorized and circulated by traveling poets called 'skalds'.

23 This is the first reference to the 'land of the midnight sun'.

and fifty years had conquered Italy, southern France, and most of Spain.

Procopius, the historian who chronicled the Roman recovery of much of these lands, described the northern tribes in a kind of awe, calling them 'superior to all who dwelt about them.' Further migrations followed in the Gothic wake. Angles, Jutes, and Saxons, tribes originating from Denmark and northern Germany, invaded Britain, and, by the time Procopius wrote, were well on the way to pushing the native inhabitants into Wales.

This early period, known appropriately enough as the 'Age of Migrations', were movements largely by land, not water, and aside from the Goths didn't affect the majority of the population in Scandinavia. What made the great Viking raids possible was a revolution in shipbuilding at the end of the eighth century.

The earliest Viking vessels were copied from Roman or Celtic designs and powered by oars instead of the usual paddles.[24] Like all ships of the time they were slow and prone to capsizing in rough seas, appropriate for short trips that hugged the shore. Sometime in the eighth century, however, the Vikings invented the keel. This simple addition is among the greatest of nautical breakthroughs. Not only did it stabilize the ship, making it ocean-worthy, but it provided a base to anchor the mast. A massive sail, some as large as eight hundred square feet, could now be added as the major source of propulsion. The impact was immediate and stunning. In a time when few Europeans ventured far from land, the Vikings criss-crossed the Atlantic with cargoes of

---

24   Roman sources hint that they also used small sails as early as the 3rd century, but this is not universally accepted. Undisputed use of sails doesn't occur till the mid eighth century.

timber, animals, and food, covering distances of nearly four thousand miles.

To aid steering on these long voyages, the Vikings used a special oar which they called a *Styra bord*, or 'steering board'. In deference to the dominant hand of most sailors it was placed on the right side of the ship near the stern to make the ship easier to control. From this we get the nautical term 'starboard', which refers to the right side of a vessel. The opposite term also owes its existence – albeit more indirectly – to the Vikings. When ships reached the port they would usually be docked on the left side to avoid damage to the steering oar. Over time, 'port' was used as a shorthand for 'left'.

A number of different ships were developed – cargo vessels, ferries, and fishing boats – but the warships, or longships, in particular were a brilliant combination of strength, flexibility, and speed. Built to glide over the surface of the water, the *longships* could be made from local materials, without the specialized labor needed for Mediterranean vessels.[25] The ships of the south were both costly and clunky, held together with multiple rivets and braces, and several decks. The Viking ships, by contrast, were clinker-built with overlapping planks of oak – always green instead of seasoned for greater flexibility – which allowed them to bend with the waves.[26]

Viking ships were mostly undecked, unless made to stow cargo, which made the long Atlantic crossing a brutal affair.

---

25 It was, however, still a significant investment of time. Modern estimates are that experienced Viking craftsmen could build a longship in about seven months, representing roughly forty thousand hours of work.

26 Oak is found across Scandinavia, but particularly in Denmark. A single oak trunk would make up the keel with the major branches forming the ribs. This was an advantage since the Vikings didn't use saws, but instead split the wood with the grain to give it greater strength.

During rough seas, the waves would frequently break over the sides, and there was little protection against the lashing rain or sleet other than a simple tent pitched on the deck.

But what they lacked in comforts, they more than made up for with lethal simplicity. Viking longships lacked the keels of the larger ocean-crossing ships, and their relatively shallow drafts allowed them to be beached virtually anywhere instead of just the deep-water ports required by other vessels.[27] This made it possible for a longship to navigate up rivers, and some were light enough to be carried between river systems.[28]

The Viking poets called the longships 'steeds of the waves', but they were more like prowling wolves. The hapless victims of Viking attacks took to calling the northerners 'sea-wolves', after the predators that roamed the darkness outside of human habitation. The longships could accommodate up to a hundred men, but could be handled on the open sea by as few as fifteen. They were agile enough to slip past coastal defenses, roomy enough to store weeks of loot, sturdy enough to cross the stormy Atlantic, and light enough to be dragged between rivers.

But the most frightening thing about them was their speed. They could average up to four knots and reach eight to ten if the winds or currents were with them. This ensured that the element of surprise would nearly always be with the Vikings. A fleet in Scandinavia could cover the nine

---

27   This is slightly menacing as the Vikings themselves had little need of this feature since the fjords are remarkably deep. Norway's Sognefjord, for example, reaches a depth of 4,291 feet below sea level several miles inland. The average depth of the North Sea, by contrast is 312 feet. The longships were clearly intended for foreign shores.

28   They were also quite thin. Roughly an inch of wood separated a Viking sailor from the Atlantic ocean.

hundred miles to the mouth of the Seine in three weeks, an average of over forty miles per day.[29] Under oar they were nearly as fast. One Viking fleet rowed up the hundred and fifty miles of the Seine – against the current and fending off two Frankish attacks – to reach Paris in three days. The medieval armies they faced, assuming they had access to a good Roman roads, could only average between twelve and fifteen miles per day. Even elite cavalry forces pushing hard could only manage twenty.

It was this speed – the ability to move up to five times as fast as their enemies – that made Viking attacks so lethal. With shallow draughts that could pass under bridges or up shallow rivers, fierce dragon prows, and brightly painted shields fitted onto the sides that glittered like scales, they must have been psychologically unnerving. In a single lightning attack, they could hit several towns and disappear before their opponents could even get an army into the field. Nor was there any hope for the victims of challenging Viking supremacy at sea. Between 800 and 1100 most major naval battles fought in the North Atlantic involved Vikings fighting each other.

As the ninth century dawned, all the pieces of the Viking Age were in place. The Scandinavians had an advantage at sea that was impossible to defend against, knowledge of the major trade routes, and an unsuspecting world in full view. The only thing that remained was to select a suitable target.

---

29   As Ragnar Lothbrok demonstrated in 845. In 1893 a replica of the Viking Gokstad ship, crewed by only twelve men, sailed from Bergen in Norway to Newfoundland in twenty-eight days.

Chapter 2

CHARLEMAGNE'S TEARS

"Braver are many in word than in deed."

\- The Saga of Grettir the Strong

Legend has it that in the late eighth century Charlemagne once caught sight of some Viking ships from his breakfast table while he was visiting the French coast. His hosts assumed that they were merchants, but the emperor knew better and warned that they were "full of fierce foes". The Franks rushed to the shore with swords drawn, but the Vikings fled so quickly that it seemed as if they had simply vanished. The disappointed courtiers returned to the palace where they were greeted with an astonishing sight. The great Charlemagne, Roman emperor and restorer of world order, was weeping. No one dared to interrupt him, but after a time spent gazing out to sea he explained himself.

"Do you know why I weep so bitterly, my true servants? I have no fear of those worthless rascals doing any harm to me; but I am sad at heart to think that even during my lifetime they have dared to touch this shore; and I am

torn by a great sorrow because I foresee what evil things they will do to my descendants and their subjects."[30]

Although this account is obviously apocryphal, Charlemagne hardly needed any prophetic gifts to foresee the danger the Vikings posed to his kingdom. He had, in fact, been preparing his defenses against them for years, and ironically, was at least indirectly responsible for drawing the raider's attention in the first place.

Frankish contact with Scandinavia predated him by a century or more. Viking furs, amber, eiderdown, and whetstones were highly prized in Frankish markets, and Danish merchants were common in the great imperial trading centers of Dorestad on the Rhine and Quentovic near Boulogne.[31] With Charlemagne, however, the dynamic changed. Before him, the Franks had maintained a powerful and stable kingdom in what is today western Germany and eastern France. When Charlemagne accepted the Frankish crown in 768, he immediately began expanding his frontiers in all directions. By 800 he had seized part of the Pyrenees, Bavaria, and most of northern Italy, hammering together a larger state than any seen since the time of the Caesars. On Christmas Day that year, in a carefully orchestrated move, Pope Leo III placed a crown on Charlemagne's head and named him the new Western Roman Emperor – an office that had been vacant for more than three centuries.[32]

---

30   This apocryphal story, written by a Swiss monk named Notker the Stammerer, was part of a collection of stories about the emperor composed for his great-grandson Charles the Fat - a man who was all too familiar with Vikings.

31   Modern Wijk bij Duurstede in the Netherlands and La Calotterie in France.

32   The Roman Empire in the west had collapsed in the fifth century with the forced abdication of its last emperor, Romulus Augustulus, in 476 AD.

Roman style coins were minted, imperial palaces were built, and Charlemagne even considered marrying the Byzantine empress and making the northern Mediterranean a Roman lake once again. A new *Pax Francia* seemed to be dawning under the auspices of the all-powerful Charlemagne. Little seemed to be beyond his reach or ambition. The scholar Alcuin, who had written of the first Viking raid on Lindisfarne, hinted that the Frankish emperor even had the ability to bring back the boys / monks who had been kidnapped by the raiders.

The addition of an imperial title may have burnished the emperor's credentials, but it also alarmed everyone on his borders. The Frankish tendency towards expansion mixed with Charlemagne's clear ability was a dangerous combination. "*If a Frank is your friend*", went a popular eighth century proverb "*he's certainly not your neighbor.*"

If they didn't think so before, by 804 the Danes would have agreed with this proverb. That year Charlemagne finally crushed the Saxons of northwestern Germany, concluding a war that had lasted for three decades. Franks and Danes were now neighbors, and the Scandinavians had reasons to believe that they were next on the menu.

The immediate cause for alarm was Charlemagne's plans to build a fleet, something his powerful land empire had previously lacked. His stated goal was to deny Danish pirates access to the Elbe, the river protecting the empire's northeastern flank. He had already tried to address this issue by building two fortified bridges to make it easier to move troops across at will. The other great rivers of the empire received similar treatment. A moveable bridge of pontoons connected by anchors and ropes guarded the Danube, the great eastern river that allowed access to the heart of imperial territory, and a canal was started between the Rhine and Danube to allow troops to move quickly to a threatened border.[33]

When the emperor announced the addition of a North Sea fleet, most inhabitants of the Danish peninsula correctly suspected that Charlemagne's real target was the Danish port of Hedeby, located just over the border on the Schlei Fjord. The town had become the great entrepôt for Viking goods, and a rival for even the largest Frankish markets. The Danes had set up toll booths and a mint – the first in Scandinavia – and were doing a brisk business that had begun to cut into the older, more established imperial trading centers.

The man responsible for Hedeby's growth was a Viking warlord named Godfred. Frankish chronicles called him a 'king', but he was less a ruler *of* Denmark than a ruler *in* Denmark. Many Danes may have recognized his authority, but there were rival figures with their own halls even in the Jutland peninsula that makes up the bulk of modern Denmark.[34]

Godfred – in what would become true Viking fashion – increased the population of Hedeby by importing captured merchants from Frankish towns he raided. To defend it against Charlemagne he began constructing the *Danevirke*, a massive earthen wall topped by a wooden stockade that would eventually extend across the neck of the peninsula from the North Sea to the Baltic.

---

33 For many of these projects, Charlemagne's ambition outstripped the technical abilities of his engineers. The canal was soon abandoned, and the ineffective fleet was left to rot in its harbors by his successor.

34 Some historians speculate that Godfred's attempts to consolidate his power in Denmark pushed out weaker rivals who turned to piracy, thus in part inspiring the early Viking raids.

Safe behind these ramparts, Godfred began to harass his powerful neighbor. He sacked several Frankish towns and forced one of Charlemagne's allies to switch their allegiance. In response, a small Frankish army marched north and the Danevirke was put to its first test. Godfred's soldiers held their ground, and Charlemagne, who was occupied with revolts elsewhere, decided to buy peace.

The two sides agreed that the river Eider would form a permanent border, and an apparently chastened Godfred sent hostages to the imperial capital of Aachen as a sign of good faith.[35] This, however, turned out to be a ruse. When Charlemagne left with his army for the campaigning season early the next year, Godfred led two hundred longboats on a plundering raid of the Frisia – what is today the Netherland's coast. His price for leaving was a hundred pounds of silver, collected from the beleaguered merchants and peasants, and whatever portable wealth his Vikings could stuff into their ships. As a final note of defiance, he announced that he was claiming the northern stretch of the Frisian coast for himself.

Despite the huge number of ships involved, the raid itself was relatively minor, and Charlemagne was too experienced to believe that any of his borders were permanent. The treaty would have been violated eventually; what really stung Charlemagne was the appropriation of a part of his empire.

It wasn't immediately apparent how he should respond. The few ships he had were woefully inadequate for an attack, so naval operations were out of the question, and a land invasion carried its own risks. Charlemagne had just finished a bruising thirty-year war with the Saxons and, now in his late sixties, had no desire to get bogged down in another slow-burning war.

---

35   Now the westernmost city of Germany.

The first order of business, in any case, was to contain Godfred. The coast had to be protected, and since the Franks lacked a true fleet, the Vikings themselves would have to provide one. Independent groups of Danes had been raiding the Frankish coast for more than a decade, and the larger ones were more than happy to take Charlemagne's gold in exchange for the promise of protection. While they protected him from the sea, Charlemagne gathered his army to storm the Danevirke.

The expedition never left. That summer, as the final preparations were being made, Godfred was cut down by one of his own men. In the chaos that followed, the identity of the killer was obscured. Some later claimed that it was his disgruntled son, angry that Godfred had recently married another woman, and others that the assassin was the king's housecarl, but either way, the threat vanished.[36] Charlemagne was apparently annoyed to be cheated of his revenge. His biographer Einhard claimed that the emperor remarked, *"woe is me that I was not thought worthy to see my Christian hands dabbling in the blood of those dog-headed fiends."* As it turned out, Charlemagne never got the chance to wash his hands in northern gore. He expired four years later and was succeeded by his son Louis.

Without a strong hand at the helm, Charlemagne's empire began to fall apart. At first the decay was barely noticeable. His son Louis seemed to be a younger, more cultured version of Charlemagne. The court took to calling him 'Louis the Debonaire', both for his refined court and his continued patronage of the arts. Even on the battlefield, he appeared to live up to his famous predecessor. During his

---

36   A member of the king's bodyguard.

father's reign he had been entrusted with the security of the southwest frontier, and had been vigorous in its defense. He imposed Frankish authority over Pamplona and the Basques of the southern Pyrenees, and sacked Muslim-controlled Barcelona. All threats to his authority were ruthlessly suppressed, especially if they came from his own family. At his coronation he forced all his unmarried sisters into convents to avoid potential threats from brothers-in-law.

The promising new reign took an unexpected turn in 817, when Louis suffered a near fatal accident. A wooden gallery connecting Aachen's cathedral to the imperial palace collapsed while he was crossing it after a church service, leaving many courtiers maimed or dead. Badly shaken, the injured Louis began plans for his succession, naming his eldest son Lothair as senior emperor, and splitting the rest between two other sons and a nephew.

The emperor recovered, but news of the planned partition had reached Italy where his nephew Bernard – currently ruling as king – discovered that he was to be demoted to a vassal. He immediately revolted, but when Louis suddenly appeared in Burgundy with an army, the unprepared Bernard surrendered without a fight. He agreed to meet with his uncle to beg his pardon, and hopefully retain Italy. Louis, however, was not in a particularly forgiving mood. Bernard was hauled back to Aachen and put on trial for treason as an example to any other family members who were considering revolt. He was found guilty, stripped of his possessions and sentenced to death.

As a sign of his clemency, Louis commuted the penalty to blinding, and two days later the procedure was carried out. The soldiers tasked with performing the blinding weren't overly gentle. They used their heated iron rods so forcefully that Bernard didn't survive the ordeal, dying after two days in agony.

Louis was never quite the same after the death of his nephew. Deeply religious to begin with, his guilt drove him to ever more lavish public displays. Members of the clergy became prominent advisors, and so many churches and monasteries were endowed that he acquired the sobriquet by which he's most known – Louis the Pious. When even this failed to alleviate the guilt, the emperor took the extraordinary step of staging a public confession of his sins before the pope and the assembled ecclesiastics and nobles of the empire. As admirable as this conspicuous humility may have been, however, it had the effect of badly undercutting his own authority.

Contemporary society was dripping with blood. The vast frontiers were surrounded by hostile peoples who could vanish into their forests or out to sea before the imperial army appeared. A good emperor was forced to set off on at least one large military campaign a year, and failure to do so would be interpreted as weakness.

Where the emperor failed to show the mailed fist, violence flared up. Rebellions had to be met with brutal force. Captured enemies were routinely blinded, maimed, tortured, or hanged. At Verdun, Charlemagne had beheaded forty-five hundred Saxon nobles as a punishment for revolt, and relocated entire populations to pacify them.

All of this was accepted as necessary behavior to impose order. When Louis, therefore, humbly bowed before the Pope and recited a laundry list of sins that included even minor offenses, it diminished the emperor in the eyes of both his subjects and his enemies. This was not the way an emperor was supposed to act. Charlemagne had wanted to bathe in the blood of his enemies; his son seemed to want to join a monastery.

On the northern frontier, the Vikings were well aware of this situation. Charlemagne's defenses, particularly the fortified bridges and army, were still formidable enough to blunt a large attack, but there were ominous signs that the situation would soon change. A Frankish bishop traveling through Frisia found help from 'certain northmen' who knew the routes up the rivers that flowed toward the sea. The Vikings were clearly aware of both harbors and sea routes, and the empire lacked a fleet with which it could defend itself.

The Franks, however, seemed oblivious to the danger. Life was more prosperous than it had been in many generations, and they were enjoying the benefits of imperial rule. The archbishop of Sens in northern France, confident in the protection of the emperor, had gone so far as to demolish the walls of his city to rebuild his church. The towns on the coast were equally vulnerable. A lively wine trade had developed along the Seine between Paris and the sea, and the coast of Frisia was dotted with ports. Thanks to the Frank's access to high quality silver – a commodity largely absent in Scandinavia – coins had replaced bartering and imperial markets were increasingly stockpiled with precious metals.

The only thing preventing a major attack was the confusion of Louis' Viking enemies. The Danish peninsula had been in turmoil since the death of Godfred. A warrior named Harald Klak had seized power, but after a short reign had been expelled by the slain Godfred's son Horik. Harald Klak appealed to Louis for help, slyly offering to convert to Christianity in exchange for aid. The emperor accepted, and in a sumptuous ceremony at the royal palace of Ingelheim, near Mainz, Harald and four hundred of his followers were dipped in the baptismal font. Louis the Pious stood in as Harald's godfather.

It was a triumphal moment for several reasons. Louis was clearly not the soldier his father was, but here was an opportunity to neutralize the Danes for the foreseeable future. If Harald could be installed on the Danish throne, and then Christianize his subjects, it would pacify the northern border.

The first part of the plan worked seamlessly. Harald was given land in Frisia and tasked with defending it against marauding Vikings, while an expedition to restore his throne was gathered. With a Frankish army at his back, he was able to force his rival, Horik, to recognize him as ruler. He then invited Louis to send a missionary to aid in the conversion of the Danes. The emperor chose a Saxon preacher named Ansgar, who immediately built a church in Hedeby.[37] At this point, however, Louis' grand policy began to collapse.

The Danes weren't particularly interested in Christianity, at least not as an exclusive religion. Nor it seems, were they interested in Harald Klak. After a year, he was again driven into exile by his adversary Horik, a stout pagan. To add insult to injury, Harald returned to his Frisian lands and took up piracy, spending his remaining years plundering his godfather's property.[38]

With the expulsion of Harald Klak, a dam seemed to break in the north, and raiders began to spill out over the Carolingian coast. Dorestad, the largest trading center in northern Europe and a main center of silver-minting, was

---

37 Ansgar was eventually canonized for his efforts and is known as the 'Apostle of the North'.

38 Louis' rebellious son Lothar later rewarded Harald Klak with an island for 'doing so much damage to his father.'

sacked every year from 834 to 837. Horik sent an embassy to Louis claiming that he had nothing to do with the attacks on Dorestad, but did mention that he had apprehended and punished those responsible. The latter claim, at least, was probably true. Successful raiders were potential rivals, and Horik had no desire to repeat Harald Klak's fate.[39]

Individual Vikings out for plunder needed no invitations from the king to attack. The Frankish empire was clearly tottering. Louis' tin-eared rule – exacerbated by an ill-thought out plan to include a son from his second marriage into the succession – resulted in a series of civil wars and his deposition at the hands of his remaining sons. Although he was restored to the throne the following year, his prestige never recovered.

The damage it did to his empire was immense. Not only were there lingering revolts – he spent the final years of his reign putting down insurrections – but the distractions allowed the Vikings to arrive in greater numbers. Multiple groups began to hit the coasts at the same time, burning villages, seizing booty, and carrying away the inhabitants, leaving only the old and sick behind.

In 836 Horik himself led a major raid on Antwerp, and when several of his warriors died in the assault, he had the nerve to demand *weregild* – compensation for his loss of soldiers.[40] Louis responded by gathering a large army, and the Vikings melted away, but only as far as Frisia where they continued to raid. In 840, the emperor finally ordered the construction of his father's North Sea fleet to challenge them, but died a few months later without accomplishing anything.

39 Ironically, however, it was this very policy that doomed him. He was assassinated a few years later by a nephew whom he had expelled for treason.

40 In modern day Belgium

Instead of unifying against the common threat, Louis' sons spent the next three years fighting for supremacy as the empire disintegrated around them. On occasion they even tried to use the Vikings to attack each other. The eldest sibling, Lothar, welcomed old Harald Klak into his court and rewarded him with land for raiding his brother's territory. This turned out to be an exceptionally bad idea, as it gave the Vikings familiarity with and access to Frankish territory. Harald, and streams of like-minded Vikings, happily plundered their way across the northern coasts of the empire.

These attacks depended on speed, not overwhelming force. By the mid ninth century the typical Viking "army" consisted of a few ships with perhaps a hundred men. Some men would be left to guard the ships while the rest fanned out to plunder. In these early days they weren't interested in prisoners, and would kill or burn anything that couldn't be taken.

The small numbers were a vulnerability, but this was made up for by the speed of the attacks. Most Vikings were reluctant to travel far from the coasts of the sea or river systems, and generally avoided pitched battles. Their equipment was more often than not inferior to their Frankish opponents; Vikings caught in open country were usually overwhelmed. This was partially because they lacked the armor common in Europe at the time. Frankish chronicles referred to them as 'naked', and they had to scavenge helmets and weapons from the dead since several Frankish rulers sensibly forbade the sale of weapons to the Vikings on pain of death.

The one exception to this general inferiority was Viking swords. The original design was probably copied from an eighth century Frankish source, a blacksmith named *Ulfberht* whose name soon became a brand. The Vikings quickly learned to manufacture the blades themselves, and weapons bearing the inscription Ulfberht have been found all over Scandinavia. They were typically double edged, with a rounded point, made of multiple bars of iron twisted together. This pattern welding created a relatively strong and lightweight blade that could be reforged if broken. They were clearly among a warrior's most prized possessions and were passed down as heirlooms and given names like "*Odin's Flame*" and "*Leg-Biter*".

Aside from their swords, the Vikings' main advantages lay in their sophisticated intelligence gathering and their terrifying adaptability. They had advance warning of most Frankish military maneuvers, and could respond quickly to take advantage of political changes. Most formidable of all, was their malleability. 'Brotherhoods' of dozens or even hundreds could combine into a larger army, and then re-dissolve into groups at will. This made it almost impossible to inflict a serious defeat on them, or even predict where to concentrate your defenses.

The Vikings were usually also more pragmatic than their opponents. They had no qualms about traveling through woods, used impromptu buildings like stone churches as forts, and dug concealed pits to disable pursuing cavalry. They attacked at night, and were willing – unlike the Frankish nobility – to get their hands dirty by digging quick trenches and earthworks. Most of all they could pick their prey and had exquisite timing. Earlier barbarians had avoided churches; the Vikings targeted them, usually during feast days when towns were full of wealthy potential hostages.

The Christian communities didn't stand a chance. The monastery of Noirmoutier, on an island at the mouth of the Loire, was sacked every year from 819 to 836. It became an annual tradition for the monks to evacuate the island for the spring and summer, returning only after the raiding season had ended. Finally, in 836 they had enough and carrying the relics of their patron saint – and what was left of the treasury – they fled east in search of a safe haven. For the next three decades they were driven from one refuge to the next until they finally settled in Burgundy near the Swiss border, about as far from the Vikings and the sea as one could get.

A monk of Noirmoutier summed up the desperation in a plea for his fellow Christians to stop their infighting and defend themselves:

> *"The number of ships grows larger and larger, the great host of Northmen continually increases... they capture every city they pass through, and none can withstand them... There is hardly a single place, hardly a monastery which is respected, all the inhabitants take to flight and few and far between are those who dare to say: 'Stay where you are, stay where you are, fight back, do battle for your country, for your children, for your family!' In their paralysis, in the midst of their mutual rivalries, they buy back at the cost of tribute that which they should have defended, weapons in hand, and allow the Christian kingdom to founder."*

The monk's advice went unheeded. By the time the Frankish civil war ended, Charlemagne's empire had dissolved into three kingdoms, each with their vulnerabilities brutally exposed. The western Frankish kingdom became the basis of the kingdom of France, the eastern, Germany, and the third – a thin strip of land between them called Lotharingia – was absorbed by its neighbors.[41] Viking raiding groups became larger and bolder. Instead of two or three ships traveling together, they were now arriving in fleets of ten or twelve. More ominously still, they began to change their tactics. In 845 they returned to the island of Noirmoutier, but this time, instead of the usual raid, they fortified the island and made it a winter quarters. The usual practice was to raid in the warmer months, and return home before the first snows fell. Now, however, they intended to stop wasting time in transit, and to be more systematic in the collection of loot.

Launching raids from their base, they could now penetrate further up rivers, putting more towns and even cities in range. Rouen, Nantes, and Hamburg were sacked, and Viking fleets plundered Burgundy. The next year they hit Utrecht and Antwerp, and went up the Rhine as far as Nijmegen. These raids all paled, however, before one that took place in 845 at the direction of the Danish king. He had not forgotten the Frankish support for his rival Harald Klak. Now Horik finally had his revenge.

---

41 Virtually the only remnant of it is the name of the modern French territory of Lorraine.

Chapter 3

RAGNAR LOTHBROK

"A cleaved head no longer plots"

\- Edda of Sæmund the Wise

Ragnar Lothbrok was undoubtedly the most colorful member of Horik's court. His surname *Lothbrok* means 'hairy breeches', a reference to a curious pair of hide leggings that he wore into battle and which, he claimed, offered him some sort of magical protection. According to one legend, he made them to win his first wife, who was being held prisoner by a dragon-like serpent. To save himself from its venomous bite he boiled a pair of leather pants in pitch, and rolled them in sand. This unorthodox garment protected him long enough to dispatch the beast and claim his bride.

Ragnar's actual origins are unknown.[42] He became the hero of so many later Viking sagas that his historical accomplishments have become obscured. Stories were told to fill in the gaps, most of them charming, and almost all certainly false. His second wife Aslaug – a woman so beautiful that bakers would let their bread burn while staring at her –

---

42 Although Ragnar is a historical figure, some historians consider 'Lothbrok' a creation of legend.

was, according to these stories, his equal in cunning. Ragnar, still grieving the death of his first wife, agreed to marry her if she could visit him 'neither dressed nor undressed, neither fasting nor satisfied, and neither in company nor alone'. She won his heart by appearing naked, but covered by her long hair, having eaten an onion the previous night, and with a sheepdog for company.

These stories would undoubtedly have pleased Ragnar. He claimed to be a direct descendant of the god Odin, which – since Horik claimed the same – was an oblique way of asserting his fitness for the throne. Rule in the Viking world, however, was a question of prowess more than ancestry, so in 845 Ragnar led a force of Vikings in an attack on Paris.

Ragnar was not a simple pirate. He was one of the first 'sea-kings'; a Viking who gained enough wealth and power through raiding to be recognized as a virtual king. A measure of the respect in which he was held was the size of his force. In a time when 'armies' were numbered in hundreds of men, Ragnar commanded over five thousand warriors in a fleet of a hundred and twenty longships.

Sailing south from Denmark, it took the sea wolves just over a week to reach the Seine river estuary. From there, they rowed upstream and pillaged Rouen and Carolivenna (modern Chaussy), roughly nine miles from the wealthy Abbey of St. Denis. His men helped themselves to whatever riches they could find and systematically plundered the fertile districts within easy reach of the river. Rumors of each fresh attack panicked the locals, and they and the monks of St. Denis fled, carrying their relics and valuables with them. However, they were met by the Frankish king Charles the Bald, who tried to stem the flood of refugees by ordering them back to their homes and churches. He had raised an army to confront the raiders, and advanced cautiously.[43]

Ragnar presented the king with a difficult choice. The Viking was well known for his blitzkrieg-like tactics to keep his enemies off balance, and only fought when the odds favored him. If Charles approached on one bank of the river, Ragnar and his men could just slip to the other side and avoid a battle. Since he wanted to force a showdown, the king split his forces and advanced along both banks.

Unfortunately for the Franks, Charles' army was not the premiere fighting force it had been in Charlemagne's day. Standards had fallen to such a degree that it now regularly fell into confusion, and was well known for its carelessness and inefficiency. Ragnar attacked the smaller section of the Frankish forces with his entire army, easily slaughtering it as the horrified Charles watched impotently from the other side of the river. Worse was to come. The captured Frankish soldiers – a hundred and eleven of them – were transported to an island in the Seine and hung in full view of Charles' army as a sacrifice to Odin.

This was equal part religious observation and equal part calculated strategy of psychological terror. To modern eyes, the Vikings appear appallingly brutal, but there were limits to their violence. They seldom willingly destroyed harvests and despite routine plundering never disturbed the vineyards of Aquitaine. There was much more money to be had in extortion. As far as the execution of prisoners, Charlemagne had done far worse with his Saxon captives at Verdun, where he had beheaded forty-five hundred of them as punishment for a revolt.

---

43 Louis the Pious' youngest son.

Ragnar's display had the desired effect. The Franks were unnerved, and easily routed when Ragnar charged at them. Charles was forced to withdraw with what was left of his army to the abbey of St. Dennis, which he vowed to defend at all costs. The presence of an army at his rear would normally have been worrying, but Ragnar had measured its quality and tellingly saw no reason to delay his approach to the now relatively undefended Paris.

In many ways, medieval Paris was the ideal Viking target. Not only was it rich, but it was largely confined to the Ile de la Cité, an island in the middle of the Seine. The first sight of the city, however, must have been momentarily disappointing. Despite Ragnar's strategy of attacking on a holy day when churches would be full of potential victims, news of their approach had preceded his army, and most of the population had already fled. The Vikings flooded in, spreading out through the streets in search of plunder. They had been raiding Europe for the better part of five decades, but never had they looted such a prize.

Thanks to advance warning, which enabled the monks to remove most of the valuables, the Abbey of St. Germain managed to escape most of the destruction. When they returned six weeks later, they found several of the outbuildings burned and superficial damage to the abbey church. The only real casualty was the wine-cellar, which the Vikings had managed to break into and empty.

The city itself proved to be as frustrating for the Vikings as the Abbey of St. Germain. Much of the expected treasure had been carried away into the surrounding countryside by the frightened inhabitants. They could send out raiding parties in search of it, but that opened them to the possibility of ambush or an assault by Charles' army.

In fact, every moment Ragnar spent in Paris, his situation worsened. The Frankish king had been collecting reinforcements, and was now at the head of a considerable army in a position to block the Viking escape. Even more worryingly was the fact that the Vikings were beginning to show signs of dysentery, which further reduced their fighting ability. From the deserted monastery of St. Germain-des-Prés, Ragnar reached out to Charles, hinting that he was willing to leave if offered a suitable tribute.

The Frankish king was in the mood to negotiate. Despite the size of his army, he had no confidence in its quality or in the loyalty of its commanders. He also had the headache of rebellious vassals, ambitious family members and chronic revolts. Ambassadors for both sides met in the monastery of St. Denis, and the Franks offered extraordinary terms. Not only could the Vikings keep their plunder and depart unmolested, but they would be paid nearly six thousand pounds of gold and silver for their trouble.

This is the first recorded example of what the English called *Danegeld* – literally 'Danish Money' – a series of increasingly ineffective bribes by desperate monarchs to get the Vikings to go away. Most of the money to pay for it would be commandeered from the church and then later from the people by means of a special tax. The very people who were bearing the brunt of the Viking attacks were now called upon to pay their tormentor's bribes. To add insult to injury, the Danegeld tended to increase rather than prevent Viking raids, since the offer of protection money simply attracted other Vikings. No matter how expedient his reasons, Charles was unwisely trusting gold to do the work of steel.

The only silver lining for the Parisians – although it must not have seemed so at the time – was that it took Charles nearly two months to raise the necessary money. During that time, dysentery took a serious toll on Ragnar's army. So many Vikings died, that the Parisians viewed it as a miracle, claiming that saint Germain was (belatedly) punishing the Norsemen for defiling his abbey.

As soon as Ragnar was paid, the spoils were loaded onto the ships, along with a heavy iron bar from the city gate to prove that he had taken the city. He proceeded in easy stages down the Seine, taking the time to plunder the trading and fishing ports along the coastline. He and his men arrived in Denmark fantastically wealthy, and with reputations to match. Ragnar himself presented the loot to king Horik, boasting about how easy it was to obtain. The only resistance he met, he reportedly said, was from the long-dead saint Germain. The implication was clear. The days of Charlemagne were gone. There was nothing now to fear from the Franks.

Ragnar may have been right about Charles the Bald, but not every Frankish ruler was weak. Charles' powerful half-brother, Louis the German, the immediate southern neighbor of Horik, was not amused by Viking raids, and had immediately sent a delegation to the Danish king to demand the return of all Frankish goods. This was no idle request. A word from Louis would send an imperial army flooding into Denmark, in numbers and quality that Horik couldn't hope to resist. Embarrassingly for the Viking king, these east Frankish delegates had been present for Ragnar's little speech, and they made it clear that if Horik wanted to prevent a war he would have to accept Louis the German as his overlord.

Horik had no choice but to give in. As galling as it might have been for him to submit, there was at least one upside.

He now had an official excuse to confiscate the spoils that had made Ragnar dangerously popular in Denmark. The Parisian loot was soon on its way to Louis the German along with all of the Dane's Christian prisoners, and although Horik had no control over individual Viking raiders – most of Ragnar's men seem to have left his territory – he did withdraw his official support for their attacks to mollify Louis the German. This submission seems to have been serious on Horik's part. Not only did he send regular gifts and embassies for the duration of his reign, but in a clever political move to get rid of potential rivals, he allegedly rounded up the few of Ragnar's men that had stayed in Denmark and had them executed.

Ragnar himself seems to have survived the purge, although accounts differ as to what exactly happened to him. The Franks claimed that he died of dysentery, but this is probably wishful thinking since he is mentioned by later English and Irish chroniclers as successfully raiding the shores of the Irish Sea as well as northern Scotland and the Western Isles.[44]

His exile, whether self-imposed or as a result of official banishment, provided fodder for his myth to grow; a legendary warrior haunting the shores of the Atlantic seaboard like an early Francis Drake. His wealth must have been the stuff of Viking dreams. In the twelfth century an inscription to him was carved into the wall of an ancient tomb in the Orkneys, an archipelago in northern Scotland by a traveling scholar: "*This mound was raised before Ragnar Lothbrok's (tomb)... His sons were brave, smooth hide men*

---

44 This has given rise to the theory that death by diarrhea was the origin of the nickname 'Lothbrok'. His feces-stained breeches, blackened and sticky, would have looked as if they had been boiled in pitch.

though they were... It was long ago that a great treasure was hidden here. Happy is he that might find it."

That reference to his sons, four boys who would follow in their father's footsteps, did not seem to have brought Ragnar much comfort. According to a thirteenth century Icelandic Saga, he admitted that his desire for fame and fortune was partly out of fear that his sons – especially his oldest, Ivar the Boneless – would eclipse him. Perhaps it was this that drove him relentlessly on.

In any event, the family was soon allowed to return to Denmark. In 854, Horik and most of the royal household were slaughtered by a disgruntled nephew, and the exiles were welcomed home. Ragnar may or may not have made the trip; his end is as obscure as his beginning. Almost all the stories, however, agree that he died as a proper Viking should: while raiding. Several stories are told of his demise, from being killed by a botched attack on the Isle of Anglesey, to dying in turf war with other Vikings off the coast of Ireland.

The most famous story, however, is that he was shipwrecked off the English coast in a freak storm. The Anglian king Aella of Northumbria, whose lands had been a favorite target of Viking raids, overwhelmed the survivors as they scrambled up the beach, and seized Ragnar. Relishing the opportunity to dispatch his tormentor, the king came up with a unique form of execution. Ragnar was thrown into a pit of vipers and left to die.[45] When his famous breeches protected him from the bites, Aella hauled him out, had him stripped, and threw him back in again. The old fox, now lying naked and mortally wounded, looked up at Aella unbowed, and sang a Viking battle hymn:

---

45 This would have been difficult, as England does not have a ready supply of poisonous snakes.

"It gladdens me to know that Odin makes ready the benches for a banquet. Soon we shall be drinking ale from the curved horns. The champion who comes into Valhalla does not lament his death. I shall not enter his hall with words of fear upon my lips. The Æsir will welcome me. Death comes without lamenting. Eager am I to depart. The Valkyries summon me home. I laugh as I die."

The Thirteenth century Icelandic Saga of Ragnar Lothbrok

His final words, gasped out as he was dying, were a warning to Aella. "*When the boar bleats, the piglets come.*"

The story is undoubtedly apocryphal, but it is true in at least one respect. Lindisfarne and Iona had only been a taste of the Viking storm that was about to break on England. When Ragnar's son Bjorn Ironside heard of his father's death, he supposedly gripped his spear so tightly that it left an impression in the wood; his younger brother Halfdan crushed a chess piece so forcefully that it made his fingers bleed. If the Northumbrian king did indeed kill Ragnar, then hopefully he enjoyed his triumph while it lasted. The piglets were on their way.

Chapter 4

THORGILS THE DEVIL

"The sea spewed forth floods of foreigners over Ireland, so that no haven, no landing-pace, no stronghold, no fort, no castle might be found, but it was submerged by waves of vikings and pirates."

– The Ninth century Irish chronicle, Annals of Ulster

The great Viking invasion of England originated at least partially in Ireland. Men of Horik and Ragnar's generation had looked to the Frankish kingdoms for their raids, but their children began to look for greener pastures to the west.

It wasn't that the Franks were getting any better at defending themselves, rather, the seemingly inexhaustible supply of Frankish gold was starting to dry up. Within fifteen years of Ragnar's raid on Paris, all the main rivers of western Francia had been visited by Viking raiders. At first they had conducted smash and grab maneuvers, seizing whatever communion vessels or reliquaries were on hand. Quickly, however, they had realized that there was more money to be had in extortion. The Abbot of St. Denis, for example, was ransomed for six hundred and eighty six pounds of gold and three thousand pounds of silver – quite a nice haul for a single prisoner.

Others found windfalls in mercenary activity. When some Vikings began raiding on the Seine, a Norseman named Weland offered to drive them off in exchange for two thousand pounds of silver and some livestock. Charles the Bald accepted, but took such a long time raising the funds that Weland upped his price to five thousand pounds. After it had been paid, he dutifully confronted the Seine raiders, but instead of attacking, he agreed to let them depart in peace for six thousand pounds of silver. Without unsheathing a sword, Weland had made himself a wealthy man.

By the end of the century more than forty thousand pounds of silver had been poured into Viking pockets, and Frankish kings were starting to debase their coinage. The coasts were beginning to be deserted as populations moved inland, and some religious communities were seeking refuge in more protected areas. Even worse, from the Viking perspective, was the fact that local resistance was beginning to stiffen.

To his credit, Charles the Bald had finally applied himself. His two main palaces were in northern France, near Picardy, and he began a systematic campaign to defend them. Fortified bridges were built across the Seine and the Loire, drastically diminishing the Vikings' ability to strike. The bridges acted as choke points on the river; they could be easily defended and prevented the Viking ships from moving further up rivers. The only way past them was to take them by seige, something which the typical lightly armed Viking raider was not equipped to do. Castles were built near the most threatened areas. These precautions didn't stop the attacks, but they succeeded in turning the tide, and the Vikings, faced with diminishing returns, began to look for easier targets.

In the years after Lindisfarne, most Viking attention had been directed toward the Frankish empire, but now it shifted back to the British Isles. While not as wealthy as the Frankish kingdoms, England, Scotland, and Ireland were politically divided and well stocked with monasteries. Ireland in particular, with its abundance of monastic houses was a tempting target. The island was overflowing with precious materials that had been exported to most of northern Europe. It had rich deposits of gold, silver, and copper, as well as emeralds, sapphires, amethysts, topaz, and freshwater pearls. High quality metalwork had been produced by Irish craftsmen since at least 2000 B.C., and 'Kerry diamonds' – glittering stones that could be found along the rocks of the coast – were used to adorn reliquaries, jewelry, and even book covers.

This native prosperity, coupled with Gaelic religious devotion, had produced a great cultural flowering. Ireland was in its golden age. Irish monasteries were bright centers of learning in an otherwise darkening Europe, producing gorgeous illuminated manuscripts and brilliant scholars who exported Irish learning to all corners of western Europe.

Politically, the island was slowly drifting towards a kind of unity as well. Tribal warfare was vicious, but over time a number of petty kingdoms had formed. These were loosely formed into two main confederations. The sub-kings of the north looked to the king of Tara, while those of the south were dominated by the kings of Munster. Traditionally, Tara was the more powerful of the two, and occasionally its sovereign was recognized as *Árd Rí*, or 'High King'.

This proto-unity, however, failed to prepare it for the Viking onslaught, because there were severe deficiencies when it came to defense. Most of the petty kings only paid lip service to their superior and even under a strong High King, the army was essentially uncontrollable. Any force that was fielded consisted of a number of tribes, each commanded by its own chief and acting as an independent unit rather than a cohesive whole. However brave or skilled individual soldiers might be, such an army was unreliable against a more disciplined opponent. Even if it could win a victory, it would be unable to exploit it.

While the Danes were busy pulling apart Charlemagne's empire, their Norwegian cousins rounded northern Scotland and hit Ireland. Just two years after the Lindisfarne raid, they sacked the great island monastery of St. Columba on the northwestern coast of Scotland. The communities of Skye, and Kells forty miles north of Dublin, were plundered in quick succession. The monks were slaughtered, the buildings were burnt, and most of the livestock was carried away. Within a decade the Vikings had rounded the northern headlands and begun plundering their way down the west coast bays.

These early raids, like their counterparts in England and the Carolingian Empire, were usually small, no more than two or three ships testing the resistance of the locals. They followed the by now familiar practice of favoring victims who were isolated and within easy reach of the sea. Even the most famous of Irish monasteries could be raided and left before any local fighting men showed up.

The success of the raids drew increasing numbers of Vikings and the next two decades saw a glut of assaults that sent the brilliant Irish renaissance up in flames. Even remote Skellig Michael, a seemingly impregnable monastery eight miles off the southwestern Irish coast and five hundred feet above sea level, was vulnerable. In 821 a group of Vikings managed to scale its craggy face, sack the gold-rich cloister, and kidnap the abbot.

Although this particular group of Vikings amused themselves by starving the holy man to death, others began to copy the Danes and look for ransoms. This extended to non-human objects as well. The first raiders had been drawn primarily to the gold and silver encrusted cases created for holy objects. The things they contained were of no use; relics were tossed aside, and the jeweled covers of books were pried off. The mutilated manuscripts were then tossed into fires, discarded in the mud or dumped into the sea.

Gradually, however, the Vikings realized that the Irish cared more for the relics and gospels than their coverings, and that they were willing to pay exorbitant sums to retrieve them. Even more valuable, were the Irish themselves. Those who were not important enough to be ransomed could be sold as slaves in Baltic or Islamic markets. Viking ships now began targeting human quarry. When the village of Howth, at the head of Dublin Bay, was attacked, the Vikings specifically targeted women, dragging off a large number to their ships. Attacks on Kildare brought in two hundred and eighty captives, while Armagh yielded a thousand.[46]

The psychological impact of these new tactics so thoroughly unnerved Irish monks that they began to pray for bad weather. In the margins of a commentary on Latin

---

46 The most famous example of a Viking slave is probably the Irish saint Findan. He was captured by the Vikings twice but managed to escape when they stopped in the Orkney Islands. He wandered through continental Europe, eventually settling in Switzerland where he lived out the last two and a half decades of his life.

grammar, a ninth century monk in the Irish monastery of St. Gall wrote: "*The wind is fierce tonight, it tosses the sea's white hair. I fear no wild Vikings crossing the main.*"

As miles of undefended coastline were plundered, rumors of richer prizes further inland began to reach Viking ears, and their raids became more daring. In 828 they reached Ireland's east coast, venturing up the Boyne river into Louth where they captured a local king.

Not all of these raids were successful. While exploring the west coast, the crew of one ship was massacred, and another was driven off by angry monks. But instead of winning the beleaguered defenders a respite, these failed attempts were always followed by attacks in greater numbers. When the monks of one monastery sent troops to defend their property, it merely alerted the Vikings to the presence of treasure. The next year saw three raids in a single month, all of which were successful.

Attacks began to shift from sporadic, unorganized hits on the monasteries of the coast, to large scale, efficient penetrations up rivers to inland targets. On Christmas Eve of 836, a group of daring Vikings travelled more than twenty miles inland through the difficult terrain of the Avonmore valley to sack the central monasteries of Glendalough and Clonmore. That same night, a hundred and sixty miles away in the north-east, another party of Vikings hit Connacht, seizing the monastery's most valuable relics which had been brought out for high mass.

That year also saw the appearance of Thorgils, the most notorious of all Viking raiders.[47] The Irish called him Turgeis, the Gaelic form of his name, and he arrived with

---

47 The Old Norse name was Thorgísl which can be rendered either as Thorgest or Thorgils.

so many ships that Irish chroniclers referred to them as a 'royal fleet'. He seems to have had dynastic connections in Scandinavia, and was accepted as the leader of all the Vikings in Ireland. In 839 he set his sights on the island's holiest shrine.

The Irish version of Jerusalem was Armagh in northern Ireland. St. Patrick himself had chosen it as the spiritual center of Gaelic Christianity, had been appointed as its first Bishop, and had died and was buried there. Many of his personal effects were kept as relics, and over the years the area around his tomb had developed into a massive complex of schools, monasteries, and a cathedral.

Thorgils personally led the attack, slaughtering the monks and students who had been unable to escape in time. The altars were shattered, the tombs and reliquaries were hacked open, and the relics torn apart in the search for valuables. As an encore, Thorgils smashed his way into St. Patrick's cathedral and conducted a sacrifice to Odin on what was left of the high altar.

The outrage ensured that the Viking sea-king became the most despised figure in Ireland. To the Irish he was a cruel and monstrous servant of Satan, a blasphemous tormentor who must be stopped at all costs. Thorgils, however, was unlike any other Viking that they had as yet faced. He had greater plans than simply grabbing loot. He anointed himself 'King of all Foreigners in Erin' and it seems that he aimed at the outright conquest of the entire island.

His timing couldn't have been better. The sub-king of Munster had attempted to claim the high-kingship, but had only succeeded in plunging central Ireland into chaos. By capturing Armagh, Thorgils had found the resources necessary to make a sustained push into the interior. Instead of simply plundering the monastery, however, he set himself up as its new master, and started collecting the customary duties. The holiest site in Ireland to all intents and purposes now had a pagan abbot.

Viking fleets were sent up rivers and along the shoreline to weaken resistance. So many of his ships prowled the coasts that monks began to complain that there was no place without a fleet of Vikings.

While his forces were busy eroding the strength of the native Irish kings, Thorgils began looking for a more defensible location to base his operations. On the east coast of Ireland, in a sheltered bay of the Irish Sea, he built a *longphort* – a shore fortress – and spent the winter in Ireland. It was an ideal location, easily defended and offering immediate access to the sea. Located on a splendid natural harbor at a spot that offered a convenient fording place across the Liffey River, it lay within direct reach of both the interior of Ireland and the west coast of Britain. The local name for the spot was "the black pools" – "Dubh-Linn" in Gaelic – and it stuck. Thorgils laid down heavy timbers for the streets and built houses in the Viking fashion with wickerwork and mud-daubed walls. Surrounding these was a thick, earthen wall, topped with a wooden palisade. Dublin was not meant to be a simple base of operations. It became the center of the first Viking state established in western Europe, with Thorgils as its 'king'.[48]

From these headquarters, Thorgils stepped up his attacks. In 844 he led sixty ships up the Shannon River to present day Limerick. From there he split up his forces to sack sacred sites throughout central and western Ireland. Thorgils himself burned the monastery of Clonfert and then attacked

---

48 The northern district of Dublin is still called Fingall, meaning 'place of the Fair Foreigners', the Irish name for the Vikings.

the abbey of Clonmacnoise, famous throughout Europe for its seminary.

Here Thorgils seems to have repeated his earlier behavior at Armagh. After killing the monks and looting the abbey, he brought his wife Ota into the main church. Wiping off the splattered gore, Thorgils helped Ota to climb on top of the shattered high altar. She was known as a *völva* or prophetess, and from her perch she amused the assembled Vikings by demonstrating her gift of prophecy in a ceremony to Odin.

The ritual defilement of the two holiest places in Ireland was not a coincidence. Thorgils was asserting the supremacy of the Viking gods, and doing so in a manner which would have shaken the faith of the medieval Irish mind. A monk in the south lamented that "many of the Irish forsook their Christian baptism and joined the 'fair foreigners' in plundering churches."[49]

By the end of the decade, Ireland was in serious danger of being completely overrun. Its petty kings were too involved with their own feuds to unite, so clerics began to take the field. The abbot of Terryglass was killed leading the local militia, and the abbot of Armagh was captured together with the relics of St. Patrick. It seemed only a matter of time before the Vikings would have the entire island in their grip.

It came as a profound relief, both spiritually and physically therefore, that in 845 Thorgils was captured by the high king of Tara, Mael Seachlinn. How the king managed to do this remains somewhat of a mystery. It's only recorded that Thorgils was seized through trickery and

49 The 'Fragmentary Annals of Ireland', a tenth century chronicle from the kingdom of Osraige, present-day County Kilkenny.

not battle. The hated Viking was tied up, weighed down with stones, and thrown into a river to drown.[50]

The death of Thorgils ended the Viking dream of ruling a united, pagan Ireland, and it also shattered the Vikings themselves. The first raiders had been Norwegian, but now Danes were beginning to show up in increasing numbers, and tensions between the two groups had reached boiling point. The death of Thorgils removed the lone figure respected by both sides, and in 850 a Viking civil war broke out over the control of Dublin.

The Irish were the main beneficiaries of the struggle between the *Dubgaill* ('black foreigners' *ie* Danes) and the *Findgaill* ('white foreigners' *ie* Norwegians). In the first year of the war a Danish force managed to batter its way over the walls and sack Dublin, but the Norwegians counterattacked, slaughtering the Danes in a bloody three-day battle. Adding to the chaos was a third group, the offspring of mixed marriages between Irish and Vikings who were called *Gallgoidel* or 'foreign Irish'.[51] The Gallgoidel fought for whichever side offered them a better deal, and most often as mercenaries for themselves.

Gradually, the native Irish began to drive the distracted Vikings back to the coasts. The High King, Mael, crushed a Viking army attempting to enter his territory, leaving seven hundred dead on the field. The same year, one of the king's allies caught a raiding party of two hundred and wiped them out. King

---

50   This was a dissatisfying end to Ireland's great tormentor, so the Irish made up a much better story. The High King lured the Vikings onto an island in the middle of the Lough Owel river by promising Thorgils and fifteen of his men beautiful brides - in reality young Irish soldiers in drag. When the Vikings went to embrace their new wives, the 'women' threw off their disguises and stabbed the Vikings to death.

51   The modern area of Galloway in Ireland derives its name from this word.

Mael even reached out to Charles the Bald, seeking a military alliance against the Vikings.

While the Vikings were entrenched enough to defend themselves against native assaults – Dublin was attacked six times, each with disastrous results for the Irish – the real threat to their security came from within. The leader of the Norwegians was Olaf the White, the son of a Norwegian warlord who had arrived in Dublin the year of Thorgils' death. The Danes, on the other hand, were led by his distant kinsman Ivar the Boneless, eldest son of Ragnar Lothbrok.

It's unclear when exactly Ivar reached Ireland, but the Danes rallied behind him. Of all of Ragnar's children, Ivar the Boneless was the most enigmatic. The Vikings themselves had contradictory legends about the meaning of his nickname. Some claimed that he was born completely without bones, but had supernatural strength and height, others that his legs had only gristle, forcing him to be carried into battle on a shield.[52] Since it's highly unlikely that the Vikings would have respected a handicapped person, or that he would have had such a long and successful career of raiding with such a disability, a more likely explanation is that he was double-jointed. Such flexibility would be useful on the battlefield, and given his family's connection with snakes – his brother was named Sigurd-snake-in-the-eye – it would have been an apt description.

What all the Sagas do agree on, however, is that Ivar was remarkably cunning. "It is doubtful", Ragnar's Saga claimed, "if anyone has ever been wiser than he." His actions in Dublin seem to support this. Arriving in Dublin in force,

---

52   This was supposedly due to a curse. His mother Aslaug had been told by Odin to wait three days before consummating her marriage. Ragnar, however, wouldn't wait and as a result his son's bones were replaced by cartilage.

he offered to split command of the city with his rival rather than weaken both of them in a protracted struggle. Olaf agreed, and the two of them took the joint title of king.

Neither Viking ruler was interested in pursuing Thorgils' old dream of conquering Ireland. It had become clear that much of Ireland was practically beyond the Viking reach. The bogs and forests of the interior were too treacherous for bands of Vikings to penetrate, and the past several decades had warned the Vikings from wandering too far from the coasts. There were, however, more tempting opportunities elsewhere.

Since its founding around the year 841, Dublin had quickly prospered, becoming one of the busiest trading ports of the Viking world. Other Viking longphorts in Limerick, Waterford, Wexford, and Cork were also flourishing, but none as quickly as Dublin. It was already connected to the main commercial centers in Norway, England, and the Frankish kingdoms, and was a regular port of call for Vikings raiding throughout the North Atlantic.

Perhaps it was from these sources that knowledge of the rich kingdoms to the east first filtered through to Ivar. Or perhaps, he really was out to satisfy a blood debt for the death of his father. Either way, in 865 Ivar the Boneless decided to invade England.

Chapter 5

THE GREAT HEATHEN ARMY

"Pagans from the northern regions came... like stinging hornets and spread on all sides like fearful wolves."

- Anglo-Saxon Chronicle

Unlike its unfortunate neighbors to the south and west, England had hitherto largely escaped the attentions of Viking raiders in the ninth century. There had been sporadic raids since the attack on Lindisfarne, but these had been relatively small and limited operations. Most monasteries were on the alert, and when one was raided, the other communities would usually scatter, ruining the chances of the Vikings obtaining further loot. In 825, for example, word reached the monks of Iona that there were raiders in the area. Most of the community fled, carrying the relics of St. Columba and the other portable treasures with them. Only the abbot and a handful of monks stayed behind to tend to the priory church. A few days later the Vikings struck, bursting into the church in the middle of a Mass. The monks were butchered immediately, but the abbot was kept alive and questioned as to where he had hidden the valuables. When he refused to divulge the secret, the Vikings hacked off his limbs on the steps of the high altar and left him to die.

As brutal as these attacks were, however, they had been mercifully rare. This was at least in part due to the fact that the English were more politically organized than their Irish neighbors. Political organization, however, had not kept Charlemagne's empire safe, and it could only deter major Viking attacks in Britain for so long. In the 830's the raids began to intensify. The first years of the decade saw Vikings off the Kentish coast where they overran the island of Sheppey. For the next fifteen years, the Vikings used this as a base to raid and interfere in English politics. When Cornwall revolted against the West Saxons, the Vikings assisted them, eroding the power of Wessex. The West Saxon king, Egbert, raised an army to confront them but was soundly defeated. After brushing aside another army of Wessex men, the Vikings ravaged East Anglia and Kent, and sacked the city of Rochester. In 844, they extended their reach into Northumbria, restoring an ousted king by killing his rival.

In 850, their tactics – as they had elsewhere – abruptly changed from seasonal raiding to outright conquest. That autumn they seized the island of Thanet off the Kentish coast, and wintered there. The presence of 350 ships at the mouth of the Thames so alarmed the West Saxon king Aethelwulf that he sent his son Alfred to Rome to petition God's support.[53]

Fortunately for Wessex – in the short term at least – the Vikings decided to target the other major state, Mercia which had absorbed most of its smaller neighbor Essex. Several hundred of them stormed Canterbury and burned London, forcing the Mercian king Berhtwulf to muster his army. Normally, the Vikings avoided pitched battles, but

---

53   The future Alfred the Great

this time they had the numbers to feel confident. After a brief struggle, the Mercian shield wall broke, and Berhtwulf and his army fled.

Instead of continuing deeper into Mercia, however, the Vikings crossed into Surrey to break the power of Wessex. Yet, this time, instead of an overwhelming victory, they suffered a crushing defeat at the hands of king Aethelwulf and his sons. The Anglo-Saxon Chronicle gushed that it was "*the greatest slaughter ever heard of.*"[54] It must not have been too crushing, though, for the next year the Vikings tried again. This time they attacked the West Saxon capital of Winchester, but were again driven off.

The campaign taught the Vikings several valuable lessons. The first was that there was much plunder to be had. London and Canterbury in particular had been rich targets, and there were sure to be more such cities further inland. Second, it also revealed the relative strengths of the four English kingdoms. A Viking force could stand against a royal army in the field and come out the victor. They had failed only because they had lacked a unified strategy, and had been severely outnumbered. Ivar's attempt would correct these mistakes.

In 865, Ragnar's son launched the largest invasion of the British Isles in recorded history. He sailed from Dublin with two of his brothers, Halfdan 'of the wide embrace' and Ubba, as well as his colleague Olaf the White. Navigating their way along the southern coast, they landed in East Anglia without opposition. The locals immediately raised a sum of money to bribe them to go away; the first example of Danegeld in England. Ivar took their money, but had no intention

---

54 Not surprisingly, the French were less impressed. A Frankish chronicle reported rather laconically that the Vikings were 'beaten with the aid of Christ'.

of leaving. He had command of a force so massive that the English referred to it simply as "the great heathen army".[55]

Unlike previous Viking forces, this was not just a collection of war bands, but was under the unified command of a single leader and his ruthless lieutenants. It was highly mobile and could break into component parts and reform according to terrain or need.

Tremendous planning had gone into the creation of the army. Men had been recruited from the Norwegian fjords, the Frisian islands, the western Baltic, and Denmark. They were drawn both by the lure of wealth and, now for the first time, the possibility of acquiring land. Ivar seems to have intended to settle on English soil and to rule as a major king to rival the warlords in Scandinavia. His colleague, Olaf the White, would most likely return in Dublin once the fighting was done. In fact, Olaf quickly broke off from the main army and confined himself to the western Scottish and Welsh coasts, territory which could be safely controlled from Ireland.

Ivar's plan was to pick off the Anglo-Saxon kingdoms one by one. His first order of business was to gather supplies for the coming campaigning season. In its entry for the year 865, the Anglo-Saxon Chronicle compactly describes his success in intimidating the locals into giving him what he needed: "*A great heathen army came into England and took up winter quarters in East Anglia; and there were supplied with horses and the East Angles made peace with them.*"

The Vikings stayed in East Anglia well into the next year, systematically stripping the surrounding countryside of its food. When the autumn harvest approached, Ivar

---

55 Modern estimates put it around three thousand fighting men – although the numbers would vary dramatically over the years.

commandeered it, then finally (after accepting yet another round of bribes) ordered his men to ride north along an old Roman road.

Intriguingly, considering the legends about how Ivar's father had met his end, the Viking's target was the kingdom of Northumbria. The Northumbrians had recently driven out their king and replaced him with a tyrant named Aella – the man who had allegedly killed Ragnar Lothbrok. Now Ragnar's sons had come for a reckoning.

Ivar, however, wouldn't have needed to march north out of filial loyalty. The Vikings were well acquainted with the northernmost kingdom. Its main city of York, positioned on a tributary of the Humber, led directly to the North Sea, and had been a site of trade between England and the rest of Europe since ancient times. Over the years, an international merchant community plying wine and other perishable commodities, had grown up in the city, and by the mid-ninth century it probably had its share of Scandinavians who had arrived as merchants since the city was too well fortified to be taken by the usual small Viking party. Capturing the city had clear benefits; surrounded by rich farmlands, and located half way between Dublin and the coastline of north-west Europe, it was also connected to ports on the west coast by the well maintained Roman roads. If the Vikings took York, they would have access to multiple trading centers and be able to avoid the treacherous six-hundred mile sea route around the north of Scotland.

The great heathen army arrived before York's walls on All Saint's Day, November 1, 866. Deciding that discretion was the better part of valor, Aella fled, withdrawing to the territory of his ousted predecessor so the two could pool their resources. Unfortunately for York, it took more than four and a half months for the joint army to reach the city, and by that time the Vikings had firmly dug in.

It was at York, that Ivar the Boneless first showed his cunning. Instead of marching out to meet the two kings, he lured them into the city by purposely neglecting a section of the walls. The Anglo-Saxon army poured in, only to find a labyrinth of carefully prepared traps, and confusing dead-ends. In the street fighting that followed, the English were wiped out and both kings were killed. What was left of the royal court fled north to Scotland.

If Aella really did kill Ragnar, then Ivar must have relished the opportunity for revenge. The Anglo-Saxon Chronicle merely states that 'the kings of Northumbria were slain', but the Norse sagas recount a more grisly end. Aella was captured alive and brought before Ivar who ordered that he be subjected to the dreaded 'blood-eagle' as a sacrifice to Odin.[56] The king was stripped to the waist and tied down to the ground. A Viking warrior hacked at his ribs, breaking them and cutting a deep incision down either side of the spine. The lungs were then pulled out through the wounds and allowed to quiver like a pair of blood-stained wings until the writhing king expired.

The stories tend to get more lurid with each telling – the latest version had Ivar pouring salt in Aella's wounds – but Northumbria certainly suffered the most of any English kingdom under Viking domination.[57] Ivar clearly saw it as

---

56 There is considerable debate about the blood eagle. Since no contemporary account of its use exists, some have concluded that it is the fanciful invention of later writers.

57 The brutality extended to both sides. Several towns in southeastern England supposedly upholstered their church doors with the flayed skins of captured Vikings. Although it is almost certainly false, even Westminster Abbey in London at one time boasted decorations of Viking hides.

a launching pad for a systematic destruction of the other three kingdoms. To lessen native resistance and free his army up for a sustained push south, he installed an Englishman named Egbert on the throne. Although he had the title of king, Egbert was nothing more than a glorified tax collector for the Vikings. Those who refused to voluntarily contribute to their coffers simply had their land and money seized.

With the north more or less pacified, the Vikings turned on the neighboring kingdom of Mercia. The city of Nottingham fell with barely a struggle, and as he had done at York, Ivar began to fortify the walls in order to use the city as a base. As a measure of his confidence, the Vikings spent that winter in the camp away from their ships.

When news of the invasion reached the Mercian king, Burghred, he wisely asked the king of Wessex, Athelred, for help. The two kingdoms were used to working together. Their military alliance had been sealed fourteen years before when Burghred had married Athelred's sister, and had given a Mercian wife to Athelred's brother, Alfred. When the appeal for aid came, both brothers responded, leading Wessex's large army to assist Mercia.

The next spring, the royal partners marched immediately to Nottingham and attempted to take it by storm. This was the Anglo-Saxon's best opportunity to defeat the Vikings. The English army was considerably larger than Ivar's force, and were fighting to defend their homes. The Vikings, on the other hand were looking for plunder - and intended to survive to enjoy it. At the first sign that they might lose the battle they would run, not make some noble last stand. Even better, from the English perspective, Ivar had foolishly left his ships, and was now cut off from reinforcements or communication with other war bands. Without the ability to replenish his forces, each Viking casualty would seriously degrade his ability to continue.

Ivar was now presented with a difficult choice. If he attacked, the risks were obvious. Although his outnumbered troops were undoubtedly of higher quality than the English, even the best-case scenario involved heavy casualties. If, on the other hand, he stayed behind his walls, he flirted with starvation and disease.

The issue of supplies is the unappreciated lynchpin of any campaign. As Napoleon said, "*an army travels on its stomach*". To sustain a force of a thousand men, Ivar had to come up with at least two tons of unmilled flour, and a thousand gallons of fresh water per day.[58] Supplying his animals made it even more difficult. The five hundred English horses that he had commandeered were smaller than modern cavalry ones, but each would have had a daily requirement of twelve pounds of grain and at least thirteen pounds of hay, adding up to more than six tons per day.[59] There were also serious hygienic concerns with keeping five hundred animals within the confines of the fort. Although horses eat and drink large amounts, they retain very little of it. If properly fed, Ivar's animals would have produced at least two hundred and eighty gallons of urine, and a ton of manure per day.

Despite these obstacles, Ivar cleverly chose to stay behind his walls. The English had similar problems of supply, and since there were more of them, it was likely to become acute rather more quickly. Additionally, the Anglo-Saxon militia was composed of peasants who had limited terms of service under arms, and couldn't stay away from their farms indefinitely. If Ivar could come

---

58 It should be noted that this diet is a bare minimum. Daily meals of nothing but cold gruel and water wouldn't have kept morale very high.

59 They had been brought over by the Romans in the Claudian invasion of AD 43.

up with enough food to bide his time, the English army would simply melt away.

Fortunately for Ivar the tactic worked brilliantly. The Wessex men were needed for the urgent business of bringing in the harvest, and as the days passed the levies began to drift home. Ivar had gambled that his professional warriors could sustain restricted diets longer than their peasant opponents, and had demonstrated superior administrative skills in rationing supplies than the unwieldy Anglo-Saxon army.

The Mercian part of the army grimly hung on, but it was suffered from desertions, and morale was low. When it had been softened up enough, Ivar proposed a truce. The terms aren't known, but the Vikings withdrew to York, probably with a payment and some sort of acknowledgement of Burghred's client status.

Ivar seems to have had pressing business in Dublin because he left the army under his younger brother Ubba's command, and crossed the Irish Sea. Without him, the great heathen army confined itself to securing its grip on Northumbria. A year of relative peace followed, allowing the fleeting belief that some sort of stability had been achieved. One English kingdom had been conquered and another maimed, but perhaps the Viking assault had been checked. In 869, however, Ivar slipped back into England and rejoined the army with fresh plans.

Of the two remaining independent kingdoms, East Anglia was the more tempting prize. Control of its coasts would give Viking ships shelter from the North Sea, and its rivers – most notably the Thames – gave access to the great river systems that penetrated deep into central England. Ivar opened the campaign by splitting his forces in two. While his brother Ubba led the army down the Roman road from York, he sailed along the coast, wreaking havoc in towns along the way. His objective was to link up with Ubba at the East Anglian capital of Thetford, and force the submission of its king.

Thanks to the Roman road, which was still in good repair despite the five centuries that had passed since its construction, Ubba made good time. He reached the city of Peterborough in early autumn and burned it, taking special care to slaughter any clergy he found.[60] From there he headed into the Fens, a large, nearly impassable marsh, which separated Peterborough from the strategically vital cities of Thetford and Cambridge.

Thetford was a kind of religious and political capital – the East Anglian king Edmund had a palace there – but Cambridge was undoubtedly more important. As far back as the first century A.D., it had been recognized as a crucial spot: the surrounding area is boggy, but Cambridge rises to firm ground and provides the most practical crossing of the Cam River for many miles. The Romans, recognizing the superb location, connected the road from London in the south to York in the north through Cambridge. In addition to its trade and military value on land, the city was also an important port since the river is navigable all the way to the North Sea. Cambridge, therefore, dominated both the land and sea communications of the entire border.

King Edmund probably called up his peasant levies as soon as he heard of the sacking of Peterborough, but they did not have the time to arrive. While he had been focused on the Viking land army, Ivar the Boneless had arrived with the fleet. After a short skirmish between the king's

---

60 According to the local chronicle there was only one survivor. He was captured, but managed to escape while Ubba was distracted.

housecarls and the Vikings, Edmund managed to escape to his stronghold in the city.

Ivar sent a messenger to the king with the usual request – a healthy bribe and acknowledgement by Edmund that he was now a client king. Edmund foolishly, if bravely, refused, adding that he would submit only if Ivar would accept Christianity. The king was negotiating from a position of weakness, a point which was soon made brutally clear. Ivar sent more men and this time Edmund was seized, bound in chains, and beaten severely with iron rods.

The king, now naked and bleeding, was dragged before Ivar, but still refused to submit, calling on Christ to deliver him. This annoyed Ivar to such an extent that he ordered Edmund to be tied to a tree and instructed his men to see how many arrows they could shoot without killing him. When he was 'bristling like a hedgehog' Ivar finally put him out of his misery by decapitating him. The body was left where it fell, but the head was thrown into a nearby wood.[61]

The kingship of East Anglia devolved to Edmund's younger brother, Edwold, but he sensibly fled and became a hermit, ending the royal line. Ivar again appointed a native client king, and collected tribute. By this time, he had shattered three of the four English kingdoms; only Wessex remained.

Ivar, however, decided not to take on Wessex immediately since he was needed elsewhere. His old Dublin colleague, Olaf the White, had requested his aid in storming Dumbarton Rock in Scotland, so Ivar left his brother, Halfdan, in

---

61   According to legend, Edward the Martyr's head was found by some locals who were assisted in finding it by the howls of a large wolf. They found the head safely between the beast's paws, and were allowed to retrieve it and reunite it with the body. Unfortunately the head's human guardians were not as capable. It was stolen in the thirteenth century by some French knights.

command of the great heathen army and returned to Northumbria with his Irish Vikings.

The fortress of Dumbarton was the capital of Strathclyde, an ancient native kingdom covering most of modern southwest Scotland. Over the years it had repulsed numerous attempts to take it by storm since its garrison had access to a deep well and could therefore outlast most besieging forces. Therefore, when the Vikings arrived at the end of the summer, the defenders could realistically hope that worsening weather would drive them away before their supplies ran out.

The two Viking allies reached Dumbarton from opposite directions. Olaf's fleet had sailed up the Firth of Clyde while Ivar had taken the overland route from York.[62] The Norwegians and Danes had no trouble making common cause, especially since Dumbarton offered much plunder if it could be taken. As it turned out, the siege was unexpectedly short. Somehow, the Vikings figured out how to draw off the well water, and within four months the parched defenders surrendered.

They regretted their decision immediately. The Vikings had come for loot, and were not in a ransoming mood.[63] Most of the garrison was killed and the citadel was thoroughly plundered and then razed. So much wealth was gathered that some two hundred ships were needed to haul it off. The unfortunates that survived were transported to Dublin where they were packed onto slave ships and sent to the Islamic markets of Spain.

62　He had stopped long enough to raid a monastery. The nuns, in an attempt to preserve their virginity, supposedly cut off their noses and upper lips. Ivar set fire to the building, nuns and all.

63　The exception was the king of Strathclyde who was taken back to Dublin while a suitable ransom was raised. Unfortunately for him, it was offered by a political enemy – not to rescue but to murder him.

Ivar returned to his Irish capital in triumph. By now, he was the most famous Viking living, the greatest of the sea-kings. In 871 he took the unwieldy but impressive title '*King of the Northmen of all Ireland and Britain*", and Olaf seems not to have contested it. As Ragnar Lothbrok had long ago feared, Ivar had surpassed his father. Two years later he died peacefully, having had, as Winston Churchill put it, "the best of both worlds" – unconquered in war, and immensely rich.

It isn't clear where he died, but at least one legend claims that he wanted to be buried in England – a plausible enough story since it was the site of his most famous triumphs.[64] His death left a leadership void, but there were plenty of able candidates. Olaf the White was his natural successor in Dublin, and his brothers Halfdan and Ubba would continue the work in England. In fact, they had already started. Even before Ivar had conquered Strathclyde, the final assault on Wessex had begun.

---

64   His corpse was allegedly transported from Dublin and interred in English soil. In the seventeenth century a grave was found in Repton containing the intact skeleton of a remarkably large man - supposedly nine feet tall - surrounded by the disarticulated remains of two hundred and fifty Vikings. Since it dates from the right time, and is clearly a figure of importance, some have speculated that the bones are - ironically given his nickname - the remains of Ivar the Boneless.

Chapter 6

ENGLAND UNDER SIEGE

"One who sees his friend roasted on
a spit tells all he knows."

- Edda of Sæmund the Wise

The only remaining independent English kingdom was tottering. King Aethelwulf of Wessex, an unambitious and unimpressive ruler, had died in 858, leaving four surviving sons to succeed him. None of them seemed particularly inspiring. The eldest, Aethelbald, married his widowed step-mother to shore up his credentials, but died two years later. The crown then passed to the second son, who, after a short rule, had the good fortune to expire the year the great heathen army landed in England. That left the last two brothers, Athelred and Alfred to face the Viking onslaught.

They both had experienced Viking opponents first hand at the siege of Nottingham three years before, and had learned two valuable lessons. The first was that peasant armies make reluctant soldiers unless they are defending their own homes. Their unwillingness to stay and fight in Mercia had dictated the retreat more than any command given by king Athelred. The second lesson was one of logistics. Calling up an army was much easier than provisioning it, and neither brother had the administrative experience yet to pull it off. In

871, therefore, news that the great heathen army under the command of Halfdan Ragnarson had crossed into Wessex territory, probably sent a ripple of fear through the kingdom.

Halfdan had spent the previous winter gathering supplies, probably linking up with other Vikings who had crossed from the continent and were ravaging Kent. In the late autumn he marched west in search of the royal army of Wessex, intending to break its will in a single battle. The two brothers dispatched a local *fyrd* (peasant levy) to occupy them while the entire army was mustered.

The English force surprised one of Halfdan's foraging parties near Reading and after a short skirmish, the Vikings withdrew. The Saxons, believing that they had forced the entire heathen army to retreat, now moved in for the kill. Athelred and young Alfred jointly led the army to Reading where they found only a light guard outside the walls. Seizing the moment, they attacked.

Alfred's biographer, a Welsh monk named Asser, recounted what happened next in his *Life of King Alfred*: "*When they had reached the gate (of Reading) by hacking and cutting down all the Vikings they had found outside, the Vikings fought no less keenly; like wolves they burst out of all the gates and joined battle with all their might. Both sides fought there for a long time and fought fiercely, but, alas, the Christians eventually turned their backs, and the Vikings won the victory and were masters of the battlefield.*"

The loss was shattering to morale. Athelred and Alfred only evaded capture by slipping across a little-known ford of the Thames. The English army was scattered. The Vikings, as the fleeing king and his brother could now appreciate, were experts at defending fortified camps. They had demonstrated this at York and Nottingham in opposite ways, and now had used Reading's multiple gates to stage a lightning counterattack.

The only silver lining was that the Wessex army had fled, rather than been destroyed. Halfdan, who had already spent more than a week at Reading, had to keep moving. He needed to break the Saxon army in order to crush Wessex, and that meant hunting Athelred and Alfred. He also needed to strike quickly while morale was low and before reinforcements could arrive.

Athelred regrouped his forces at Abingdon Abbey, where there were fresh supplies and spiritual support for the shaken army. Unless they traveled by water, it would have been nearly impossible for Halfdan to disguise his movements, and he seems to have made no effort to do this. Just four days after the battle at Reading, Athelred was informed that the Viking army was moving towards him along an old Roman road.

Out in the open, Halfdan wanted to avoid a serious battle unless he was sure of victory. For this reason he was staying close to the Thames river and access to his ships. The English brothers moved to intercept him, positioning their army at Ashdown, near an old Roman road.

The Vikings reached the Saxon lines just before noon. Seeing that his enemy held the high ground, Halfdan split his forces in two and attempted to outflank the English. Alfred, who had been watching for just such a maneuver, asked his brother for permission to split their army in the same way and fall on both halves at once. He appeared to have given quick permission for his brother to act, for Alfred's division immediately threw themselves at the Vikings.

The fury of the attack seems to have caught the Vikings completely by surprise. Just four days earlier they had scattered this same army with ease, but now they were being driven steadily back. Motivated by the defense of their own farmlands, the English fought with desperate courage. As the Vikings retreated up a hill, Alfred charged 'like a young boar' after them, shattering the Norse shield wall. The Vikings, now hopelessly disorganized, turned and fled.

To the English, it was a miraculous victory of crushing significance. Alfred's biographer gushed that "...*many thousands on the Viking side were slain... over the whole broad expanse of Ashdown, scattered everywhere... The Christians followed them until nightfall, cutting them down on all sides.*"

Although the numbers claimed are obvious exaggerations, the list of earls killed illustrates the high casualties of the battle in the bloody hand-to-hand fighting. What Asser fails to mention, however, is that this was true for both sides. It was a victory for the English, but it was a pyrrhic one, since the Saxon army was also mauled.

This high casualty rate was actually a greater problem for the Saxons than for the Vikings, since the royal army was drawn from local forces. Each shire would send its contingent of men who would in turn be commanded by the local lord or ealdorman. However, these subunits were most interested in defending their own territory, and when a shire was overrun its service was lost to the king. Perhaps a few of the professional soldiers would stay loyal, but most peasants would understandably return home to be with their families. As the Vikings advanced therefore, the pool of available men kept shrinking. The more victories the Vikings piled up, the less Saxon resistance was possible.

From the perspective of manpower, therefore, the victory was almost indistinguishable from a defeat. The local forces had been exhausted and could no longer be counted on in the case of a fresh Viking attack. Halfdan, on the other hand, had no such problems. There was also a continuous stream of raiders arriving from Ireland, France, and Scandinavia to boost Viking numbers.

At least military supplies were no longer a problem since the English held the field. This was, as Hannibal had dryly remarked after the battle of Cannae in 216 BC, almost as good as the victory itself. A harvest of weapons and armor was waiting to be claimed, replenishing items lost or damaged during the struggle.

The English would soon have need of their weapons. Halfdan retreated to Reading and built up his strength, unleashing waves of roving war bands to harry the surrounding lands. Two weeks after Ashdown, one of these groups caught the Saxon army and, in another bruising battle defeated them. To make matters worse for the English, this was followed by the arrival of a large fleet led by a Viking named Guthrum. The new addition nearly doubled the size of the Viking army. The Anglo-Saxon Chronicle calls Guthrum's force 'the great summer army', and its arrival at Reading solved any manpower issues Halfdan might have had. The two leaders took joint control and in March of 871 left their base to plunder Wessex. Just before Easter they met the English army and this third time proved decisive.

The Anglo-Saxon Chronicle reports simply that there "*was great slaughter on both sides... The Danes had possession of the battlefield.*" One of the casualties appears to have been King Athelred. He was either mortally wounded during the fighting, or was simply worn out by the exertions of his five year reign. The crown should have gone to his young son, but with the national emergency it passed to his twenty-three year-old brother, Alfred.

The new king understood better than most how desperate the situation really was. The army was putting up a brave resistance, but had already effectively lost control of eastern Wessex, and the first months of his reign seemed to promise the loss of the west half as well. While he was burying his brother the Danes attacked again, causing what was left of the English army to flee. Alfred managed to raise a fresh one, but this too was pushed back in a series of skirmishes which left the Vikings in control of the battlefield.

Alfred sued for peace. His army hadn't been able to stop the Danish advance – or even prevent a group of Vikings from plundering his brother's grave. Surprisingly, Halfdan and Guthrum agreed. Despite their success, the Vikings had suffered heavy casualties as well, and there were elements within the army pushing for a settlement. The point of raiding was to live to enjoy one's plunder, and the uncharacteristic pitched battles that Halfdan had been fighting had probably damaged morale. Accepting a large payment of Danegeld, and the designation of eastern Wessex as a kind of Danish 'protectorate', Halfdan pulled back to his base at London.

He had been reassessing his priorities for some time. The death of his brother, Ivar, had loosened the family's hold on both Ireland and Northumbria. In the former, the Norwegians had once again gained the upper hand, and in the latter, there was a full-scale rebellion against Viking rule. He spent a year in London gathering supplies, then marched north to reestablish control over Mercia. Burghred, the Mercian king, didn't wait around for him to arrive. Slipping out of his capital before the Vikings got there, he escaped to Rome where he spent the rest of his life as a pilgrim.

With that last victory, the Great Army began to fracture. Its organization was always fluid since it was less a proper 'army' and more a collection of war bands with aligned goals. That unity, however, had been fractured by the arrival of Guthrum and the heavy losses in Wessex, and at the conclusion of the Mercian campaign the army divided in half. The Lothbrok brothers peeled off and headed north, leaving Guthrum to finish off Wessex.

Halfdan's portion of the army was probably made up of veterans who had been steadily campaigning for a decade. What they wanted now was land, and Halfdan himself probably was thinking about establishing himself in a permanent location. He may have intended this to be London and had gone so far as to mint coins of his own there in imitation of Wessex. The Lothbrok base of power had always been in the north though, so Northumbria was a more suitable choice. As soon as he had pacified it, he started deeding land to his soldiers, like some Anglo-Saxon monarch. His veterans, for their part, seem to have eagerly abandoned swords for plows.

The life of a sedentary king, however, didn't quite suite Halfdan, and the old sea-wolf couldn't resist the temptation for one last adventure. In 875 he launched an invasion of Dublin, losing the support of most of his soldiers and eventually his life, during the two-year campaign. He seems at least to have gone down fighting. Of the various accounts of his death, the most believable is that he was killed in a sea-battle with the Norwegian king of Dublin.[65]

The departure of the Lothbrok brothers gave Wessex some much needed breathing room, and Alfred used it to reassemble his army. Expecting an attack, he kept the army

---

65 The most colorful account has Halfdan fighting his way to Russia, only to be captured by a Slavic tribe. When asked to choose how to be executed he rather bizarrely selected burning.

in the field, attempting to block the fords across the Thames. The canny Guthrum, however, evaded the Saxons by splitting his forces in two. A small, mounted field army slipped across the river at night and seized the port of Wareham, while the main forces sailed along the coast. By the time Alfred was aware that Guthrum had left Cambridge, the Vikings were already dug in.

The main Viking army had not arrived yet, but experience had taught the Saxon king of the dangers of attacking entrenched Vikings, so he offered to buy them off instead. Guthrum, after some initial reluctance accepted, and the two leaders exchanged hostages as a show of good faith.

Guthrum, however, had no intentions of making peace. As soon as the Saxon army withdrew, he had all of his hostages butchered, and then seized the much more defensible fortress of Exeter. The Vikings were now established in the heart of Wessex. If they could hold that position, commanding the Thames River valley, they would dominate both the economic and spiritual heart of the English kingdom.

From his stronghold, Guthrum ravaged the south, building fortified camps and breaking morale. His fleet, meanwhile, reached Wareham and began to plunder its way along the coast. If the two linked up, there was little hope for Wessex of avoiding a Viking triumph. Alfred would be forced to his knees, Danegeld would be paid, and Wessex would be compelled to admit the supremacy of a Viking overlord.

Since Alfred lacked a fleet, there was little he could do but watch the campaign unfold. Guthrum had maneuvered his forces brilliantly, but just as he was on the verge of victory, the weather stole his triumph. As the Viking longships were rounding some headlands they were wrecked by a severe storm, along with nearly four thousand men. The would-be conqueror was now trapped at Exeter, massively outnumbered, and deep in enemy territory. Guthrum sued for peace, and Alfred, realizing how close he had come to defeat, was magnanimous. The Vikings, properly chastened, were allowed to cross the Thames with what was left of their army.

Once again, Alfred had miscalculated his enemy's weakness. The Vikings had consistently shown a remarkable ability to replenish their forces in a short amount of time. Within five months, Guthrum had brought his army back up to fighting strength and had launched his final invasion.

All of the favorite Viking tactics were on display. Not only did Guthrum attack Alfred's stronghold of Chippenham during the winter, but he waited until Twelfth Night – a time when most of Alfred's army would be either home celebrating Christmas with their families, or deep into their wine. The lightning blow caught the king completely by surprise. He had dismissed the field army for the holiday, and was protected only by his personal guard. They were quickly overpowered, and Alfred himself barely escaped. He fled to Athelney, a wooded island in the marshes of Somerset, with the few of his bodyguard who had survived.

Guthrum had shattered the power of Wessex, bringing almost all of England under Viking domination in the process. It would take some time to mop up the last resistance, but even as the Vikings took command of Chippenham, reinforcements arrived. They were commanded by Ubba Ragnarson, younger brother of Ivar the Boneless and Halfdan. He brought with him the Raven banner, a fearful totem that the Vikings believed carried the favor of Odin. Supposedly woven in a single day by the daughters of Ragnar Lothbrok, it was a triangular canvas with the image of a raven sewn on it. If its wings were seen flapping, victory would soon follow.

Of course, Wessex had not admitted defeat, and it still had a surviving king, but that was a mere technicality. Under the twin hammers of Guthrum and a Lothbrok son, it would crumble soon enough.

Chapter 7

THE LAST KING OF ENGLAND

*"When ill seed has been sown, so an
ill crop will spring from it."*

- Njáls Saga

In the early months of 878, Alfred must have cut a sorry figure for a king. Driven into exile in his own kingdom, abandoned by most of his subjects, and constantly on the run, there must have seemed little hope of ever regaining his throne. There are a number of charming stories that originate from this period, the most famous of which involves him taking refuge with a peasant couple. The wife assigned him the task of watching some cakes by the fire, but the distracted king, weighed down with his troubles, let them burn. Having failed to recognize her sovereign in his ragged and dirty clothes, the wife berated him for neglecting his duty. The husband, who immediately recognized Alfred, begged the king's forgiveness, but Alfred good-naturedly admitted that she was right. In another tale, Alfred snuck into Guthrum's camp disguised as a traveling minstrel. As he entertained them, he overheard their plans, enabling him to win a victory the following day.

While these stories are almost certainly invented, they do manage to capture Alfred's character. He had an ability to inspire and connect with his subjects that his brothers and father did not. He was also starting to form a strategy to defeat the Vikings.

His experience in battle had taught him to avoid a head-on collision with a Viking army. Their usual tactic was to seize a fortified position or a high point and mass their infantry into a shield wall. They would then provoke the English into attacking. This could usually be repelled – the Vikings who invaded Wessex were veterans – and as the English fell back in disarray, the Vikings would storm forward and sweep the Saxons off the battlefield.

This strategy had won almost all of England for the Vikings, and seemed unassailable. During his time of exile, however, Alfred had realized the flaw in the Viking armor. Despite having great ability to replenish their forces, they were still vastly outnumbered by the English. The only way they could overpower a kingdom was to destroy its army, and until they did so they would be vulnerable. All Alfred had to do was to wear them down with skirmishes and not offer a conclusive battle. For the next three months he waged a stubborn guerrilla war from his swamp, always one step ahead of the pursuing Danes, and by Easter of 878, he was ready to go on the offensive.

He had prepared the ground well. Without an enemy to strike, the Vikings had been forced to spread out their forces to control Wessex. Alfred's raids had slowly chipped away at their strength and provided a rallying point for English resistance. The greatest blow to Viking morale, however, had been an unexpected bit of luck that had nothing to do with Alfred. After his success in capturing Chippenham,

Guthrum had sent Ubba on a raid in Devonshire, and the latter had stumbled into an English army commanded by a local noble. In the ensuing struggle, Ubba was cut down and the Raven banner was captured. When Alfred left his marsh, the English were energized and waiting for their call to arms.

The king mustered the forces of three shires, and when he was confident that they were ready, he marched north to Edington. His army was probably around four thousand strong, slightly smaller than the Viking force commanded by Guthrum.

This was the battle that both sides had wanted, and it was clear before it began that it would be the decisive conflict of the war. Both armies formed a shield wall and advanced. This was a brutal contest of sheer muscle and will, each side shoving forward, trying to hack and smash their way through the opposing line. The fighting was bloody and exhausting, and neither side could gain an advantage. Finally, after many hours of hard fighting, the Viking line broke.

As with all medieval battles, once the shield wall collapsed, the end came quickly. The Vikings abandoned their positions and fled, taking refuge in their base at Chippenham. The Saxon army followed close behind, and Alfred settled in for a siege of his former residence.

The loss was particularly devastating to the Vikings because Guthrum had probably expected an easy victory. He had anticipated facing the demoralized, half-beaten army that had fled some four months before, and wouldn't have risked a pitched battle. The defeat at Edington, however, was decisive on another level; not because of the loss of men – Guthrum could always find more – but because of the realization that Alfred was not going away.

There were some veterans in the Viking army that had arrived with Ivar the Boneless a dozen years before. They, like most of the Vikings, had come not just for plunder, but for land. Wessex might eventually fall to them, but it would take years of bloody struggle, with every inch contested. There were easier pickings across the Chanel and to the north. Wessex may simply not have been worth it.

If he needed convincing, it took only three weeks for Guthrum's army to persuade him to come to an agreement with Alfred. The terms were generous, and reflected a desire by both parties to ensure a lasting peace. Alfred agreed to pay Danegeld, and to respect the Viking conquest of the other three English kingdoms. Guthrum, for his part had to withdraw from Saxon land, accept Christianity, and acknowledge that Wessex was an independent kingdom.

Several weeks later, Guthrum and thirty of his most distinguished men arrived at Alfred's marshy stronghold in Athelney, and was baptized. Alfred stood in as his godfather, and christened him Athelstan in memory of his eldest brother. The newly minted Christian monarch then agreed to a permanent division of territory.[66] Wessex and the western portion of Mercia would belong to Alfred, while eastern Mercia and East Anglia would belong to the Vikings. Wessex would be governed by English law and custom, while the Vikings would abide by Danish custom.

Guthrum's portion, known thereafter as the *Danelaw*, maintained its identity until the end of the twelfth century. What was left of the great heathen army – somewhat less heathen by this point – settled in Mercia or left to raid the continent. Guthrum appears to have lived out the remaining years of his life in peace, dying in East Anglia in 890.

---

66 Within a generation, the descendants of the Vikings who had killed king Edmund were venerating him as a saint.

The victory over his great antagonist would have been enough for most men, but Alfred was playing a long game, and knew that peace with one Viking commander – no matter how important – did not mean the end of Viking raids. He had to place the kingdom on a firmer foundation to enable it to fend off the next attack when it inevitably came. Wessex must be turned into a fortress that could withstand another great heathen army.

The Vikings' mobility had been the key to their success, so Alfred took it away. Towns, bridges, and roads were fortified, and strongholds were built throughout Wessex to deny roving bands any sanctuary. Within fifteen years, the kingdom was bristling with fortresses allowing the English to strike at any future raid from numerous points. Next, Alfred reorganized the army, training a professional, permanent force supported by taxes, to replace the unreliable peasant levies. He even attempted to challenge the Viking monopoly of sea power by beginning work on a fleet, although the results proved disappointing.[67]

To stabilize things internally, he also reformed the currency. At his coronation, English coins had had very little silver in them and were nearly worthless. Somehow he was able to increase the silver content, whether by using treasure confiscated from the Vikings, opening some old Roman mines, or discovering some buried loot. He never explained how, and historians have been wondering about it ever since.

Within a decade, Alfred was secure enough to start expanding his territory. He drove the Vikings out of London and signed a final treaty with Guthrum renegotiating his exact border with the Danelaw. It wasn't

---

67 One encounter had nine English ships pursuing six Viking longships. Three escaped, two were beached, and only one was captured. When an actual Viking fleet appeared, the English ships usually didn't bother going to sea.

just the reorganization that had strengthened Alfred's army. The king had realized that a literate force – or at least an officer corps who could read – would give him an advantage. He couldn't be everywhere at once, so it was vital that he could communicate exact and detailed plans to his underlings. With that in mind he issued a command that all commanders should 'be able to read and write or else surrender their offices of worldly power.'

This directive was profoundly shocking to a warrior culture that was almost completely illiterate, and Alfred had to modify it so that his sheriffs could appoint a literate deputy to read for them.[68] But he remained adamant that schooling should increase in Wessex. Although he had received no education, he was very conscious of what he'd missed and understood that exposing himself to minds more vast and subtle than his own was an enriching experience.

With that in mind, he composed a list of books that every educated man should know and – at least according to legend – personally translated some of them from Latin into the vernacular. A particular favorite was Boethius' *The Consolation Of Philosophy*, from which he chose his own epitaph: "*I desired to live worthily as long as I lived, and to leave after my life, to the men who should come after me, the memory of me in good works.*"

The revival of learning that Alfred championed was accompanied by a spiritual revival, since churches and monasteries were the vehicle of education. Religious foundations were rebuilt and re-endowed, and monks began copying manuscripts again. The law code was rewritten, and trade began slowly to pick up.

---

68 This would be a bit like telling modern politicians that they had to pass a test in advanced Calculus or they'd be relieved of duty.

Unfortunately, all of this made Wessex a target for more raids, and in 892 Alfred's reforms were tested by another invasion. The Viking army, led yet again by a son of Ragnar Lothbrok, arrived in two waves and struck from different directions. They had brought their women and children with them, obviously expecting to settle permanently in Wessex. Neither group, however, had much success in establishing themselves. After several months Alfred confronted the smaller of the two groups and managed to buy them off, while his son Edward ran down the larger one near Essex. Two years later, the Danes tried again, but this time were spotted by Alfred's coastal guard sailing down the Thames. His army was able to blockade them and burn the ships while they were beached.

Alfred died in October of 899, aged fifty – a ripe old age for the time – having accomplished the impossible. He had checked the irresistible Viking tide and prevented England from becoming a Viking colony. By simply surviving, he had taken a huge step toward the creation of a single English state. Thanks to the Vikings, he was the only remaining native king, a fact which ensured that the eventual unification of the country would occur under the crown of Wessex. Along the way he had revived literacy, reorganized the economy, and created a stable base for the future kingdom. Without him, Anglo-Saxon civilization may very well have been extinguished.

The achievement has led to an unparalleled reputation which remains intact today. Alfred was hailed as the 'Solomon of England', Alfred the 'Wise', and most commonly, Alfred the 'Great'. We need not necessarily agree with the historian Edward Freeman who, in a gush of patriotism, called Alfred 'the most perfect character in history', but he certainly earned his epithet of 'Great'. The inscription under his statue at his birthplace of Wantage, in the modern British county of Berkshire, erected in 1877 by Victorian admirers, provides a fitting epitaph:

"Alfred found learning dead, and he restored it. Education neglected, and he revived it. The laws powerless, and he gave them force. The Church debased, and he raised it. The land ravaged by a fearful enemy, from which he delivered it. Alfred's name will live as long as mankind shall respect the past."

Chapter 8

A VIKING KINGDOM
IN THE IRISH SEA

"The overpraised are the worst deceivers."

- The Saga of Grettir the Strong

Perhaps the greatest tribute to Alfred's success was that the Danelaw never became a kingdom of its own. At the time of his death it accounted for roughly half the land area of the modern kingdom of England. Its main city was York, a city which owes its location and much of its existence to the Vikings. In AD 71, the Ninth Legion of the Roman army had built a wooden fort at the confluence of the rivers Ouse and Foss which they named *Eboracum.*[69] The Anglo-Saxons, however, had moved the settlement inland and renamed it *Eoforwīc,* or 'wild boar town'. It remained a smaller royal center until the Viking conquest, when its new masters moved it back to the bank of the rivers, transforming it into a major port city. Their name of *Jorvīc* or York stuck, and by the eleventh century it had grown to around ten

---

69 Legion IX had a distinguished history. They fought for Caesar at Pharsalus and for Augustus at Actium, two of the most important battles in Roman history. They also served with distinction in the Claudian invasion of England.

thousand people, representing perhaps a sixth of the existing population of the Danelaw.

Under the Vikings, York flourished. It was at the western end of the great northern trade arc that they had been developing, and was a major center for the export of food and metals to markets from Ireland to Russia. In the other direction came aromatics, glassware, silks, and silver, along with other refined products from eastern markets.

The lure of English wealth glittering just over the Irish Sea was irresistible to the Vikings of Ireland, and they kept returning to it, like moths to a flame. But the repeated attempts to seize its riches – especially the great invasion of England – nearly proved the undoing of Viking settlements in Ireland. The Gaelic Vikings had been facing a serious manpower shortage since 870 when the discovery of Iceland had diverted immigrants to the north, and they could ill afford to lose men in fruitless adventures in England. The drain of available forces left them exposed, and in 902 a High King had managed to drive them out of Dublin itself. The Irish victory proved fleeting, however. In 914 a grandson of Ivar the Boneless named Sitric One-Eyed, sailed into Dublin's harbor and crushed the High King's army. With that triumph, the Irish fell back, allowing the Vikings to reoccupy their old settlements.

Sitric One-Eyed, who was pragmatic to the point of ruthlessness, made the strategic decision not to spend his efforts conquering Ireland.[70] Instead he wanted to capture the lucrative northern trading routes, by linking Dublin with York. His ambition was to rule a kingdom made up of bits of the coasts of Ireland, England, Scotland, and Wales.

---

70   He had already murdered one brother who had gotten in his way.

This dream was born of a typically Viking outlook. They saw the world in terms of the sea, not land masses, and it made perfect sense to connect the major crossing points. Dublin was cut off from the interior of Ireland by bogs and forests, while northern Britain was divided by the Pennine mountains. By sea, however, which the Vikings could cross easily and quickly, these areas could be knit together into a single kingdom straddling the Irish Sea.

The only serious resistance he faced was from the Irish. In 918 a coalition of petty kings tried to drive him out of Dublin, but were heavily beaten. The next year they tried again with even worse results. In what was probably the most catastrophic defeat ever inflicted on the Irish by the Vikings, Sitric One-Eyed crushed the army, killing several kings.

The victory ensured that Dublin would remain Viking, and reinforced the dominant Viking position in Ireland. With his flank secured, Sitric One-Eyed left Dublin in the hands of his cousin, and sailed across the Irish Sea to claim York as well. The family of Ivar the Boneless had always thought of York as their patrimony, and the feeling seems to have been reciprocated. He was accepted as king, and spent the next six years methodically expanding the size and influence of Viking Northumbria.

By 926 it looked as if Sitric's dream had become a reality. Dublin and York were the twin centers of an unlikely realm spanning the Irish Sea. He had even made enough of a nuisance of himself that the English king, Athelstan, had bought him off by giving him a royal bride – the king's own sister. The following year, however, Sitric One-Eyed died, and his Hiberno-English realm collapsed.

The next two decades saw York ruled by a succession of Viking kings, each trying to fend off Athelstan and put

Sitric's possessions back together. His son, Olaf Sitricsson, came the closest, conquering York in 941, and leading an ambitious invasion to bring the entire Danelaw under his control. If he could convince the Danish population of the north to make common cause with him, England would be divided between rival kingdoms.

It appeared at first as if the English nightmare would become a reality. When confronted with the Hiberno-Norse army, the people of Northumbria pledged their loyalty to Olaf. When Edmund arrived, however, they switched their loyalties again, and Olaf was forced to withdraw. The English pursued them all the way to York where Olaf admitted defeat and came to terms. He accepted the English as his overlords, and was baptized with king Edmund standing in as his godfather.

Olaf would probably have tried again, but in 944 he was expelled by the people of York, and forced to flee to Dublin. Bad news continued to plague him, as that year Dublin was sacked by the Irish High King, and Olaf only just managed to maintain control. With Dublin badly weakened, the Viking grip on York waned, and the English seized control of the city.

As the Vikings of Ireland entered a period of relative weakness, other Viking adventurers began to cast interested eyes on York. The most ambitious of these was Erik Bloodaxe of Norway. He was one of at least twenty sons of the first Norwegian king, Harald Fairhair, and according to later accounts, showed tremendous potential as a Viking from an early age. When he turned twelve, he left Norway to go adventuring, and spent the next decade raiding up and down the coasts from France to northern Russia.

These exploits won him the affection of his father, who made it known that he wanted Erik to succeed him. That didn't sit well with Erik's older half-brothers, but when two of them protested, Erik resolved the issue by murdering them with an axe. Two other siblings marshaled armies to depose Erik, but he brutally suppressed them as well, and they met the same fate. Erik – now called 'bloodaxe' for his method of fratricide – was accepted as king of Norway. Unsurprisingly, he was unable to keep the throne for long. The brutality he had shown in cutting his way to the crown was a prelude to how he would rule, and the increasingly despotic reign lost the support of both commoners and nobles or *jarls*. After only a brief time on the throne, Erik was run out of Norway by his youngest brother Håkon the Good.

Erik seems to have resorted to what he was best at – raiding – and while pillaging in the north learned that York had expelled its king. Using the dissatisfaction with English rule, which had already alienated the Danish population, he managed to get himself crowned king of York.

He quickly found himself between a rock and a hard place. The new English king, a capable warrior named Eadred, had no intention of letting another Viking establish himself in York, and induced the Scots to raid Northumbria. At the same time the English sovereign moved north, promising the inhabitants of Northumbria severe punishment if they didn't expel Erik. Once again, the Danish population refused to rally around a Scandinavian monarch, and Erik was run out of England.

That cleared the way for Olaf Sitricsson to return from Dublin, but he quickly squandered any goodwill and was driven back to Ireland by his own subjects after only three years. By that time it was clear that the constant changing of power had eroded whatever support there was in the north for Viking rule, and doomed Sitric's old dream of a united York and Dublin. The Danes of Yorkshire may have still gone by Viking names and abided by Viking law, but they no longer considered themselves Vikings. For the most part they had accepted Christianity and developed a settled, landed class. They no longer viewed the adventurers from Norway or Ireland as kinsmen, seeing them instead as disruptive forces, if not outright enemies. They preferred the stable, Christian kings of Wessex to the violent sea-kings of the north, and that realization marked the first real assimilation of the Danelaw into the kingdom of England.

This failure of a Scandinavian kingdom to take root was by no means inevitable. The first generation of Vikings may have been too restless to be good administrators, but their successors undoubtedly would have learned. Both Ivar the Boneless and Guthrum had given land to their veterans and styled themselves as Anglo-Saxon kings. Over time, the Viking population adopted the religion, fashions, and even the farming techniques of the English, a process which should have resulted in a strong Viking state in the north, similar to that which developed in Normandy.

It didn't only because Alfred and his two successors were shrewd enough to allow the Vikings of the Danelaw to maintain their traditions, while building up a strong, centralized English state. In the end, the fading Norse language and cuisine wasn't enough to maintain a Scandinavian identity. Once the population of the Danelaw realized that they had more in common with their neighbors to the south than with the immigrants from the north, it was only a matter of time before the region was swallowed up by the English king.

Viking York still had one gasp of life left in it. In 952 Erik Bloodaxe stormed back into England at the head of a small Viking army. He smashed a combined Scottish and Welsh army and was accepted as king in York. A man with the nickname 'bloodaxe', however, was hardly the one to win over a population that was disillusioned with Viking rule. After two years of Erik's increasingly harsh reign, he was thrown out by the people of York and assassinated while trying to recruit another army.[71] York was absorbed permanently into the English kingdom and never again had a Viking king.

---

71 The later saga Eriksmal has a grand description of Bloodaxe entering Valhalla and being welcomed by the gods.

Chapter 9

THE BATTLE OF CLONTARF

"Many have been brought to death by overconfidence."

- The Saga of Grettir the Strong

Across the Irish Sea, the kingdom of Dublin was also faltering. In some ways, the repeated attempts to conquer and hold on to York had drained Viking Ireland of its energy. The potential conquest of Ireland had been sacrificed for the mirage of a watery empire, and now Dublin would pay the price.

After he had been driven from York, Olaf Sitricsson tried to expand his power in Ireland, but ran into serious resistance from the growing strength of the High King Máel Sechnaill mac Domnaill of Meath, an area directly west of Dublin. In 980, Olaf, by now in his late sixties, decided to put an end to the threat by recruiting Vikings from the Scottish coast and the Hebrides to help him cow the Irish into submission. The two armies met near the hill of Tara, traditional seat of the High King.

The battle resulted in the worst Viking defeat ever suffered in Ireland, and effectively ended Dublin's role as a dominant power on the island.[72] Olaf's oldest son and successor was killed, and the Viking army disintegrated. The victorious Irish occupied Dublin and forced its citizens to pay a heavy tribute. Olaf either abdicated or was forcibly removed from power and – in a moment rich in irony – joined the monastery of Iona where he lived out the remainder of his life as a simple monk. From that point on, the Vikings in Ireland were a subordinate power, used as allies by feuding kings, but no longer a credible threat to the native Irish.

King Máel was the big winner in the long struggle with the Vikings. Meath emerged as the dominant kingdom, and established a virtual lock on the office of High King. Meath's only real competition came from Munster, an area in the remote southwest, whose ambitious king, Brian Bóruma, had won a reputation by clearing the Vikings out of western Ireland.[73]

Brian was a parvenu, a second rate minor lord from a backwater kingdom, but he had already shown something approaching brilliance for the equally bruising worlds of politics and war. The youngest of twelve sons, Brian had survived a Viking attack in his youth and had been educated in a monastery in Munster where he learned to play the harp; after his death the instrument was adopted as a symbol of Ireland in his honor. He became proficient in several languages, including both Latin and Greek. His study of the life of Julius Caesar in particular stayed with him, as he was struck by the great general's ability to keep his enemies off

---

72 The Vikings of Ireland were assimilating in a similar manner as their English counterparts. Vikings allies from the Hebrides fought on both sides, and the 'native' Irish Vikings had started calling themselves 'easterners'.

73 He supposedly killed Ivar of Limerick - probably a great-grandson of Ivar the Boneless – in single combat.

balance, as well as his habit of memorizing battle plans to prevent them from being intercepted.

When he inherited the kingship of Munster, he put this into action by using the Viking's tactics against them. He sent his armies on lightning raids into the interior, often using captured Viking ships to lead the way. With this unorthodox combination of naval and land attacks, he steadily imposed his authority throughout the southwest. Recognition of this remarkable achievement came in 997 when he forced Máel Sechnaill, the reigning High King, to share power with him. Máel would retain the title of High King, but Brian would independently control the south. For all practical purposes, there were now dual High Kings.

However creaky the new alliance was, it allowed the main powers in Ireland to unite for the first time against the Vikings. This was put to a serious test in 999 when Sitric Silkbeard, the last great Viking figure of Irish history, joined the men of Leinster in a revolt against Brian. The two High Kings led a joint campaign, trapping the rebels in a narrow valley and slaughtering most of them. Dublin was occupied again, and Sitric only kept his throne by swearing fealty to Brian.

The victory strained the alliance almost more than a defeat. It was galling enough for Máel to share power with a jumped-up nobody, but the next year Brian inflicted a worse humiliation by claiming the High Kingship for himself, thereby demoting Máel. This set in motion a series of intrigues – convoluted even for Irish history – to bring down the meteoric Brian Bóruma.

The plan was hatched in Dublin by Sitric Silkbeard and aided in secret by Máel Sechnaill who was still smarting from his demotion from High King.[74] They were joined in 1005 by other Irish warlords who were alarmed by Brian's naked ambition. In that year, Bóruma had taken a pilgrimage to the tomb of St. Patrick at Armagh and left twenty ounces of gold on the altar. He had then instructed a scribe to sign his name in the cathedral's record book with the title *Imperator Scottorum* – Emperor of the Irish. His grand vision, he now revealed, was to hammer together the divided tribes into a single nation, ruled over by a *single* king.

This meant a demotion for every other ruling figure in Ireland, and – as Bóruma steadily made it a reality over the next decade – drove a number of sub kings into the arms of Sitric's alliance. By 1014, Sitric felt strong enough to openly defy the High King. To bolster the rebel forces he called in Viking allies from the Isle of Man led by their earl Brodir, mercenaries from Iceland, and even the famed adventurer Sigurd the Stout of Orkney who brought with him a dreaded Raven banner of Odin.[75]

This grand alliance of rebels, however, never really got off the ground. The size of the army that Brian Bóruma mustered unnerved Sitric, and he quietly withdrew from his own rebellion. His counterpart Máel came to the same conclusion, and decided to remain on the sidelines and throw in his forces with whatever side seemed to be winning.

Even without the two protagonists that had initiated the revolt, the remaining allies decided to go ahead with the

---

74 Some historians credit Sitric's mother Gormflaith as the true mastermind of the rebellion. A ferocious Irish princess, she was either married to or directly related to every major participant.

75 According to tradition, both Brodir and Sigurd were recruited by Gormflaith. Brian had imprisoned her and she had promised to marry whichever hero killed Brian and liberated her, giving them Dublin as a dowry. Sitric's thoughts on the matter aren't recorded.

rebellion. As planned, the army assembled in Dublin, which proved somewhat awkward for Sitric since he was now attempting to play the part of loyal vassal of Brian. The two sides met on the morning of April 23, 1014, on the plain of Clontarf, just west of Dublin.

The Battle of Clontarf, fought portentously on Good Friday, has been hailed as the most significant event in Irish history. It is traditionally said to be the defining moment in two centuries of resistance to Viking invasion, the great victory of Christian Ireland over the pagan Viking horde. Brian Bóruma, the great secular figure of Irish history, is celebrated as the man who united the country, drove out the northern invaders, and secured Irish independence.

The reality, however, is a bit more complicated. Clontarf wasn't fought to drive out the Viking invader, but to decide who would be High King in Ireland. There was, in fact, no longer much difference between the Norse of Dublin, and the native Irish. Sitric Silkbeard was probably more Celtic than Viking, and as Christian as Brian.[76] He built the first cathedral in Dublin, minted coins with the sign of the cross, and made at least two pilgrimages to Rome. He may have called in pagan Viking allies like Brodir of Man to fight for him, but Brian did the same. Brodir's brother Ospak fought for the High King, as did several Viking companies. Furthermore, Brian Bóruma himself – now in his late eighties – played no part in the battle. He retired to a hill above Clontarf to pray, delegating the task of leading the army to his son, Murchad.

Medieval war was the job of the young. The two armies, evenly matched, formed into long rows, men shoulder

---

76   In addition to his Irish mother he may have had three Irish grandparents.

to shoulder with their spears raised and their shields overlapping. From then on it was only a question of who would break first as the lines slammed into each other. It was an exhausting form of combat with men heaving against the opposing shields, hacking from the front or attempting to stab underneath the unyielding wooden wall.

The brutal contest lasted all day, as both shield walls bent, but neither broke. The allied army had more to lose, and at first held the upper hand, driving Brian's forces back. But in the murderous hand-to-hand fighting that followed, they were in turn forced to retreat toward the small bridge that spanned the Liffey River.

Two of Brian's grandsons were killed in the assault, but they forced the Viking, Brodir of Man, to flee, badly weakening the allied army. Fortunately for the rebel cause – at least according to a colorful Viking account – Sigurd the Stout managed to rally them by waving the Raven banner. This was a considerable act of courage for the Vikings believed that the banner would bring victory to whomever held it, but at the price of the holder's death.[77]

In a scene worthy of the best Norse sagas, Sigurd was confronted by Brian's son Murchad. The prince – who given his father's age was at least in his early sixties – carried a sword in each hand and was riding a white horse like some figure out of early Irish legend. With one sword he knocked Sigurd's helmet off, and with the other he slashed his throat, killing him instantly. One of Sigurd's men struck Murchad in the belly, spilling his intestines, but before he died, Murchad managed to pull the Viking's chain mail over his head and stab him three times in the chest.

---

77 Such courage was to be expected from Sigurd who was a son of the terrifyingly-named Thorfinn Skull-Splitter.

As with all medieval battles, the end came quickly and bloodily. When Sigurd fell the allied shield wall broke, and Bóruma's forces swept them from the field. Men were cut down as they attempted to flee or drowned as they tried to cross the Liffey. Roughly two thirds of those who took part were killed, and more Vikings died than in any other single battle in Irish history. Any Viking mercenary who was caught was killed, although Dublin itself was spared since Sitric had the foresight to abandon the coalition before the fighting started.

But the losses on Brian's side had been appalling as well. The High King's eldest son and heir had died, along with two of Brian's grandsons, a nephew, a brother, and innumerable other clan leaders of his allies. In perhaps the cruelest twist, the High King himself had also fallen. From his vantage point above the battle Brian Bóruma had witnessed the Viking line splintering and had withdrawn to his tent to pray, attended by a single servant. There, alone and virtually unattended, the victorious emperor of Ireland had been killed by a group of fleeing Vikings.

The most common version of his death, says that it was Brodir of Man who dispatched him. The Viking chief stumbled on Brian's tent with two companions as they tried to escape the carnage of the battlefield. His men mistook the king – holding a crucifix and kneeling in prayer – for a priest, but Brodir recognized Brian. With a single stroke of his battle-axe he split the old man's skull, then fled, leaving the High King dead behind him.[78]

As time passed, it became clear that the victory at Clontarf had been a pyrrhic one, and that Brian's great dream of a

---

78 According to a Norse saga, an Irish warrior named Wolf the Quarrelsome hunted down Brodir and enacted a terrible revenge. A slit was made in Brodir's stomach and one end of his intestines was nailed to a tree. The dying Viking was then dragged around until his entrails were looped around the trunk.

united Ireland had died with him. His younger son inherited the 'empire', but he lacked the charisma of his father and was unable to hold it together. Within a few years his control barely extended to the old kingdom of Meath, the endless petty wars had resumed, and Máel Sechnaill had recaptured the title of High King. For those who lived through them, the decades of Brian's rule must have seemed like a mirage. They had started with Máel as High King and Sitric as ruler of Dublin, and now that he was gone, nothing at all had changed.

Although Dublin kept its Viking kings for the next century and a half, it was reduced to a minor role, dominated by the nearby kingdom of Leinster. In any case, it had long since ceased to be purely Viking, and was well on the way to being completely assimilated. Its last king, Ascall mac Ragnaill, was killed by Henry II's forces when the English invaded Ireland in 1171.

The Viking legacy in Ireland is a tangled one. They founded the island's first commercial cities – Dublin, Cork, Limerick, Wexford, and Waterford – but they also fully justified their reputation as destructive raiders by wrecking an Irish culture that was in its prime.[79] Monasteries and churches were plundered, homes were destroyed, and countless innocents were either killed or dragged off into slavery.

It is the latter sin that is most held against them today. Although slavery existed in Ireland before the first Viking came – St. Patrick himself had been captured by Irish slavers – it had died out by the eighth century. The Vikings reintroduced it, at first taking their slaves or *thralls* back to Scandinavia or selling them in Islamic markets, but later

---

79 This should not, however, be pushed too far. It was a violent age. In the first quarter century of Viking raids, Irish sources record twenty-six attacks on monasteries. In the same period they list eighty-seven assaults by fellow Irishmen.

retaining their captives to serve them in Ireland. The Irish understandably considered this a mortal insult, so they retaliated by starting a slave-trade of their own – using only captured Vikings. Before long, it became a status symbol to own slaves, and as the Vikings faded, their place was taken by native Irish.

The Church railed against the practice, citing the words of St. Patrick whose own horrified experience had convinced him of its evils, but if anything, the slave trade increased. By 1171 it had reached such a pitch that when Ireland was invaded by English armies – the start of centuries of oppression – an Irish cleric drew the damning conclusion that God had sent the English to end the slave trade.

The real Viking legacy in Ireland is the city of Dublin. After the time of Sitric it might have been reduced to a minor political power, but the same period saw its steady growth as a center of trade. It was especially well-known for its luxury goods, and became an international hub of gold, silver, weapons, silks, and horses. It was the Vikings of Dublin who introduced the first coinage to Ireland, and gave the island its first distinct class of merchant traders.[80] Thanks to the Vikings, Dublin became one of the most profitable ports in Europe, with access to the great trading routes of the Viking world.[81]

That it did not also become the capital of a Viking kingdom, was because Viking society was as tribal as the Irish. One of the chief traits of the Vikings was their adaptability, both in battle and in the areas they settled. They would generally try to build on the existing political order, modeling their realm on whatever had come before. In England they had found

---

80   The Irish word for penny, 'pingin' is a Viking word.

81   It also had the largest slave markets in western Europe since the fall of Rome.

a tradition of strong centralized government, but Alfred and his son and grandson had been too strong to allow a Viking kingdom to take root. In Ireland, they faced the opposite problem. There were only embryonic communities and petty kings, so Dublin became another petty player on the eternally shifting ground of Irish politics.

But if England was too strong, and Ireland was too chaotic to found a lasting state, France proved just right. The Carolingian Empire provided the Vikings with fertile ground, where the centralized but decaying monarchy provided both a template for a strong state and the inability to contest it. All that was needed was a sea-king who was willing to settle abroad.

Chapter 10

ROLLO THE WALKER

"He has need of his wits who wanders wide."

              - Edda of Sæmund the Wise

Very little is known about the ancestry of the man who would eventually found one of the most powerful states in western Europe. He was most likely of Norwegian extraction, and is known to posterity as 'Rollo', the Latinized version of the name *Hrolf* or possibly *Hrolleif*.[82] The most comprehensive account of his life comes from a later Norman historian named Dudo of St. Quentin, who had been commissioned for that purpose by Rollo's grandson, Richard I. According to Dudo, young Rollo was the son of a trusted companion of Harald Fairhair, the first king of Norway. Despite their friendship, however, Rollo's father is described as fiercely independent, a man who "never lowered the nape of his neck before any king."

Perhaps he should have. In the last years of his life Harald Fairhair turned over the kingdom to his favorite son Erik

---

82   His ancestry is still disputed, although most accept it as Norwegian. Sources that refer to him as Danish usually don't bother to distinguish between different groups of Vikings, while pro-Danish historians like Saxo Grammaticus are tellingly silent.

Bloodaxe, who took a rather dimmer view of stubborn nobles. As soon as the old man died, Bloodaxe invaded and seized his farm. Rollo's brother was hacked to death in front of him, and Rollo was forced to become an exile.

Like other Scandinavians who had run afoul of more powerful lords, the boy became a professional Viking, spending his formative years raiding in England and the Frisian coast – what is today the Netherlands. Thanks to his prodigious size – apparently he was so large that the undersized Viking horses couldn't bear his weight, forcing him to walk everywhere – he soon attracted a company of Danes to fight with him.[83] Whatever the truth about Rollo's parentage or size, he clearly had a knack for pillaging, and he and his company crossed the English Channel and joined a great surge of Norsemen heading for the Frankish Empire.

The flow of raiders back into Frankish territory had started in the wake of King Alfred's victory over the Great Heathen Army. In the summer of 885, the largest raid yet seen on the continent headed toward Paris, with seven hundred ships carrying as many as forty thousand men.[84] "*The rage of the Northmen*" one French cleric wrote, "*was let loose upon the land.*" Unlike the horde that had besieged England, however, there was no single accepted leader of this Viking army. When the Parisians attempted to parley by sending out a Viking who had settled there, he couldn't find anyone with the authority to speak for the group. When he asked who they were and what there intentions were, their reply – according to Dudo – was that they were Danes and

---

83   The Norse sagas call him Hrolf Granger – Hrolf the Walker.

84   According to the Normans, Rollo was a part of this raid. There is no compelling reason to doubt the traditional claim, although Rollo doesn't reliably appear until twenty-five years later. He would have been in his early thirties in 885.

had come to conquer France. When the messenger asked who their king was, they drew themselves up proudly and said, '*We have no king, for we are all equal.*'

This exchange may be fiction, invented by a Norman writer trying to emphasize his own Duke's independence from the French crown, but it captures nicely the independent streak of the ninth century Vikings. They put great stock in freedom of speech and action – not as concepts, but as stubborn facts. Most of them had no king because they were outlaws of some form or another, looking to carve out a name and some wealth for themselves. They were inspired by plunder, not patriotism or feudal obligations, and were only loosely held together by clan or family ties.

If there was one man who was respected more than others it was Sigfred, a Viking who had probably served with the Great Heathen Army. A year after Alfred and Guthrum had come to terms, he had crossed the North Sea with a large army and sacked several cities of the Frisian coast. For several years they had their way with the eastern Frankish kingdom, raiding Maestrict, Cologne, Aix, and Trier until the Frankish emperor, Charles the Fat, decided to rid himself of the troublesome raiders by buying them off.

Sigfred was happy to oblige, and spent the next three years raiding Picardy and Flanders. In the spring of 885, he returned to Charles' domains and asked for a hefty bribe. When Charles refused, Sigfred led his fleet into the Seine estuary, brushed aside a Frankish army, and sacked Rouen. It was here that he was joined by the bulk of war bands, and by November the entire army had reached Paris.

In the ninth century, there were only two bridges connecting the Île-de-France with the Seine riverbanks. The northern one was narrow, but made of stone and strongly fortified with large, garrisoning towers at either end. The southern bridge was also protected by towers, but was a flimsier structure made of wood.

Everything depended on these two bridges. If the Vikings could destroy them, they would not only cut off Paris, but have access to the rich country beyond. If, on the other hand, the Parisians held the bridges, the Vikings would be cut off and exposed to a relieving army.

Sigfred first tried to negotiate his way past them. There were only two hundred armed men inside Paris, and he promised to leave the city unmolested if they would agree to pull down both edifices. The Parisians refused, saying that their emperor had charged them with protecting the bridges, and they would do so to the last man. The next day the siege began.

Sigfred threw everything against the tower on the north bank of the Seine protecting the stone bridge, hoping to catch the Parisians by surprise. But after fighting for an entire day and suffering heavy casualties from the boiling pitch and oil poured down on them, they had managed to accomplish nothing and the Vikings withdrew. The second day they tried again, only to find that during the night the defenders had added another story onto the top of the tower, further increasing their advantage. The Vikings tried to counter by bringing up a battering ram and heavy catapult, but were again driven off with horrendous casualties.

By the end of the second day of fighting, the Vikings realized that they needed either new tactics, or better siege equipment. They constructed a palisade and spent the next few weeks collecting supplies, and planning their strike.

On the last day of January, 886, they attacked the bridge itself in a furious, sustained assault. The protecting moat was filled up by throwing everything they could think of into it – including branches and dead animals. When that still wasn't enough, they slaughtered their prisoners and tossed the corpses in as well.

This gave them access to the protecting tower of the bridge, but when they tried to set fire to it they were driven back with heavy losses. In a final effort, they filled three longships with straw and oil and set fire to them, pushing them so they crashed into the tower and bridge. But the flames licked harmlessly at the stone pilings, and the ships burned themselves out without doing any serious damage.

The failure – coming as it did with such loss of life – was a blow to Viking morale, but nature provided a boost a few days later when a winter flood did their work for them and washed away the southern bridge. The tower guarding it was now stranded, and fell easy prey to an attack. The Vikings were then free to plunder upstream, so they left a small force to continue the siege and raided all the way up to the Loire.

The Parisians sent frantic messages begging Charles the Fat to come to their assistance. The emperor was in Italy, so he sent his general Henry of Saxony with an army. He must have stressed the importance of speed, because Henry pushed his army hard. The difficult winter march across the Alps was followed by an exhausting attack on the Viking camp, which failed miserably. After that solitary attempt, Henry withdrew, abandoning Paris to its fate.

The only bright spot for the Parisians that dark winter, was that Sigfred gave up. His attempt to emulate Ragnar Lothbrok's famous siege had turned into a farce. Surely his time could be spent more fruitfully than sitting under some huge stone walls and waiting for his prey to spontaneously give up. He concluded that the siege was a fool's errand, and allowed himself to be bought off with the rather pathetic sum of sixty pounds of silver – a far cry from Lothbrok's six thousand.

Sigfred's departure did not mean the end of the siege, however. He was only one commander among many, and he was unable to convince many of his fellow Vikings to depart.[85] The siege dragged on until October when the Parisians were heartened by the news that Charles the Fat was on his way with the imperial army. This knowledge gave them the courage to fend off one last full-scale assault by the Vikings who had heard the same news and were anxious to take the city while they still could.

Those Vikings still around when Charles arrived were easily routed. Paris was garrisoned with royal troops, and Charles advanced on the Viking camp. The emperor had the Vikings surrounded and could have struck a decisive blow, but to the shock of the Parisians – and probably the Vikings as well, he opened negotiations instead.

Charles was hardly a successful warrior, and he had a rebellious vassal in Burgundy that was proving hard to put down. Here was a chance to kill two birds with one stone. In exchange for free passage along the Seine, the Vikings would be allowed into Burgundy where they could ravage to their heart's content, punishing Charles' rebellious vassal. Then, as an incentive to leave Frankish lands, they were to be given seven hundred pounds of silver.

The Parisians were furious when they heard the terms. They had performed their duty of defending Frankish territory at great cost, only to have their emperor reward

---

85   He provoked the Vikings into yet another doomed attack of the northern bridge, hoping that the failure would prove his point. Not surprisingly for the hard-headed Norsemen who had spent months dreaming about the riches behind Paris' walls, this did not prove compelling.

the Vikings with exactly what they wanted. As a protest, they refused to abide by the treaty and blocked the river, refusing to let their former enemies pass. The Vikings were forced to drag their ships overland some distance to get around the blockade.

Charles may have thought his plan a shrewd move, but it backfired disastrously. Neither Sigfred nor the other Vikings kept their word, and were soon raiding imperial territory at will. Three years later Charles was deposed, and the Parisians elected a count named Odo, – the man who had directed the city's defense during the Viking siege – as their new king.

Rollo and his war band spent their time raiding in Burgundy, where they were able to accrue substantial loot. Surprisingly, his only defeats seem to have come at the hands of the clergy. In 910 he was driven off from a city by a local bishop who had gathered a militia. The next year, he advanced against the northern French city of Chartres, but again a bishop foiled his plans. Rollo's fleet had been sighted several days before, and the cleric had time to marshal his troops.

The defenders decided not to risk a siege and marched out to confront the Vikings in the open. In the fierce battle that followed, Rollo gained the upper hand, but victory was snatched away when the bishop – who had been watching from the walls – came roaring out of the gates with a mob of citizens behind him. The boost in numbers turned the tide and by nightfall the Vikings were trapped on a hill to the north of the city.

Fighting at night was unthinkable for most medieval armies since in the darkness it was almost impossible to tell friend from foe. The Franks sensibly withdrew to their camp, posting guards to make sure the Vikings didn't slip away.

Rollo, however, had been counting on just such a reaction. The Vikings frequently attacked after the sun went down, using the chaos to their advantage by striking in prearranged thrusts and then withdrawing as the opposing army scattered.

He waited till the early morning, when all but the sentries were asleep, and sent a few men into the middle of the Frankish camp. At a signal, they blasted their war horns, as if an attack was under way. The camp came alive in a panic as men rushed half dressed out of their tents, milling about in confusion. In the chaos, Rollo and his men cut their way out, running for their ships.

The Vikings reached the bank of the Loire, but were not far enough ahead of the pursuing Franks for the entire army to board their ships. Switching tactics, Rollo slaughtered every pack and stock animal he could find, erecting a wall of their corpses. When the Frankish cavalry arrived, their horses were unnerved by the smell of blood and refused to advance. Rollo had temporarily saved the Vikings, but he was still trapped. A Frankish army under the command of King Charles the Simple had arrived upstream and was blocking the escape route. Sooner or later the king's army would move in for the kill, or the Vikings would starve. Either way there seemed little hope, but instead of attacking the exposed Norsemen, the king offered them extraordinary terms.

King Charles had been on the throne for just over a decade. He was not, despite the English translation of his nickname, a stupid man.[86] The Frankish policy of buying off Vikings had gone a long way towards bankrupting the kingdom. Roughly one third of the coins minted in France had ended up in Viking hoards, and more than a hundred

---

86   A better rendering would be Charles the 'Straight-forward', as in not flowery
        or verbose.

and twenty thousand pounds of silver had been paid out. There was little money left to defray the tremendous cost of keeping the royal army in the field, and in any case Charles was well aware of the limitations of his authority. While he could defeat individual bands of Vikings in pitched battle, there was no hope of checking their lightning raids across the entire breadth of his kingdom. He had to defend the vital core and delegate the coastal defenses to others.

That meant not only tolerating a Viking presence on the Seine, but actually encouraging one. If he could convince the Norsemen that it was in their best interests to defend rather than raid the coast, Charles would provide first-rate protection to his kingdom's shoreline. There was only one guaranteed way to do this and that was to make the Vikings landowners.

This bold tactic had already been tried by his cousin Charles the Fat some twenty years before. The Vikings had been swarming over Frisia for more than half a century, and had been the de facto rulers for nearly as long. In an attempt to stabilize the area, Charles the Fat had contacted one of the Viking leaders named Godfred, offering to give him most of Frisia in exchange for his conversion to Christianity.[87] Godfred had accepted and been duly baptized, but Thor was not so easily washed away. Instead of consolidating his holdings into a unified state, Godfred left to go pillage Saxony. When Charles the Fat reminded him of his duties, the Viking demanded to be given some wine-districts along the Rhine as a condition of peace. Clearly the experiment in Viking protection had failed, so Charles the Fat had Godfred assassinated.

It is to Charles the Simple's credit that he realized that the plan to establish a Viking buffer backfired not because it

---

87   His partner was Sigfred who would later lead the attack on Paris.

was impossible for the Norsemen to settle down and become loyal citizens, but because Godfred had been the wrong man for the job. In Rollo, however, he had unwittingly found the perfect candidate.

The Viking had probably first gone to sea as a young teenager, and after a life spent raiding, was now in his mid to late fifties. Judging from the number of men who followed him he was already wealthy, and had reached the age where a man thinks about enjoying the fruits of his labor. Here was a chance to settle down and reward his followers with that most precious commodity – land.

The two sides met on the highroad from Rouen to Paris and signed the treaty of St. Clair-sur-Epte. The terms were much as they had been for Godfred. In exchange for becoming a Christian, Rollo was to be granted the lands of the Seine basin from Rouen to Évreux, to be held in fief from the king. He pledged to keep peace with the Christian king, defend the lands he had been given, and provide military assistance when required.[88]

Rollo was baptized with his entire army, which proved somewhat embarrassing for all involved. When his men realized that they would get a fresh white tunic after the ceremony, several of them were caught being baptized multiple times. Despite scandalized whispers, an incident was avoided. The same could not be said for the ceremony of homage, however. According to a dubious later Norman source, Rollo balked at the traditional kissing of the king's foot. No Viking warlord was ever going to grovel in public, so he delegated it to one of his men. The hulking Norseman

88 Interestingly enough, he was given tacit permission to continue plundering Brittany - perhaps as an outlet for any residual Viking tendencies. Charles the Simple was determined not to repeat his cousin's mistakes.

yanked up Charles' foot to his mouth, upending the surprised Frankish monarch.[89]

Regardless of the difficulties in getting through its ceremonies, St. Clair-sur-Epte was one of the most important agreements in medieval history. The treaty created the *Terra Normanorum*, the 'land of the Northmen' which today is better known as Normandy. From the beginning, Rollo took his duties seriously. He rebuilt the abbeys and churches that the Vikings had plundered, built up the defenses of Norman towns, and put together a legal code to protect his citizen's lives and property. Most important of all, he divided up the land among his most important followers, transforming a mobile Viking aristocracy into a landed class.

Rollo also seems to have remained loyal to Charles the Simple. When a revolt deposed the king in 923, Rollo dutifully led his army against the rebel. Neither Rollo nor his immediate successors stopped harboring Vikings – the Normans would continue to offer them sanctuary until the eleventh century – but Charles the Simple's experiment was a success. After Rollo, there were no further major attacks on the Seine, and Normandy itself began to adopt French customs.

Much of this was established by Rollo's own example. He adopted his baptismal name of Robert, married a local woman that he had captured, and encouraged his men to take native wives as well. Within a generation, most of the Scandinavian language and traditions had faded away, replaced by French.

---

89   It could be said that this was a fitting metaphor considering the relationship of later Norman dukes and their nominal French overlords.

Rollo himself may only have been Christian in name, but his descendants emerged as the faith's most able defenders.[90] From a Viking foundation, there emerged a hybrid state with the culture and religion of the Franks and the ferocious energy of the Norsemen. It was perhaps the most successful of the Viking creations.

Rollo's triumph, however, was also a sign that the world was changing. The old hunting grounds of western Francia, England, and Ireland were closing off. The century of Viking raids had either exhausted their wealth or provoked a strong native response. If the Viking way of life were to continue, more fertile territory had to be found. The great age of Viking discovery had begun.

---

90 In the last glimpse we have of him, he is hedging his bets for the afterlife. He donated a hundred pounds of gold to the Church and sacrificed a hundred prisoners to Odin.

THE EXPLORERS

Chapter 11

VIKINGS ON THE RIVIERA

"They raised the standards, spread the sails before the wind, and like agile wolves set out to rip apart the Lord's sheep, pouring out human blood to their god Thor."

- William of Jumieges

If Rollo was indeed present at the siege of Paris, he served alongside the first significant Viking explorer, Hastein. By 885, Hastein was near the end of a colorful career, having served in nearly every major Viking campaign of the ninth century. He had been one of the leaders of the Great Heathen Army when it attacked Alfred's kingdom, and had crossed over to France after the treaty of Wedmore. Although his ancestry is disputed, he was either the son of Ragnar Lothbrok, or had been recruited by him to toughen up Ragnar's youngest son Bjorn. Either way, he had fulfilled the latter request admirably, by leading the twelve-year old on a wild raid up the Loire river.

Hastein had already made a nuisance of himself along both banks of the river. The Norman monk, Dudo of Saint-Quentin, described him as '*accursed, headstrong, extremely cruel, and harsh*", and then, perhaps fearing that his audience wouldn't get the point without further elaboration, continued " *destructive, troublesome, wild, ferocious, infamous, inconstant, brash, conceited and lawless, death-dealing, rude, a rebellious traitor and kindler of evil, a double-faced hypocrite, and ungodly, arrogant, seductive and foolhardy deceiver, a lewd, unbridled, contentious rascal".* Clearly Ragnar had chosen his son's mentor well.

Hastein and Bjorn made themselves such a nuisance in northern France that King Charles the Bald tried to buy him off by handing over control of the city of Chartres. Since the Viking had no use for a city, he sold it to a neighboring count and continued raiding.[91]

This time, however, he wasn't careful and was surprised by an army led by Duke Robert the Strong.[92] Hastein only managed to avoid destruction by barricading himself and his men inside a church. Not wanting to destroy a sacred building, Duke Robert decided to starve them out and settled in for a siege. Since it was a hot day, he removed his armor, only to have Hastein – who had been watching discreetly from a window – charge out with his entire force. In the melée, Duke Robert was killed, and the Vikings escaped.

Preying on the Loire valley proved lucrative, but in 859 Hastein and Bjorn dreamed up an even more audacious plan. There were untold riches to the west, beyond the borders of Christendom. The Moorish kingdom of Spain, once part of a vast caliphate that extended east across north Africa to Iran, was dripping in gold.

They had obtained the idea of attacking Spain from a failed Viking expedition a dozen or so years before. The raid had gotten off to a good start in 844 when thirty ships had

---

91 A far more useful bribe was offered by the Count of Brittany who gave Hastein five hundred cows to stop attacking his territory.

92 Robert was the great-grandfather of Hugh Capet, and therefore the ancestor of the Capetian line of kings which ruled France from 987 until 1328.

reached the city of Seville, where they managed to pull down a section of the walls. After dispatching what little resistance they found the Vikings settled down to the important work of plundering the wealthy homes of the many aristocrats and silk merchants. The fittest and most attractive citizens were loaded on to ships and sent to the busy Muslim slave markets to the west.

Instead of leaving Seville, the Vikings decided to make it a base, and for the next six weeks they struck targets as far away as Lisbon and Cadiz. If there were plenty of riches for the taking, however, there were also dangers. Most of the Vikings of the 844 expedition never made it back to their ships. They spent so long stripping the surrounding country of valuables that the Moors were given time to arrange a counterattack and the emir of Cordoba managed to catch the Vikings by surprise. So many of them were captured that the local gallows couldn't accommodate them all, and the surplus had to be hung from the surrounding palm trees. The heads of the leader and two hundred of his men were then sent as a gift to an emir in Tangier.

Despite the inglorious end, the expedition had proved that Spain was vulnerable, and if one was willing to risk these dangers, even more fabulous treasure awaited in the lands beyond. The Spanish route would give the Vikings entry into the Mediterranean, and allow them access to the wealth of legendary Rome. This was too tempting to pass up for Hastein, so in the summer of 859 he loaded twenty four hundred men on sixty-two ships, and launched the raid that would cement his reputation.

It got off to a rocky start. Hastein and Bjorn sailed to Seville, hoping to repeat the success of the previous raid. Unfortunately for them, in the fifteen years since the first attack, the local emir had built a fleet of his own and established a chain of look-out posts along the Atlantic coast. He was well aware of the approaching threat, and had fortified the city as a result. As the Viking longships neared the walls, the Moorish garrison used primitive flame-throwers to spew a burning, oily pitch onto the decks below.[93]

A humiliating retreat followed, and Bjorn and Hastein decided to bypass Spain's northern coast except for the occasional light raid to pick up supplies. After rounding the headlands of what is today Portugal, they came ashore at the Spanish city of Algeciras. Here they burned a local mosque and captured a few slaves and supplies, but were disappointed by the lack of plunder.

Bad luck continued to plague them. A storm initially prevented them from entering the Straits of Gibraltar, driving them down the western coast of Africa but they eventually managed to salvage most of the fleet and cross through the Straits to the north African city of Nador. Once in the Mediterranean their luck turned. They spent eight days raiding the beaches of Nador, capturing exotic 'blue' and black slaves.[94] They then crossed over to the Spanish coast, stopping along the way to raid the Balearic islands of Formentera, Majorca, and Minorca.

With winter approaching, Hastein began looking for a suitable base in southern France where they could sit it out. Sailing up the Ter river, they sacked the monastery at Perpignan and attacked several more cities before coming up against a defensive Frankish force at Arles which required

---

93 This was the Moorish version of 'Greek Fire', the Byzantine super weapon.

94 The 'blue' men were probably Tauregs, a Berber tribe that tatooed themselves extensively. The 'blacks' were most likely sub-Saharans who had been captured by the Moors.

them to find winter quarters on an island in the Côte d'Azur of what is today the French Riviera. The Scandinavians enjoyed the climate, which was warm even in the winter.[95] When the spring arrived, they crossed over into Italy and sacked Pisa. It was from the captives of this raid that Hastein probably learned that he was near Rome.

The chance of sacking the imperial city was the grand prize of all piratical raids, beyond the wildest dreams of most Vikings. If they could pull it off, they would cover themselves in enough glory to be remembered for generations.

The fleet slipped down the western coast of the peninsula, looking for the great metropolis. When they spotted Luna, a large city, which was the center of the Roman marble trade, they allegedly mistook it for Rome and sailed into its harbor.[96]

There was no chance that the Vikings could take it by assault. Perhaps under cover of night they could have evaded detection and slipped through the massive walls unscathed, but it would have been impossible in broad daylight. Sentries had spotted the fleet several miles away and by the time the Vikings reached the city, the alarm bells had warned the garrison and the gates to the city had been closed.

If brute force wouldn't suffice, however, there was always the famous Viking cunning. The fleet was put to anchor and under a flag of truce some Vikings approached the gate. Their leader, they claimed, was dying and wished to be baptized

---

95 The spot they were in was one of the first to be developed as a winter resort destination. In the 18th century it was the place for members of the British upper class to go. The Vikings were clearly on to something.

96 That at least is the story. Given the Viking sophistication in choosing their targets, however, and the fact that they stayed in the Mediterranean for several years, it is difficult to believe that they would have made such an error.

as a Christian. As proof, they had brought along the ailing Hastein on a litter, groaning and sweating.

The request presented a moral dilemma for the Italians. As Christians they could hardly turn away a dying penitent, but they didn't trust the Vikings and expected a trick. The local count, in consultation with the bishop, warily decided to admit Hastein, but made sure that he was heavily guarded. A detachment of soldiers was sent to collect Hastein and a small retinue while the rest of the Vikings waited outside.

Despite the misgivings, the people of Luna flocked to see the curiosity of a dreaded barbarian peacefully inside their city. The Vikings were on their best behavior as they were escorted to the cathedral, remaining silent and respectful. Throughout the service, which probably lasted a few hours, Hastein was a picture of reverence and weakness, a dying man who had finally seen the light. The bishop performed the baptism, and the count stood in as godfather, christening Hastein with a new name. When the rite had concluded, the Vikings respectfully picked up the litter and carried their stricken leader back to the ships.

That night, a Viking messenger reappeared at the gates, and after thanking the count for allowing the baptism, sadly informed him that Hastein had died. Before he expired, however, he had asked to be given a funeral mass and to be buried in the holy ground of the cathedral cemetery.

The next day a solemn procession of fifty Vikings, each dressed in long robes of mourning, entered the city carrying Hastein's corpse on a bier. Virtually all the inhabitants of the city had turned out to witness the event, joining the cavalcade all the way to the cathedral. The bishop, surrounded by a crowd of monks and priests bearing candles, blessed the coffin with holy water, and led the entire procession inside.

As the bishop launched into the funerary Mass, reminding all good Christians to look forward to the day of resurrection, the coffin lid was abruptly thrown to the ground and a very much alive Hastein leapt out. As he cut down the bishop, his men threw off their cloaks and drew their weapons. A few ran to bar the doors, the rest set about slaughtering the congregation.

At the same time – perhaps alerted by the tolling bell – Bjorn Ironside led the remaining Vikings into the city and they fanned out, looking for treasure. The plundering lasted for the entire day. Portable goods were loaded onto the ships, the younger citizens were spared to be sold as slaves, and the rest were killed. Finally, when night began to fall, Hastein called off the attack. Since nothing more could fit on their ships, they set fire to the city and sailed away.[97] For the next two years, the Norsemen criss-crossed the Mediterranean, raiding both the African and European coasts. There are even rumors that they tried to sack Alexandria in Egypt, but were apparently unable to take it by force or stealth.

By 861, they were ready to return home with their plunder. As they neared the Straits of Gibraltar, however, they found a Moorish fleet blocking their way. Hastein and Bjorn were probably not too worried. The Moors were novice sailors – this was their first fleet and it had been constructed for the sole purpose of intercepting the Vikings. The Viking ships, by contrast, were faster, more maneuverable, and

---

97   Luna was certainly plundered, but the way the Vikings got in is not known for sure. Perhaps it was by the following ruse, but a version of the same story is told about nearly every famous Viking or Viking descendant, including the Danish king Frodo, the Norwegian Harald Hardråda, and the Norman Robert Guiscard.

piloted by seasoned, veteran sailors. Confident of their skills, the Vikings closed to attack.

Most of them got an unpleasant shock. The Moors had brought with them their portable flamethrowers and had even mounted some on their ships. As soon as the first longships were in range, the Moors sprayed the burning oil over the Viking prows. The wooden decks, caulked with pitch, immediately caught fire, and the entire fleet broke up in disorder. Of the sixty ships that entered the battle, only twenty escaped the Mediterranean.

Both Hastein and Bjorn survived the disaster, but the experience had dented what had otherwise been a brilliant raid. To recoup their losses, the two leaders decided to plunder the northern coast of Spain. This time they attacked Pamplona, capital of the little Christian kingdom of Navarra. Its king, García, happened to be in the city when the Vikings attacked and was captured. He was ransomed for the tidy sum of seventy thousand gold pieces, and with this last victory behind them, the Vikings returned to the Loire.

At this point, the two leaders parted ways. Bjorn departed for Scandinavia where he lived out his life as a wealthy and famous sea-king. His colleague, Hastein, returned to his old haunts, looting the Loire valley and collecting various payments from the Frankish king, Charles the Bald. In 885 he took part in the siege of Paris, and when it petered out, he – by now in his late sixties – crossed over the Channel to invade England.

Wessex, however, was no longer the easy target it had once been, and after five years of fruitless raiding, Hastein disappears from history. His remarkable career, which spanned almost four decades of plundering, made him one of the most feared men of his times. In an age where travel was severely limited, cities from north Africa to the British Isles had learned to dread his name. His most frequent victims, the French, probably had it right when they called him "the lusty and terrifying old warrior of the Loire and Somme".

Both Bjorn and Hastein – and the other veterans who had experienced it – must have frequently retold the story of their exploits. It made for a wonderful way to pass the time on a cold northern night, and undoubtedly gained many lurid details around the warm hearth of a mead hall. It had been a daring adventure, which rightly cemented the reputations of its leaders. But unlike Ragnar Lothbrok's sack of Paris, the great raid inspired no duplicates. The western Mediterranean was simply too far away and its coasts were inhabited by too many well-armed and organized enemies. The Vikings needed to establish footholds, bases from which they could extend their reach, and neither the various Islamic Caliphates nor the Frankish empire were going to allow that.

The Mediterranean was abandoned as a site of possible raiding, and the Danes concentrated on England and France.[98] This however, was just the start of the great age of Viking discovery. Even as Hastein and Bjorn set out on their adventure, Norwegian Vikings had started the push west.

---

98   At least from the west. The Vikings would eventually reach it again via Constantinople in the east.

Chapter 12

THE FRONTIER REPUBLIC

"It is a still and silent sea that drowns a man."

- Edda of Sæmund the Wise

Most Viking discoveries were made by island hopping. Sometime towards the end of the eighth century, the Vikings discovered the Shetlands, an archipelago located roughly sixty miles north of Scotland. This uninhabited cluster of more than three hundred rocky islands was probably found by Norwegian Vikings since it lies almost directly west of Bergen, Norway's largest western port. The Vikings used them for stock raising, mostly sheep and cattle, to resupply ships headed south.

About fifty years after the discovery of the Shetlands, Viking explorers found the Faeroe Islands a hundred and seventy miles to the northwest. These seventeen treeless islands were used for the same purpose as the Shetlands, namely the production of wool and salted meat.

They had no reason to keep going west. The Faeroes themselves, were well out of the way of the main target of the British Isles, and any further rocky little islands would have been too remote and – given the sudden storms and frequent fogs of the North Sea – too dangerous to be worth visiting.

The first Vikings to reach Iceland, therefore, did so purely by accident. Viking sailors reckoned through careful observation, and trial and error, not sophisticated navigational tools. Land was found by noting changes in the color of water, differences in the flight patterns of birds, and the presence of driftwood. The Vikings calculated latitude by the midday sun during the day, and by the stars at night. If neither of those two options was available, they relied on instinct. Skippers were notoriously pragmatic. The Laxdæla Saga tells the story of Olaf the Peacock who got hopelessly lost in a fog and drifted for days. When it finally lifted, there was a heated debate about what direction to go. The crew voted for a particular direction and informed Olaf of their choice. The grizzled captain ignored them and told his veteran navigator to pick the direction. '*I want only the shrewdest one to decide*', he said, '*because in my opinion, the council of fools is all the more dangerous the more of them there are.*'

Around the middle of the ninth century, a Norwegian named Naddodd got lost on his way to the Faeroe Islands, overshooting his destination by four hundred miles. When he finally spotted land, he had the crew fan out looking for human settlement to try to figure out where they were. When they could find none, he scaled a mountain and looked into the interior, seeing nothing but a vast icy plain of glaciers and frozen fields. There was no smoke from hearth fires – a sign that at least this part of the land was uninhabited – so Naddodd returned to his ships, just as a heavy snow began to fall. It seemed appropriate to give this new country a name, so Naddodd chose 'Snowland' after its chief characteristic.

The landing party was undoubtedly disappointed that there were no monasteries to raid, but when they returned to Norway, Naddodd and his crew told how there was good land for the taking to the northwest. Word eventually spread to Sweden where a merchant named Garthar decided to find it for himself. With a bit of good luck he managed to retrace Naddodd's route and landed on the east coast of the new country.[99] Instead of coming ashore, however, he sailed along the coast to find out large it was. By the time he had concluded that it was an island the weather was worsening, so he and the crew beached the ships and built a house on the northern coast, staying alive through the bitter winter by harvesting seagull eggs and other marine life. Since there were no predators, and it was seemingly uninhabited, Garthar named the island 'Gartharsholmi' after himself and returned to Scandinavia.[100] At least one of his men was impressed enough to want to stay behind. A free man named Nattfari (Nightwalker), remained on the homestead with a male and female slave for company, becoming the island's first settlers.

They soon had company. A Norwegian named Flóki set out at the end of the ninth century with the explicit attempt to colonize the new land. Story has it that he brought his family with him, along with cattle and other settlers, and navigated with the aid of three ravens. His plan was to release them periodically, and if one didn't return, he would know that land could be found in that direction. When this unorthodox ploy actually worked, his contemporaries began calling him 'Flóki the Lucky' and 'Raven Flóki'.

---

99 He also seems to have lost his way in a fog.

100 The earliest Icelandic sources claim that there were some Irish monks on the island when the Vikings arrived. They got there - in what must have been a terrifying experience - by skin boats, tiny crafts without keels which would skim along the top of the waves. They had come in search of a refuge from the world, and wisely fled when the Vikings arrived.

The little group set up a camp on the western coast at a place called Vatnsfjordur, and built a farmstead. The summer was a delightful one, with the midnight sun so bright that they could 'pick lice off their clothes at night'. There was plenty of grazing land for Raven Flóki's stock animals, and even some birch trees for constructing homesteads. Unfortunately for the settlers, however, the winter was brutal. They had neglected to store up enough hay, and all their animals died. When they tried to move, they found that icebergs and glaciers choked the fjords. Only when the summer had begun did the ice clear enough to allow them to leave.

The disillusioned Flóki sailed away as soon as he could, leaving most of his crew behind. When he returned to Norway, he reported that the land was worthless, calling it 'Iceland'. Yet his failed attempt at colonization and demoralized comments didn't deter anyone.[101] Just a year or two after his return, a Norwegian named Ingólfur Arnarson repeated the attempt, and this time it worked.

Only a Viking would have found Iceland enticing! For a ninth century European, the island was at the remote end of the world. Just below the Arctic Circle, it is habitable – but only barely. The western, southwestern, and parts of the northwest coasts are livable thanks to the moderating waters of the North Atlantic Drift, but many of the fjords and coastlines are blocked by icebergs and ice floes for much of the year.

These icebergs made any approach to the island treacherous. Only an inch of wood separated Viking sailors from the Atlantic Ocean, and even a small iceberg could rip through the hull. Nor was there much wood for repairs if they then managed to land. The island, nearly

---

101 Including Flóki himself. He later returned and spent the rest of his life in Iceland.

forty thousand square miles, is larger than England, Wales, and part of Scotland combined, but is mostly treeless. The interior, a vast central plateau of volcanoes, snowfields, and glaciers, is nearly three hundred miles across and completely uninhabitable. Only the coasts – roughly fifteen percent of the total land area – are capable of supporting a human population.

The first Norwegians who looked into the interior probably thought they were seeing a preview of Ragnarok. In that last battle, the primeval ice giants and fire demons would be released, plunging the world into a freezing and fiery twilight. Iceland, with its volcanoes and glaciers, and its winters of lasting darkness, must have seemed a vision of things to come.

The island straddles the Mid-Atlantic Ridge – the division between the Eurasian and North American tectonic plates that is responsible for both its many hot springs and active volcanoes. The latter regularly unleash lava floes that melt glaciers and spew ash across the surface of the entire island.[102] This in turn, stunts the growth of any plant life, and wreaks havoc on attempts at raising stock. When the animals eat the ash-covered grass, the sulfides damage the teeth and gums, and most of them die. A Viking population would be forced to slaughter and preserve what they could, eating well one year and starving the next.[103]

From the start, Iceland was a forbidding landscape, even for Scandinavians who had experience surviving along the

---

102 The last several centuries have seen an average of one eruption every five years.

103 This happened as late as 1783. An eruption of the craters around Mt. Laki killed 50% of all cattle, 80% of all sheep, and 75% of all horses. Within three years a third of the population had starved.

fjords of the North Atlantic. It demanded full cooperation between all of the colonists, and ruthlessly weeded out the weak. To paraphrase a later settler in a different colony, 'those who didn't work, starved.'

The reasons the Vikings came were varied, but can loosely fall into two categories. They were either fleeing oppression at home – King Harald Fairhair was busy imposing his will over Norway – or were unable to resist the attraction of free land. Occasionally it was a bit of both. The founder of the first permanent settlement, Ingólfur Arnarson, had become involved in a blood feud (a distressingly common occurrence among the Vikings) and was looking to escape to greener pastures. Hearing about Raven Flóki's island, he sailed with his stepbrother, wife, and entire household.

His stepbrother Hjörleifur, had a checkered past as well. After killing a man in Norway, he decided to go raiding in Ireland until tempers cooled down at home. He returned with ten Celtic slaves, and a sword that he had found in an Irish barrow that had once belonged, he rather dubiously claimed, to Ragnar Lothbrok. Famous sword or not, the family he had insulted was still out for blood, so he joined Ingólfur on his trek to Iceland.

When they came in sight of land, Ingólfur decided to let the god Thor choose where he would establish his homestead. He had brought with him a pair of wooden poles and now cast them overboard, vowing to build wherever they washed ashore. He then beached the ship and sent two slaves to find the poles. The current carried them into the small bay of a fjord on the southwestern coast. Steam from nearby hot springs partially obscured it, so Ingólfur named it Reykjavík, which means '*Smoky Bay*'. He built his hall on the spot, positioning the two poles on either side of his own seat at the head of the main table.

Ingólfur's kinsman Hjörleifur was not so fortunate. He was not about to let the whim of the gods choose anything and selected the first spot that looked promising to build his hall. Although he picked a fine spot, he paid for his arrogance a short time later when his slaves revolted, and he was killed in the resulting skirmish. To the Vikings, the lesson was simple. Honor the gods, and prosper, or disregard them and fail.

The choosing of a settlement became a religious ceremony for those first settlers, and many of them emulated Ingólfur by letting the currents choose a site for them.[104] The god of choice for nearly all of them was Thor. He controlled the storms at sea, the mist, rain and skies, and his favor was therefore critical. This was true even of those who adopted Christianity. When asked what god he worshiped, an early tenth century Icelander, Helgi the Lean, replied, '*On land I worship Christ, but at sea I always invoke Thor*'.[105]

Thor's help, or at least a good deal of luck, was needed. The trip to Iceland took seven to ten days from the west coast of Norway, a distance of some six hundred miles. The usual route involved island hopping, from the Shetlands to the Faeroes, and then to Iceland, a treacherous and often stormy route.

The ship used for such a journey was called a *knörr*. It was roughly eighty feet long and could accommodate several

104 Although some Icelanders believe it, there is reason to doubt the story of the founding of Reykjavík. In 1974 during the millennial celebrations, more than a hundred marked pillars were thrown into the ocean along the southeastern and southern coast. None of them made it anywhere near Reykjavík.

105 A huge number (some say up to a quarter) of all Icelanders were named in honor of Thor during the Viking age. This has declined in modern times, but there are still plenty of Thors, Thorgills, Thorbergs, and Tors, etc

dozen passengers. In addition to food and water for the journey, the first settlers would have also carried horses, pigs, sheep, and cattle, along with farming tools and weapons. They wouldn't have needed building materials as there were some scrub forests of birch that could be harvested.

Although it was a hard land, there were some advantages. Along the coasts there was plenty of pasture land, no predators, and virtually no insects. Seals, walruses, and other mammals were plentiful, and flocks of seagulls, puffins, and great auks nested on the coasts. Vast schools of North Atlantic cod could be found in the nearby waters, and its meat could be frozen and broken into chunks to be consumed on long sea voyages. Fruits, grains, and vegetables all had to be imported – a vulnerability the Vikings never solved – but it was possible to carve out a home of some sort.

One settler, Aud the Deep Minded, illuminates the power a woman could hold in Icelandic society. She was the wife of Olaf the White, co-ruler of Dublin with Ivar the Boneless. After her husband and son died, Aud outfitted a ship of twenty men, and captained it herself, managing the impressive – and highly praised – feat of landing with crew and cargo intact. When she arrived, she claimed a huge plot of land, freed her slaves, and divided the property between herself and them. She acted as a clan chief, presiding over her own hall and its celebrated feasts. As a mark of the respect she was held in, she was given a complete Viking ship burial when she died. Nowhere else in Europe at the time, would a woman be allowed to own land much less rule over it.

This limited equality was possible because the harsh conditions created a society that was both rugged and stubbornly independent. Most of the settlers had come to Iceland to escape being told what to do, or to find a new life, and they didn't intend to create a new tyranny on their free island. This was a remarkable experiment, a kind of frontier republic on the fringes of human existence. There were no towns or cities, no army or taxes, no king, and virtually no government. There were only isolated farmsteads, extended families living together in groups as small as fifteen and as large as several hundred.

When mediation between individuals was needed, both parties turned to the local *Gothi*, a man who was respected for his reputation, knowledge of the traditional law, and his generosity. Despite the respect he was held in, the Gothi was no chieftain. The Icelanders were very conscious of creeping despotism, and were determined to stop it. The *Gothar* were not lords or nobles; theirs was not a hereditary position, and if they failed to do their job adequately they were replaced. There were no peasants and nobility. All free men were equal.[106]

When group decisions needed to be made for a local area, it was done in the ancient Germanic manner of a *Thing*. The free Icelanders would gather at an assembly and vote, with the majority carrying the day. If there was ever a need for foreign policy, or a decision affecting the whole island, a great assembly called the *Althing* would meet. Each farmstead would send a representative and again a simple vote would determine the outcome.

The closest thing they had to a national figure was the Lawspeaker, a particularly respected Gothi who was elected for a three-year term. Each year he would stand on a special

---

106 The Vikings had three social classes: Slaves (thralls), freed slaves, and free men. The middle group did not have all the rights of free men.

rock at the Althing and recite from memory one third of Iceland's laws with the other Gothar around him making sure he didn't make an error. Any Icelander who wanted to announce the settlement of farm, or a marriage, or business contract would do so here, in the presence of the assembled free men.

The feat of memory, being able to recite the entire law code, was a testament to both the simplicity of Iceland's laws and the capability of Icelandic memories. This was a skill perfected during the long Arctic nights, when there was nothing to do except weave entertaining stories to pass the time. During the Viking Age, Iceland's main export was its poetry. Icelandic *Skalds* – traveling poets – became famous for their ability to bring tales of Viking heroes to life. Any king, or would-be adventurer had to have a skald on hand in their hall to tell of their exploits. Many Icelanders found fame and even wealth by telling their stories across the Scandinavian world.

The island was resource poor, but it had a society that only the Vikings could have pulled off. Since travel across the interior was impossible in some places, the only way to maintain contact and a sense of mutual identity, was by sailing around the coasts. Life was certainly hard, but the idea of a self-regulating society was wildly attractive. Iceland held out the promise of good land where a lowly Norwegian or Irish Viking could settle and live as a jarl, without having to risk life and limb fighting fierce Anglo-Saxon or Celtic opponents. Within a generation it had filled up.

Fifty years after Ingólfur Arnarson's landing, the population had risen to around ten thousand and there was no more available land to claim. Iceland remained a popular destination, especially for exiles from Norway, but its initial promise had dimmed. Men began looking out to sea again, perhaps following schools of fish further and further from shore, in little journeys of discovery. Glimpses of misty land masses far to the west began to filter back, and there were always restless men who found even Iceland's frontier society too constricting. For them, the lure would always be westwards.

Chapter 13

THE WESTERN ISLES

"It is best to search while the trail is new."

- Edda of Sæmund the Wise

The discovery of further islands to the northwest was a replay of the discovery of Iceland itself. Tradition holds that the first Viking to site fresh land was the Norwegian Gunnbjørn Ulfsson in the early ninth century. He was caught in a storm on a trip from Norway to Iceland and after a long journey, saw previously unknown rocky islands that he named after himself – Gunnbjørn's skerries. He also caught sight of a much larger landmass to the west, but when he reported his findings, no one was interested since Iceland still had available land.

Nearly a century later, Iceland was becoming over populated – at least by Viking standards – and in 978, Snæbjörn Galti, decided to go and search for Gunnbjørn's mysterious land and colonize it if he could. After putting together a crew, he sailed to Gunnbjørn's skerries to gather information about what lay beyond. By this time the skerries were thinly populated with men who wanted to escape the crowds of Iceland, and they confirmed that there was indeed something to the west.[107]

Snæbjörn's persistence paid off, and a few days sailing brought him to the eastern shore of Greenland, a massive volcanic island larger than all of Scandinavia put together. He set up his colony, but disaster struck almost immediately. The site he chose was a difficult one since the eastern coast of Greenland is largely not suitable for human habitation. More damaging, however, was the internal quarrelling which soon had the colonists at each other's throats. Some violent argument erupted – the precise issue is unknown – both sides drew weapons, and Snæbjörn was killed in the fighting. Without its leader, the colony collapsed, and only two survivors returned to Iceland.

Although the attempt at the colonization of Greenland had been a spectacular failure, it had proved that the new land existed and could be reached from Iceland. Only four years later a second attempt succeeded. This time the expedition was led by a hotheaded Norwegian named Erik Thorvaldsson, better known as Erik the Red. Recklessness seemed to run in the family. His father, Thorvald, had been exiled from Norway for manslaughter, and Erik continued the family tradition a few years later, getting banished for the crime of '*some killings*'. He fled to Iceland for refuge and claimed a farm on the northwest coast hoping to settle down.

Everywhere he went, however, trouble seemed to follow. At his first farmstead, two of his slaves inadvertently started a landslide and damaged some of his neighbor's property. In

---

107 At their height they boasted eighteen farms. What made even this possible was the presence of hot springs which the colonists used for bathing, dressing their meat, and baking their bread. Unfortunately, this geothermal activity proved the colony's undoing. In 1346 a volcanic eruption destroyed them completely.

the ensuing demands for payment, Erik killed a man – the delightfully named Eyjolf the Foul – and was forced to flee again. This time he settled on one of the islands off the coast of Iceland, safely out of reach of Eyjolf's kinsmen.

His new farm was even less successful than the first. Within a short time he was again quarreling, this time killing not only his neighbor, but the man's sons as well, a crime which finally got him exiled for three years.[108]

Erik was running out of places from which he could be banished, and he clearly needed a place without existing laws, so he bought Snæbjörn's ship – and the services of the surviving crew – and headed west. The old sailors managed to repeat their earlier trip, and Erik spent the three years of his exile exploring the coast looking for a suitable spot for a colony. Rounding the ice-bound southern tip of what is now Cape Farewell, he discovered two habitable fjords on the western coast at roughly the same latitude as Iceland.

Erik was probably not aware that he had reached an island since the ice floes prevented him from sailing around it, but he noticed that there were no predators – either human or animal.[109] Convinced that he could make a colony work, he sailed back to Iceland and began to recruit settlers.

Like all good salesmen, Erik recognized the value of publicity, so he called the new land 'Greenland' to make it more attractive. The pitch worked dramatically, as more than five hundred Icelanders agreed to make the trip. This was due at least in part to Erik's powers of persuasion and his description of Greenland's plentiful reserves of fish and fowl. The old lure of an empty land for the taking certainly played

---

108 This was the lighter of two possible sentences. The worst crimes were punished by death.

109 The Inuit population wouldn't arrive till the fourteenth century.

a part as well, all the more so because the days of claiming good land in Iceland were gone. The island was beginning to show the first unmistakable signs of ecological decay. In the search for ever more pastureland, the settlers had cut down all the birch forests and the deforestation was starting to erode the uplands. Not only was there no new land, but some of the newest farms were failing as the soil deteriorated.

In 985, Erik set off with twenty-five ships, loaded down with all the supplies needed to start a new life on the frontier. The journey was a difficult one, and those who went knew they were risking everything in a thousand mile journey through stormy seas. Eighteen of the twenty-five made it to Greenland, and when they pulled up their ships on the beach, there was probably a palatable sense of disappointment.

Now they discovered by just how much Erik had oversold the place. If Iceland was barely habitable, Greenland was downright hostile. Lying mostly above the Arctic Circle, it was at the very edge of the technical and survival abilities of the Vikings. While there was plenty of land – the eight hundred and forty thousand square miles of Greenland makes it the largest island on earth – nearly all of it was uninhabitable. A vast glacier covers the interior, leaving only a bleak, mountainous strip of coast barely fifty miles wide. There is almost no timber or iron, and the warmer months are too short for growing wheat or other staple crops. If they ran out of any vital supplies, they would have to import it from Iceland, a difficult, and unreliable prospect in the tenth century.

Fortunately, there was enough marine life available to supplement their diets. Luxury goods like sealskins, walrus ivory, and the fur of Arctic fox, hares, and polar bears could all be harvested in small amounts. They were in high demand in markets at home and could even be brought to the continental centers of Europe.

The colonization got off to a good start. Erik had probably selected a spot for himself during his three years of exile, and knew exactly where to go. He planted his farm at the head of several long fjords, and called it *Brattahlíð*, meaning 'the steep slope'. It was an exquisite estate. Protected from the frigid arctic waters by the banks of the appropriately named *Eriksfjord*, it still boasts some of the best farmland in Greenland today. The maze of necks and islands in the fjord allowed enough meadow grass to start raising stock animals – the Viking version of wealth – and the rest of the settlers spread out around him.

Thanks to some clever Viking innovations like using irrigation as cold protection for their crops, the colony eventually swelled to four thousand inhabitants.[110] So many settlers arrived that a decision was made to establish a second colony a hundred and seventy miles to the northwest.[111] Erik was naturally chosen as the Gothi of the Eastern Settlement, and established a meetinghouse for an island-wide 'Thing' at Brattahlíð.

In the summer months, when the warmer weather made travel more palatable, some of the colonists would journey nearly a thousand miles to the north in search of walrus,

---

110　When water freezes a small amount of heat is released - roughly 80 calories per gram of water frozen. The Vikings noticed that if they continuously watered a plant it would survive through even the most brutal winter.

111　These are referred to as the 'Eastern' and 'Western' Settlements, which can be confusing since they are both on the west coast of Greenland. 'Northern' and 'Southern' would be more appropriate. A third colony may have been planted between them, but it's not clear if this was just a part of the Western Settlement.

seals, and beached wales to harvest.[112] These voyages resulted in enough of a yield that even accounting for the vagaries of sea travel, Erik became a wealthy man.

Trips back to Iceland and Norway were not frequent, but enough ships made the voyage in both directions that contact was maintained. In addition to the continuous trickle of immigrants who had left Scandinavia and found Iceland overcrowded, there were also relatives who would come to visit, or colonists who gave up and returned.

Although Erik himself never left Greenland again, his children inherited his wanderlust and made several trips back to the homelands. By his wife Thjodhildr, Erik had at least three sons, the oldest of which, Leif, made the dangerous crossing from Greenland to Norway in the summer of 999.

The purpose of his visit isn't known, but he brought his wife as well, perhaps intending to settle there. He managed to find employment with King Olaf Tryggvason as a member of the royal bodyguard. Olaf had need of such men, because he was in the middle of a campaign to forcibly christianize Norway, and there was considerable resistance. The king ultimately failed in his attempt – and lost his life in the bargain – but he made one important convert. Some time in the winter of 999 Leif accepted the new faith, and was baptized together with his wife.

Before he died, Olaf convinced Leif to return to Greenland as an evangelist and spread Christianity. Leif agreed, but on the return trip was caught in a storm and blown badly off course. When the winds died down, and the fog lifted, Leif caught sight of land, but was confused when he saw heavily wooded hills instead of the barren,

112 There is evidence that they reached Disko Bay, two hundred miles north of the Arctic Circle.

rocky coast he was expecting. Realizing that he was somewhere west of Greenland, he turned around and sailed in the opposite direction. Unknowingly, Leif Erikson had glimpsed the New World.

His attention for the moment, however, was the afterlife. When he reached Brattahlíð, he set about the business of conversion, starting with the Eastern Settlement. He found an eager audience for his message, but success came at the price of splitting his family. His mother Thjodhildr became a devout Christian, but his father Erik the Red, a proud pagan, was horrified. Tensions escalated further when Thjodhildr built a church at Brattahlíð, and informed her husband that she would no longer sleep with him until he abandoned his gods – a tactic which the sagas inform us *'was a great trial to his temper.'*[113]

Fortunately for familial relations, Leif announced a new project that diverted attention from the religious dispute. There was an undiscovered country to the west, and he was going to explore it. He invited his father along – Erik's success in Greenland had made him a sort of good luck totem – but the patriarch, already in failing health, declined.[114]

Leif Erikson was not the first Viking to spot the Americas. That honor belonged to Bjarni Herjólfsson, son of the second most wealthy inhabitant of Greenland. Herjólf had

---

113 Leif's efforts were eventually successful and Greenland was christianized, but the lack of priests led to the development of some curious practices. When a man died, for example, he was buried on his farm in unconsecrated land. A stake was driven through his chest until a priest could arrive - at times more than a year later. The stake was then removed, holy water was poured in the hole, and a funeral service was conducted.

114 According to the Norse sagas, Erik agreed to go, but fell off his horse while riding to the ship and, seeing this as a sign of bad luck, changed his mind and stayed home.

been one of the original settlers, a close companion of Erik
in Iceland. He had done quite well for himself there, but
had been unable to convince his son Bjarni to join him on
the island. This was probably because Bjarni was already a
successful merchant in Norway, and had no desire to start
over on an overcrowded island. He did agree, however, to
visit his parents each year, a promise he appears to have kept.
In 986, however, when he arrived in Iceland for his annual
call, he found no trace of his father, just a rumor that he had
left for Greenland.

Bjarni immediately decided to go after him, but was faced
with a serious navigational problem. Neither he nor anyone
else in Iceland had been to Greenland, or even knew how to
get there beyond the vague understanding that it was to the
west. There was no map, no compass, not even a description
of what the colony looked like. Nevertheless, he set out with
a volunteer crew, and not surprisingly, got completely lost
and overshot his goal.

His first glimpse of land was of rolling hills covered with
trees, a sure sign that he was in the wrong place. To men
used to Iceland and expecting Greenland, the sight of so
many trees was astonishing. They were everywhere, a vast,
unbroken green carpet from the edge of the beach to the
gently sloping hills in the distance. The Norsemen named it
Markland, 'Tree Land', and continued north, not wanting to
stop and explore.[115]

They next came to an island dominated by curious flat
stones so large that two men could lie heel to head without
touching the edges. The only sign of life they saw were
the polar-foxes that darted away from the ship when they

---

115   This was probably the Labrador coast.

neared the shore. The Vikings called this *Helluland,* 'the Land of Flat Stones'.[116]

Again, Bjarni didn't allow exploration of the island because he was anxious to find his parents. This time, his sail caught favorable easterly winds, and after four days, they finally reached Greenland. Bjarni was reunited with his father, and – probably not willing to go through the harrowing journey again – decided to stay on the island permanently. His story of a new country to the west was treated as a curiosity, but there was little interest initially in pursing it.

Even Bjarni was content to let the issue drop. He was a trader, not an explorer, interested in cargoes and profits, not setting up colonies or fighting off natives. When his father died some time later, he inherited the estate and settled down to a life of farming.

A decade later, when Leif Erikson announced his intention to sail west, Bjarni still had no interest in going along, but he sold Leif his ship, and pointed him to the surviving members of his crew – most of whom signed up for the expedition.[117] All told there were thirty-five men, a large number for a single vessel. This was to be a journey of exploration; both to find a suitable place for a colony, and more importantly, to find a source of raw materials. If the land were really as tree-rich as Bjarni claimed, then all of Greenland's resource problems were solved. Although Leif was not aware of it, the very survival of Greenland's colonies were also at stake.

---

116 Most likely Baffin Island. Viking yarn, tools, and nails have been found on the island.

117 All of the surviving sagas portray a sad end to Bjarni's life. Frontier societies are notoriously violent, but Bjarni's experience was particularly brutal. Armed intruders broke into his home, killed his only son, and abducted his wife. After handing over his ship to Leif, he supposedly committed suicide.

Chapter 14

VINLAND

"Be warned by another's woe."

- Njáls Saga

The land he was looking for was tantalizingly close. On a clear day, a man could climb the highest mountain of the Western Settlement and – provided he knew where to look – could see the cloud banks in the grey sub-Arctic sky that touched the North American continent. The crossing would be much easier for the Vikings than going back to Iceland, and Leif had the advantage of veterans who knew the way.

He decided to sail Bjarni's route in reverse. The old crew had no trouble retracing their course, and with a few days of easy sailing they cast anchor off the coast of Helluland. Leif and a small group rowed ashore, but after a quick survey realized that the land was unsuitable. There was no grass, and virtually no plants of any kind, just a gradually sloping hill of slate that reached all the way to the glaciers – which they called ice mountains – in the distance.[118]

---

118 The Inuit name for the region is Auyittuq, 'the land that never melts'.

Returning to the ships, Leif and his men had a brief discussion and decided to sail south, to see if they could find better land.[119] To the southwest they caught sight of the heavily wooded hills and white beaches of Markland, but again decided to keep exploring. Two days later, they spotted an island, and since the weather was good, rowed ashore. The sight of wild, green grass was a welcome change to the frozen coasts they were used to, and in the first rush of excitement of men who had been cooped up on a ship too long, they claimed the dew was the sweetest thing they had ever tasted.

As soon as they had found a safe place to beach their ship, Leif and his men disembarked with their hammocks, and began work setting up a camp. Although it was only the beginning of autumn, they decided to spend the winter there, and Leif proposed a plan for systematically exploring the land around them. The men were split into two groups of sixteen, with Leif floating between them. Each day one of the groups would go out in a different direction, while the other would stay at camp. The only rules were that the men were not to go so far that they couldn't return the same day, and they were to stay together at all costs.

The island, probably modern Newfoundland, was overflowing with abundance. Not only was there virtually unlimited timber, but the salmon in the rivers were both larger and in greater numbers than they had ever seen before, and the forests were teaming with game. The winters seemed

---

119 Although Leif didn't establish a colony of Baffin Island, the Viking legacy remains in the name of several of its mountains. The highest peak is Mt. Odin, overlooking the nearby twin peaks of Mt. Asgard. The most famous, however, is Mt. Thor, a massive granite slope shaped like the thunder god's hammer resting on its side. Its western face features Earth's tallest vertical drop, some 4,101 feet, the height of nearly four Eiffel Towers stacked on top of each other. The first successful attempt to climb it took 33 days.

milder – Leif claimed that there was no frost – and there was enough wild pasture to support farm animals without the need to make hay. Most astonishing of all, the Vikings noticed that winter days had more hours of sunlight here than they did in Iceland or Greenland. This was a rich country, ready to be exploited.

The most exciting discovery, however, came after Leif and his men had settled into a routine. One evening it was discovered that Tyrker, Leif's foster-father, had gone wandering off from the main group and had lost her way. The distraught Leif immediately gathered a search party of twelve men, but just as they were setting out, Tyrker appeared.

He was obviously in good spirits, and announced that he had made a discovery. He had found some type of wild wheat growing, and had then stumbled across some *wine berries*. The word he used has traditionally been translated as 'grapes', which has led to confusion since grapes don't grow that far north. The Vikings, however, referred to any berry as a 'wine berry'. Tyrker had probably come across cranberries or gooseberries. Either way, the Norsemen immediately started fermenting them into a heady wine and got rather drunk toasting themselves and their new find.

From that time on, the focus became gathering supplies to return home. The two groups no longer went exploring, instead, one gathered berries, while the other cut timber and loaded it on the ships. The new country, named *Vinland* by Leif for its berries, was far superior to Greenland or even Iceland. Not only was it lush, but it was also apparently uninhabited.

When they had gathered as much timber as they could carry, they shoved off, towing their rowboat – now filled to the gunwales with berries – behind them. They had several days of fair wind, and when they were approaching the skerries off Greenland, Leif spotted several figures clinging to the rocks. Sailing closer, he recognized that it was a group of marooned sailors from Iceland who had missed Greenland and crashed into the treacherous rocks. Somehow, he fit the fifteen survivors onboard, and even managed to salvage the remains of their cargo.

Given the relatively small number of colonists on Greenland, the absence of anyone sailing in their direction, and the sheer implausibility of someone stumbling onto their tiny skerry, the men had given themselves up for lost. The appearance of Leif out of the vast ocean, arriving within the rapidly diminishing window of time they could survive, won him the sobriquet 'Leif the Lucky' from the grateful sailors, and they spread the story throughout Greenland.

Leif undoubtedly intended to go back and found a colony, but didn't get the chance. Sometime before, probably during the winter, his father Erik the Red had died. There is some doubt about the cause, but in 1002 some fresh colonists from Iceland had brought the plague with them, and Erik was probably one of the many who died. The colony needed a leader, and Leif was the natural candidate. His duties prevented any new trips west, and he never again set foot on North American shores. The responsibility for further exploration and colonization fell to his siblings.

As a sign that he was passing the torch, Leif gave his ship to his brother Thorvald, and the latter gathered volunteers to start a colony. He was not quite as charismatic as his father or brother, and only managed about a hundred people, but hopes were high as the expedition set off.

At first all went well. Thorvald found Leif's old camp without difficulty, and spent the winter fishing and gathering timber.[120] In the spring, he equipped a boat and began to explore the western coast, taking careful notes on possible settlement sites. As he investigated one island just off the coast, however, he discovered a wooden hut that looked like it had been used to store grain. It was clearly not Viking workmanship, but there was no other sign of human habitation, so Thorvald and his men returned to their camp. It was a slightly disturbing finding. Someone had obviously discovered this land before them. The only question was if they were still there.

The answer was provided the next summer when Thorvald explored the opposite direction. A sudden squall drove their ship onto the beach, damaging the keel. Not wanting to stay there, they limped along until Thorvald spotted a suitable harbor. The site was pleasant enough to encourage Thorvad to think it would make the perfect site for a colony. As they walked back to the ship, they noticed three mounds on the beach that hadn't been there before. On closer inspection they turned out to be canoes, each with three strange looking men hiding beneath. A short struggle ensued where eight of them were captured, but one of the strangers managed to escape in a canoe.

None of the prisoners understood Norse, so the Vikings called them *Skrælings*, 'screamers' or 'screechers', for the strange noises they made.[121] After they had killed the captives, they climbed a nearby hill to look around, and noticed what looked like the huts of a small village in the distance.

While they had been exploring, the Skræling who had escaped returned, this time with 'a countless fleet of canoes'.

---

120 This is almost certainly L'Anse aux Meadows, Newfoundland.

121 They were probably Algonquins.

The two sides attacked each other, but after the first clash, the Skræling's fled. The only Viking casualty was Thorvald, who had been struck with an arrow in the armpit. He managed to pull it out, but the wound proved fatal and his men buried him – with some irony – on the same beach that he had wanted to make his home.

Thorvald's expedition had been reasonably successful, but his loss – he has the dubious distinction of being the first European killed in North America – crippled the survivor's morale. They spent that winter gathering wood and berries, and as soon as the weather improved, they returned to Greenland to report what had happened.

By this time it was clear that if Lief and his father had been lucky, the rest of the family was decidedly less so. The thought of Thorvald's body mouldering in some distant land was too much for his siblings to bear, so the youngest brother Thorstein decided to retrieve it. He set out with a crew of twenty-five, but as soon as they were out of sight of land, they got hopelessly lost, drifting for almost a month. When they were finally driven to shore in early winter, they discovered that they were still in Greenland, having only made it as far as the Western Settlement.

The rest of the crew found homes among the other settlers, but Thorstein and his wife wintered on board their ship, a brutal experience that cost Thorstein his life. After his death, there was no one willing to take up the cause.

If salvaging Thorvald's body had lost its luster, at least Vinland still remained tantalizing. The need for timber, pasture, and resources was a constant concern, and the western land promised a nearby solution. So in the summer of 1009, Leif sanctioned a second major attempt at colonization.

The expedition was led by Leif's brother-in-law Thorfinn Karlsefni, who had married the dead Thorvald's widow, Gudrid. There was always a supply of people looking for greener pastures, and Thorfinn seems to have recruited volunteers by highlighting, among other things, the alcohol that could be made with the abundant wine berries.

This turned out to be a popular pitch, as more than two hundred people enlisted to join him, making it necessary to outfit three ships to fit them all. Among the passengers was Leif's half-sister Freydis, an illegitimate daughter of Erik the Red who had inherited more of his fiery temper and dominant personality than any of his sons. Not wanting to miss the wealth or reputation that could be gained by the trip, she had browbeaten her reluctant husband into joining, and was determined to make him one of the leaders in spite of himself.

Once again, the Vikings found Leif's old camp, and moved in to exploit the nearby resources. That first winter was a particularly brutal one, killing off most of the livestock that they had brought with them. Morale was not improved by the conspicuous lack of berries. They were able to gather enough to make a small brew, but it was hardly the lavish 'banquets of wine' that they had been promised.

Virtually the only bright spot in that harsh winter, at least for Thorfinn, was that his wife Gudrid gave birth to his first child. The boy, named Snorri by his father, was the first European born in North America.[122]

When spring arrived, the colony began to split up. One group returned to Greenland, while the rest relocated to a different site.[123] Thorfinn built a stockade, probably

---

122 Five and a half centuries would pass before there was a second.

123 Thorfinn named it Straumfjord, but its exact location is unknown.

because he was aware of Skrælings in the area, but they seemed peaceful enough. After a while a group showed up wanting to trade, which Thorfinn was happy to do – with the exception of weapons which he forbade any Norseman to sell on pain of death.

The bartering was conducted amicably, but three weeks later a huge number of Skrælings suddenly burst out of the woods and attacked the stockade.[124] They quickly overran the walls, but were brought up short by two unusual sights. The first was the Vikings' penned up bull – the lone male survivor of the previous winter – that was now agitated and bellowing fiercely. The Skrælings had never seen such an animal before and were suddenly uncertain. The second sight, was probably equally terrifying. The Vikings had been caught by surprise and were wavering between resisting and fleeing. Out from her sleeping quarters, however, had come Freydis, and she stood, sword in hand and bellowing like a Valkyrie, rallying the Vikings. They formed a makeshift shield wall and charged, scattering the Skrælings.

The colony had been saved, but it was only a matter of time until it was attacked again. Thorfinn tried to avoid this by relocating, but once again the winter was brutal, and the colonists gave up. Even Thorfinn was exhausted, unwilling to stay longer. As soon as the weather cleared enough to sail, they all left.

Freydis' thoughts on the matter aren't recorded, but judging from her next actions, she was probably disgusted that her kinsman had given up. Clearly, if there was going to be a new colony set up she would have to do it herself.

---

124 Why they did so is a mystery. Perhaps the pungent Viking dairy products – unknown to the natives – convinced the Skrælings that the Vikings were trying to poison them.

Her husband, as usual, was no help. He lacked both the imagination and energy to gather a crew. Fortunately for Freydis, the same summer in which she returned to Greenland, two brothers had arrived with a crew from Norway. She invited them to her home and spent the summer plying them with stories of the easy wealth available to the west.

It took less than a month for the two brothers – Helgi and Finnbogi – to sign on. They agreed to provide a ship, and to make sure that there was an equitable division of whatever they found, all three agreed to a limit of thirty men per vessel.

Relations between them broke down immediately. The brothers arrived at the camp first and installed themselves in Leif's old hall. When Freydis angrily protested, they pointed out that she had cheated by concealing five extra men on her ship. Insults started flying back and forth until Helgi and Finnbogi took their crew and moved to a different location.

By the time winter set in, relations were so strained that the two camps stopped communicating with each other. Freydis decided to eliminate her rivals in a typical Viking fashion, equal parts ruse and brutality. Early one morning she walked to Finnbogi's longhouse and offered to make amends with him. She had decided to leave, she said, and was wondering if he would sell her his ship as it was slightly larger than hers. Finnbogi generously agreed, and Freydis returned to her own camp.

When she climbed back into her own bed, her cold feet woke up her husband who wanted to know why she had been outside. She proceeded to tell him that she had gone to make peace with the brothers, but that they had beaten her instead. Egged on by Freydis, the husband angrily gathered all his men and stormed into Helgi and Finnbogi's camp.

They were taken completely by surprise. Everyone in the house was seized, bound, and then dragged out in front of Freydis where they were killed. The only exception consisted of five women who the men refused to kill no matter how hard Freydis pleaded. She taunted her husband mercilessly for his weakness, but when he still refused, she grabbed an axe and butchered them herself.

The grisly deed may have been gratifying for the formidable Freydis, but it doomed the colony. There were simply too few to sustain another winter, let alone a permanent settlement. She and her husband returned after threatening to kill any man who talked about what happened – and the Vikings never again attempted a settlement in the new world.

There is evidence that they did periodically return to gather raw materials. An Icelandic annal records a voyage 'in search of Vinland' in AD 1121, and more than two centuries later mentions a journey to Markland to harvest timber.[125] The failure to establish a permanent base, however, also doomed Greenland. The island was simply too rugged and sparse to support a European style existence based on animal husbandry. There was not enough pasture, wood, iron, or farmland available.

Vinland would have solved this problem nicely. At the narrowest point of the Davis Strait, less than two hundred miles separates Greenland from Baffin Island. Beyond lay a vast continent teeming with greater resources than Iceland, Europe, and Scandinavia had to offer. But the Vikings simply had too few people to establish themselves against

---

125 The Icelanders were careful to preserve the stories of the new world. In 1477 Columbus, by his own account, sailed to the island to study these records about the land to the west.

a determined native population.[126] This failure threw the Greenland colony back on its tenuous lifeline of long distance trade with Scandinavia. As long as Viking sea-kings ruled their vast northern empire, that was at least possible, but even by the eleventh century, the trade routes were beginning to shift.

As Greenland began to grow more isolated, the climate started to deteriorate. Starting in the mid fourteenth century, global temperatures began to cool, further reducing the island's arable land. The glaciers advanced, and the Inuit crossed over from what is today northern Canada and began to push south.

The last years of Greenland's Viking colonies were not pleasant. A cluster of skeletons exhumed from the Western Settlement reveals a picture of a dying civilization. Half of those who survived to eighteen died before age thirty, and the average height of both men and women is less than five feet. Famine began to be more common; the Icelandic *Landnámabók* claims that the old and helpless were 'killed and thrown over cliffs.' Communication between the two settlements declined as temperatures cooled. After years of hearing nothing, an Easterner named Ivar Bardarson tried to contact the long silent Western colony. He wrote in his diary that he found "*no people, neither Christian nor Heathen, but many sheep running wild.*"

The surviving eastern settlement struggled on a bit longer. It was decimated by the Black Plague, and in 1379 the "*Skrælings* (Inuit) *raided it, killing eighteen and carrying off two boys as slaves.*" The last record we have of anyone living, is the hauntingly short mention in an Icelandic annal:

126 For comparison, Jamestown – in a far more hospitable climate and with the advantage of guns – dwindled from 381 settlers to only 90 in its third winter.

"*In the Year of Our Lord 1410... Sigrid Bjornsdatter married Thorstein Olafson.*" After that, Icelandic ships stopped going west, and there was only silence.[127]

The colonies of Greenland were sustained by trade, and ironically, that lifeline was cut by other Vikings. A source for the luxury goods that the remote island provided – the ivory, pelts, and sealskins – was found much closer to the Scandinavian markets in what is today Russia. There was no need to risk life and limb on harrowing journeys across storm tossed seas. All the exotic goods a rich sea-king could ever want, were to be had to the east.

---

127 Even Scandinavia forgot about them. In 1712, a Danish king who vaguely
     recalled reading about Greenland, realized that the Viking colony had
     probably not heard of the Reformation. He sent a protestant missionary
     to correct the situation, only to discover that the settlement had been
     abandoned nearly three centuries before.

THE TRADERS

Chapter 15

RURIK THE RUS

"They are tall as date palms, blond, and ruddy..."
- Ibn Fadlan describing Vikings

Unlike their Scandinavian cousins who pointed their longships down the coasts of Frisia and the British Isles, the Swedish Vikings looked in the other direction, to the vast forest zones across the Baltic Sea. As early as the mid eighth century – forty years before Norwegian raiders had attacked Lindisfarne – the Swedes began to explore the river systems of western Russia.

What attracted them was not plunder but trade. There were no rich monasteries or unprotected towns, just expansive birch and pine forests and beyond them the grass steppes of the east. The Vikings came at first to exploit raw materials: honey and wax from the Finns living on the Baltic, and Arctic furs and amber from the Lapps to the north.[128] The Slavic populations who lived in the interior of what is today Russia could offer little in the way of plunder, but were valuable as slaves, to be used in Scandinavia or sold

---

128 The Finns were a distinct group of people living to the east of Sweden along the shores of the Baltic.

in the busy slave markets of the south.[129] The Vikings were joined in these early slave raids by the Finns, whose name for Sweden – *Ruotsi* – became corrupted to *Rus*, the name by which the Swedes in the east eventually came to be known to the Islamic and Byzantine worlds to the south.[130]

The Vikings, regardless of which area they hailed from, were people of the water, and it was by lakes and rivers that they penetrated what is now Russia. In AD 753 they took over the outpost of 'Staraya Ladoga'. The fort sat on the edge of Lake Ladoga near the mouth to the Volkhov River, and gave access to the two great river systems of Russia: the Volga and the Dneiper.

Both rivers led to an abundant supply of silver and silks, two things in high demand back in Scandinavia. The Volga pointed east to the Islamic world, while the Dneiper led south to Orthodox Byzantium.

The Dneiper route was extremely treacherous, and the Rus are the first people we know of who successfully navigated it.[131] It required sailing south from the main Rus base of Staraya Ladoga, then up the Volkhov River to pick up the headwaters of the Dneiper. The five hundred and seventy miles of river that followed were broken up by a series of twelve dangerous falls that necessitated dragging the ship out of the water and carrying it – cargo and all – to a more navigable spot downstream. This exposed the traders to attack, a daunting proposition since the area

---

129 The English word 'slave' comes from the Greek 'Sklávos' which originally meant 'captive'. 'Slav' derives from the same root, an indication of the frequency with which they were taken.

130 The "Rowing Way".

131 When a tenth century Byzantine emperor listed the rapids along the Dneiper, he used the Viking names.

was inhabited by the Pechenegs, a terrifying tribe of eight 'hordes' who specialized in ambushes. If a merchant survived the river, he would still have to navigate the shores of the Black Sea, an additional three hundred and fifty miles away from Constantinople.

The Volga route, by contrast, was far simpler and therefore preferable. It led by gentle stages to the Caspian Sea, and from there to the wealthy markets of Baghdad. There was a tremendous amount of money to be made, but in this case it was by trade, not by raiding. The Rus were far from home, and they could only operate on the Volga by permission of the Khazars, a powerful tribe that dominated the southern end of the river where the Volga Delta emptied into the Caspian. The Khazars were a semi-nomadic people originally from central Asia who had converted to Judaism in the eighth century.[132] They commanded all trade on the southern Volga from their capital of Atil, a city near the Caspian Sea,

The Khazars provided an emporium for the northern goods that the Swedes brought, but more importantly, they gave the Rus access to the far more lucrative markets of the Muslim world where the Rus could sell their slaves. The bulk of these unfortunates were acquired by the Rus from the Slavic populations of present day Russia, and were destined for the markets of Baghdad.

The scale of this slave trade – and its profitability – can be glimpsed by the amount of silver that made its way back to Sweden. More than ten thousand Islamic silver coins have been found in various hoards, surely only a fraction of what was acquired. The Arab geographer Ibn Rustah claimed that

---

132 Their king lists read like a passage from the Old Testament; David, Joseph, Aaron, Obadiah, etc...

slaves were virtually the only thing the Rus cared to import. "*They sail their ships*", he wrote, "*to ravage the Slavs...*"

Arab opinions on the Rus were mixed. There was no doubt that they were magnificent specimens. The traveler Ibn Fadlan claimed that he had never seen people of more perfect physique. "*They are tall as date palms, blond, and ruddy*", he wrote. But, he also considered them "*the filthiest of God's creatures*" – at least by Islamic standards.[133]

By this time the Rus were beginning to act like the Khazars. Not only did their chieftains surround themselves with concubines and ape the dress and ceremonies of the Khazars, but they started describing themselves as 'Khans'.

By the mid ninth century, however, signs of trouble along the Volga route began to appear. Thanks to religious rifts, cultural stagnation, and several civil wars, Baghdad entered a period of decline, and as the silver dried up, the Rus began looking for other ways of making money. Characteristically, they resorted to the old habit of raiding and fell on the Islamic populations near the Caspian Sea without mercy. A Muslim chronicler wailed that "*The Rus shed blood, ravished women and children, plundered... destroyed and burned... Then the people prepared themselves for war... but the Rus attacked them and thousands of Muslims were killed or drowned.*"

If Baghdad's power was waning, however, that of the Khazar's was not, and any raid had to have their permission first. This was made abundantly clear in an infamous raid carried out in AD 913. A large Rus fleet – according to

---

133 Hygienic standards obviously varied considerably as in Europe at this time the Vikings' bathing habits were considered slightly unmanly. After the 1002 St. Brice's Day Massacre in England, John of Wallingford denounced the Danes for their excessive cleanliness. Among other sins, they combed their hair daily, bathed on the Sabbath, and frequently changed clothes.

an Islamic source it was five hundred ships – sailed down the Volga and cut a deal with the Khazars to split evenly whatever spoils they found. After pillaging several cities on the southern coast of the Caspian, the Rus turned north and advanced into a strange, 'burning' land.

After three days travel across the surreal landscape, they sacked the city of Baku in present-day Azerbaijan. They found enough plunder to satisfy even the most avaricious Rus. Not only was Baku a major source of naphtha, one of the main ingredients of Greek Fire – fuel for the war machines of Byzantium and Moorish Spain – but it was also a religious center. Not far from the city was a geyser of natural gas which at some point in antiquity had been ignited. The fire-worshiping Persians had built a temple which over the years had attracted a tidy pilgrim trade from as far away as India, and was responsible for much of the city's wealth.

The raid was a dramatic success, but was remembered less for the haul of slaves and gold and more for what happened on the return journey. When they reached the Volga, the Rus were ambushed by their Khazar allies and slaughtered. The disaster illustrated the dangers faced by the Rus even in war bands. They were far from home, and as likely to be victims as raiders. The deeper problem, however, greater than any double-cross, was that the Volga trade was showing diminishing returns.

There also seem to have been troubles closer to home. The Russian Primary Chronicle, a twelfth century work written in a monastery near Kiev, records that in the mid ninth century, several Slavic tribes drove the Rus out of their strongholds around Lake Ladoga. It continues – rather improbably – to suggest that the Slavs then fell into a civil war and after several years of fighting invited a Viking named Rurik to rule over them.

This unlikely story is our first introduction to the man who would eventually be known as a founding father of the modern states of Russia, Belarus, and the Ukraine. By 862, a Viking named Rurik, a form of the Norse name Erik, had installed himself south of Ladoga at a fortified market town he called Holmgård – better known today as Novgorod.

From his capital on the Volkhov River, Rurik sent two of his nobles named Askold and Dir south to secure access to the Dneiper.[134] On the west bank, where the ground rose to a prominent bluff, was the city of Kiev, dominating the river below. It served as a frontier outpost of the Khazars, and by sending his men to take it, Rurik was reorienting the Rus toward the south, a change which would have important ramifications for both Russian and European history.

The dangers of the southern route were well known. The Rus would have to cross more than eight hundred miles of hostile territory, at times frighteningly exposed to aggressive tribes and treacherous conditions. But if the risk was much greater, so was the reward. At the end of that journey was the city of Constantinople, at the time the greatest metropolis on earth. In an age of poverty it was a city of gold. While the capitals of the west counted their populations in the thousands, Constantinople's population was nearly a million.

It was the physical and spiritual center of a realm that stretched back into antiquity. No mere kingdom, it was the eastern half of the fabled Roman Empire, the final unblemished jewel in the Roman crown. It was ruled over by an emperor who was still called Caesar, by a population which still called themselves Roman. Both emperor and empress still presided in style over chariot races in an ancient Roman Hippodrome as

---

134 Askold was supposedly a grandson of Ragnar Lothbrok.

their predecessors had for five centuries. The empire's borders stretched from the island of Sardinia off the coast of Italy to the Black Sea and the northern coast of what is today Turkey, and were still defended by its formidable legions.

It was, to medieval eyes, a place of wonders. The great land walls, the most formidable defensive fortifications ever built, were pierced by nine main gates, the most famous of which was the ceremonial Golden Gate. It was a vast Roman triumphal arch with three huge doors, lined in gleaming precious metal and surmounted with statues of elephants pulling a victorious chariot. Beyond it lay a wide avenue lined with palaces of white marble, vast forums, and bazaars overflowing with exotic wares from three continents.

Everywhere one looked there were splendid mosaics and breathtaking works of art from the vanished world of antiquity. Public squares held famous classical statues, while golden and porphyry sarcophagi held the remains of legendary emperors.[135] Most awe-inspiring of all was the great cathedral of the Hagia Sophia that dominated the city's skyline.

There was no building like it in the world. In an age of squat, heavy architecture, the church of Divine Wisdom rose in graceful, elegant lines. A worshiper who entered through its enormous imperial door – a portal encrusted with silver and supposedly made from the wood of Noah's ark – would gaze in wonder at the multicolored marble walls and an interior space that beggared imagination. The massive central dome, the largest in the world for a thousand years, rose a hundred and eighty feet above the

---

135 Most prominent was the monumental statue of Athena from the Parthenon. It was moved to Constantinople some time before the tenth century.

floor, and the ceiling was covered with four acres of gold mosaic. Around the base of the dome, the builders had put windows lined with gold. As light flooded into the building, this made it appear as if the dome itself were insubstantial and merely floating, '*as if*', wrote one of the first observers, '*it was suspended from heaven by a golden chain.*'[136]

If these wonders weren't enough to fire Rus greed, there were always the busy market places. In the sixth century, the Byzantines had smuggled the secret of silk making out of China by sending two monks to tour a Chinese facility. After learning the intricacies of the trade, the clerics had managed to sneak some silkworms into hollow bamboo canes, with enough Mulberry leaves to keep them alive on the return trip. When they arrived in the capital, they planted the city's first Mulberry trees, and Constantinople's most profitable business was born.

The silk that the Rus had bought in Baghdad had been imported with the usual price increases along the way. In Constantinople, however, there was no middleman to add to the cost, greatly increasing the profit the Russ could get when they resold it at home. The route there was dangerous, but the Rus were free to develop it without asking permission from anyone, and having done so, they would reap all the rewards.

---

136 Even the Byzantines found the building miraculous. An old legend had it that an angel came up with the design while the workers were on a lunch break. Coming down from heaven, the angel found only a young boy who had been left to guard the tools. He sent the boy off with the solution, assuring him that he would stand guard until the boy returned. When the architects heard the plan, they realized the mysterious being was an angel, and banished the boy from the capital. The angel, who had promised to stand guard till the boy returned, was therefore forced to remain in the church and watch over it forever.

Constantinople, called *Miklagård* – the Great City – by the Vikings, was obviously worth braving treacherous rapids, and fighting barbarians along the way. The Rus had probably been aware of its existence for some time. The first recorded contact is of a Rus delegation in 838, and the sight of such wealth must have stunned them. The walls probably did as well. The city was protected by a triple line of defenses. The first was a moat nearly sixty-six feet wide and twenty-three feet deep, reinforced with a seven foot stockade. If an attacker managed to get past that, they would have to climb over a thirty foot outer wall, while defenders could strategically withdraw through numerous minor gates. The last line of defense was the most formidable, a massive inner wall towering forty feet high and twenty feet wide – broad enough to rush whole companies of men wherever they were needed. This final wall was reinforced with ninety-six towers, allowing the defenders to fire their lethal bolts from nearly three hundred and sixty degrees. With adequate troops manning them, the walls were quite impregnable.

To most, defenses of this magnitude were intimidating.[137] The Rus, apparently, considered it a challenge. Constantinople might be the greatest city on earth, with defenses that had shrugged off four hundred years of attacks, but it was also built on a peninsula, surrounded on three sides by water, and water was their element.

The attack was coordinated from Kiev, where Askold and Dir had been gathering and equipping a fleet of some two hundred ships. When they reached the Black Sea they

---

137 Even Attila the Hun had thought better of attacking the city when he saw them.

found it completely unguarded and managed to slip along its coast, unnoticed by any imperial patrols. On June 18, 860, just as the sun was setting, the Rus fleet drew up before the massive walls of Constantinople. Whether by good fortune or careful planning, they had timed the attack perfectly. The emperor was away, and the city sat virtually undefended.

Chapter 16

MIKLAGÅRD

"...the terror and darkness robbed you of your reason..."

- Patriarch Photius

In its long struggle with Islam, the Byzantine Empire was finally starting to see the tide turn. This was due to both a temporary decline in the strength of the Caliphate, and the careful stewardship of a series of emperors who had taken halting steps toward recovering some of the territory lost during the previous two centuries. The current dynasty had been reaping the benefits of this resurgence, but had been less than successful on the battlefield, and was eager to fend off the whispers of cowardice. When the opportunity came to gain some ground on the Arab frontier, therefore, the emperor Michael III – better known to posterity as Michael the Drunkard – marched out to fight the Muslims.

He quite sensibly took a large part of the navy with him. For all their power on land, the forces of Islam had not mustered a corresponding naval strength, and the imperial fleet could be used to resupply the army while it hugged the coasts. They were leaving Constantinople undefended behind them, but in all the years of the city's existence there had never been a credible threat from the Black Sea. When the Rus fleet arrived, the shock was overwhelming.

It was as if a wolf had suddenly materialized inside the sheep pen. As far as the Byzantines knew, the northeast was a trackless wilderness, an effective barrier to the hostile tribes beyond. There were no cities or population centers capable of supporting an army, and no dockyards on the coast for building a fleet. And yet, here were strange ships with dragon prows and menacing warriors where no ships should ever be.

With the emperor and most of the armed forces away, the task of defending the city fell to the Patriarch Photius. The city seemed paralyzed. As Photius later recounted, "*Like a thunderbolt from heaven... the terror and darkness robbed you of your reason... You, who have captured many trophies from enemies out of Europe, Asia, and Levant, are now threatened by a spear held by a brutal, barbarian hand which would make a trophy of you!*" As the Rus looted the unprotected suburbs outside the walls, the stricken population could only watch in horror. Those who couldn't get out of the way were cut down or burned as the Rus put their homes to the torch.

From the imperial harbor, the citizens could see the Rus fleet wheel towards the islands off the coast. The 'Princes Islands' were used both as spiritual retreats and prisons for exiled political prisoners. They had served as the final home of several blinded emperors and currently held Photius' predecessor. When the Rus landed, they found to their delight, that there were also plenty of monasteries nestled among the rocks.

The several weeks it took to loot the entire chain of islands, gave Photius the time he needed to mount a defense. The patriarch was a remarkable man. Not only was he arguably the most erudite man to fill his post, but he was also an adroit political animal.[138] His first order was to summon the monks guarding the city's holiest relic – a cloth worn by the Virgin Mary – and have them parade it around the city walls. While this had no discernible effect on the Rus, it did give a needed boost to the morale of the populace by reminding them that the city was under divine protection.

It certainly seemed as if it was. What happened next is unclear since our only contemporary source is silent, and later chronicles are garbled. Most likely, several imperial ships arrived on the scene and, with the help of a convenient storm, managed to scatter the Norsemen.[139] The Rus withdrew to the Black Sea in disorder, ending the expedition.

The Rus had seen just how formidable the city's defenses were. Their failure to attack the city despite the absence of the army is a testament to how impressed they were. They were also concerned about the imperial navy. This was the first time that the Rus had ever come across a power that was capable of matching them at sea. They would have to either attack it in greater numbers, or gain access to its wealth as traders and mercenaries.

For their part, the Byzantines were also shaken. The attack had served as a diplomatic wakeup call. There was a new power to the northeast that had come out of nowhere, and it had to be brought to terms. Byzantine ambassadors were sent speeding to Kiev, and a treaty was agreed to, allowing the Rus to trade inside Constantinople. If that had been the

---

138 He left a catalogue of all the books he read - most now lost - complete with his notes on what he thought of each. In effect, he created the world's first book review.

139 The Bosporus is a notoriously treacherous stretch of water, but according to a later Byzantine source, the origin of the storm was the Virgin's mantle that Photius had brought down to the sea and dipped into the water.

goal all along for the Rus – as it may indeed have been – it was a brilliant success.

On this triumphal note, the shadowy Rurik the Rus disappears from history. He had founded the first centralized state – or at least received credit for it – and would become the great ancestor of Russian dynasties. For the next seven centuries, aspiring leaders would gain credibility by how close they could tie themselves to his house.[140]

The future of his state, however, was not in Novgorod where he had ruled. His successor, Helgi, relocated to Kiev, and took the title 'Great Prince of the Rus'.[141] For the first few years, he concentrated on imposing his rule, expanding south and gaining control of the prosperous trading towns along the Dneiper.

By 907, he felt secure enough to undertake the major campaign of his reign, an attack on Constantinople. Unlike the earlier probing strike, this one was a full invasion with the full support of a 'prince'.[142] Helgi had made a careful study of the habits of the imperial navy, and skillfully managed to avoid it, reaching the outskirts of the city unopposed. The mouth of the imperial harbor was blocked with a huge iron chain, so Helgi walked his men overland and used two thousand canoes to cross over to the north side of the city.

If any spot of the land walls was vulnerable, it was the northeastern district where they dipped into a valley. Helgi brought his army there, cheekily hung his shield on the gate, and waited until the imperial army appeared. This was a

---

140 His dynasty came to an end with the death of Feodor I in 1598.

141 Today he is better known by his Slavic name, Oleg.

142 The Russian Primary Chronicle makes the absurd claim that there were two thousand ships and eighty thousand men. Byzantine sources - for obvious reasons - pretend the attack never happened.

magnificent bit of saber rattling. Helgi wasn't foolish enough to think that they could overwhelm the most formidable walls in Europe without siege equipment. His predecessor had demonstrated that the Rus were capable of commanding a threatening fleet, and Helgi had now shown the strength of an army he could put in the field.

What he really wanted was a formal treaty granting his merchants favored status, and the imperial government decided that it wasn't worth the nuisance of denying him. Specific terms were laid out for how Rus merchants could operate and they were given a privileged quarter in the city. The Rus were exempted from certain taxes and duties, although what they could sell was strictly regulated. The Byzantines even agreed to give them access to the city's baths. Most importantly, however, the Rus were given the opportunity to serve as mercenaries.

This would in time grow to be their main occupation in the east. The Rus had found in Byzantium the only state in medieval Europe that was financially organized enough to *regularly* pay mercenaries, and this employer – as they were to find out – paid extremely well. A succession of emperors used Viking soldiers – both the Rus and fresh recruits from Scandinavia – to great effect. The most famous was the emperor Nicephorus Phocas, who in 961 launched an attempt to reconquer Crete from the Muslims. Three previous tries had been made with disastrous results, but Nicephorus – a brilliant general – had brought with him a compliment of Vikings. He used them to storm the beach, and so thoroughly intimidated the defenders that they refused to engage in another battle. After a nine-month siege of the capital they surrendered.

It was a mistake, however, to think that Byzantium and Kiev were at peace. The lesson the Rus took from the treaty of

907 was that they could renegotiate better terms by invading every few years. Helgi's successor Ingvar, better known by the Slavic version of his name, Igor, launched two attacks on the city in 941 and 944.

In both cases, the Rus suffered horrendous casualties, largely due to a mysterious super weapon known as Greek Fire. It was a naphtha-based liquid which would ignite on contact, and had been a state secret of Byzantium since its invention in the seventh century.[143] The closest the Byzantines got to explaining it was emperor Leo the Wise's laconic description that it was *fire prepared with thunder and lightning*. The sons of Ragnar Lothbrok had run into a version of it when they had raided Muslim Spain, but that was undoubtedly not as effective as the real thing. The Byzantines would store it in clay pots and lob it at ships, igniting the decks as the vessels shattered, or use flame throwers mounted on their prows to spray it at opposing ships. Since it was oil based, water only made the situation worse. It would spread out in a slick over the surface, setting fire to anyone who jumped overboard.

The Byzantines used their weapon sparingly, but they knew how to deploy it to devastating effect.[144] During Ingvar's attack, the imperial fleet used submerged brass tubes to burn the Rus ships beneath the water line. To an eyewitness, it looked as if the very sea had caught fire. "*The Rus*", he wrote, *"seeing the flames, jumped overboard, preferring water to fire. Some sank, weighed down by the weight of their breastplates and helmets; others caught fire."*

---

143 They guarded it so zealously that even today we're not quite sure how it was made.

144 The fear was that overuse would allow an enemy to reverse engineer it, a worry that in the Arabs' case proved accurate.

It took almost a century of costly failures for the Rus to understand that they couldn't take Constantinople by storm or ruse. Despite the trauma that these repeated assaults caused the citizens, there was something in the dogged persistence that impressed the Byzantines. They became the mercenary of choice, and in 988, the emperor Basil II created a special corps that would in time become the most famous – and profitable – employer of the Vikings in the east.

In 988, Basil was in desperate need of effective soldiers and was on the brink of losing his throne. Although of peerless lineage – he claimed descent from Constantine the Great – the thirty-year old Basil II was facing a massive revolt by Bardas Phokas, one of the empire's most capable generals. Although he would eventually emerge as one of the empire's most ferocious warriors, in 988 he was still new on the throne with an unreliable army and a skeptical court.[145]

The rebel general marched through Asia Minor unopposed, sacking any town that displayed loyalty to the emperor. When he reached the shore of the Bosporus, the narrow strip of water that separates Asia from Europe, he had himself crowned emperor, complete with imitation diadem and the purple boots of the imperium. The population, sensing the way the wind was blowing, hurried to offer their congratulations and support. By one account, the rebel army was now twice the size it had been when it set out.

Basil, whose one previous military campaign had ended in an ambush, had only the few troops in Constantinople and a nearby field army of questionable loyalty. Things looked bleak, but the emperor kept his head. Even before the rebel army had reached the shore, his ambassadors were speeding

---

145 His nickname was Basil the Bulgar-Slayer. After one battle, he is said to have gouged out the eyes of fifteen thousand prisoners.

towards Kiev. Ingvar's grandson Vladimir, was only too happy to receive them, and he made an audacious offer. In exchange for six thousand Viking recruits from Scandinavia, he wanted to marry Basil's sister, Anna.

The ambassadors probably returned to Constantinople believing that they had failed. In the long history of the empire, a princess of the ruling dynasty had never been given to a barbarian. The proposition itself threw the court into an uproar. Not only was Vladimir a barbarian, but he was a staunch pagan to boot, who had slaughtered his own brother, raped his sister-in-law, and usurped the throne. He already had seven wives and over the years had collected some eight hundred concubines. Even in an emergency, he was not the type to be given a chaste Christian princess.

The court – and poor Basil's sister – may have been outraged, but the emperor was determined to have the extra troops.[146] He agreed to the deal, adding only the stipulation that Vladimir had to accept Christianity and give up some of his more scandalous behavior. Both sides were as good as their word. Vladimir was baptized, the protesting bride was shipped north, and six thousand hulking Vikings arrived at Constantinople.

Basil wasted no time. Under the cover of darkness he slipped across the thin strip of water separating him from the rebel army, and landed a few hundred yards from the main enemy camp. At first light he charged, driving them toward the beaches.

The rebels didn't stand a chance. Stumbling out of their tents half awake and undressed, they were confronted with a horde of screaming Vikings, swinging

146 Anna icily accused her brother of selling her like a slave.

their massive battle-axes. So many were slaughtered that before long the Vikings were doing their work ankle-deep in gore. Those who managed to escape the carnage had the equally horrid fate of being burned alive. As they fled the ruins of their camp to the water's edge, a squadron of imperial ships blanketed the beach with Greek Fire, immolating everyone.

The victory both secured Basil on his throne, and convinced him – if there were any remaining doubts – that he had been right to sacrifice his sister. Another man would have thanked his mercenaries, paid them off, and dismissed them, but Basil had other ideas. The years of turmoil had convinced him of the necessity of overhauling the Byzantine army, and he intended to use these Vikings as a new core around which to build it.

The Norsemen were loyal to gold, and there was no finer paymaster than Basil. They took an oath of allegiance to the throne, after which they became known as *Varangians* – the men of the pledge.[147] In times of peace they served as the royal bodyguard, and in times of war as shock troops.[148] They were the empire's premier fighting force, successor to the ancient Praetorian Guard of Rome, and they fought the empire's battles from Syria to Sicily.

To an ambitious Scandinavian, there was no surer way to find wealth than through service with the Varangian Guard. Signing up with the emperor ensured regular payment and the chance to raid far off lands without the rigors of

---

147 Throughout their history, the Varangians were famously loyal to the throne, not necessarily to the man on it. They were sworn to serve the current occupant not avenge the previous one.

148 They were responsible, among other things, with guarding the keys to whatever city the emperor was visiting.

planning.[149] These campaigns not only offered a better chance of survival than traditional plundering, but were extremely lucrative. One Byzantine source even claims that when an emperor died, the Varangians were entitled to one trip to the treasury where they could have whatever they could personally carry away.

Over the next few centuries, some of the most famous Vikings from across Scandinavia would spend some time under arms in the Varangian Guard. Kings of Norway, Princes of the Rus, Irish jarls, and Icelandic berserkers, all found prestige and wealth in tours of duty.

Often men who went on to other careers considered their time in the south among their greatest accomplishments. Being part of a successful campaign gave one tremendous cachet with both sexes. Bolli Bollason, a hero of the Icelandic Laxdæla Saga, is described returning from Greece like some new Adonis. Wherever he and his men took lodgings for the night, "*the womenfolk paid no heed to anything but to gaze at Bolli and his companions and all their finery.*"

Evidence of the Vikings in Byzantium is littered throughout the south. In Athens, they carved runes into the side of a marble lion that guarded the city's port of Piraeus, and in the Hagia Sophia, at least two bored guardsmen carved runic graffiti into the parapet of the second floor balcony.

The price of service can also be found recorded in runes. Many stones in Scandinavia bear the inscription *Vard daudr i Grikkium* – died among the Greeks. Some never returned because they found life in the warm climates of the south preferable. Enough 'axe-bearing barbarians' settled in Constantinople to qualify for their own quarter, often serving

---

149 This was like a more dangerous Viking version of a modern cruise. The fun of travel without all the hassles of booking hotels or planning meals.

the throne from father to son. As the Byzantine princess Anna Comnena wrote more than a century after Basil, "*As for the Varangians, who bear on their shoulders the heavy iron sword, they regard loyalty to the emperors and the protection of their persons as a family tradition, a kind of sacred trust and inheritance handed down from generation to generation.*"

As time went on, however, the Guard began to change. After 1066, there was a great influx of Anglo-Saxons who were trying to escape the heavy yoke of the Norman Conquest, and the Viking recruits began to dwindle. By the early fourteenth century, the Viking element had almost completely vanished.[150]

There was more to this change than just the arrival of different conscripts. The Rus themselves were different. It was more profound than a simple break with their nomadic, raiding past, and the adoption of a settled lifestyle around fortified cities. Although they still thought of themselves as Vikings – or at least of Scandinavian descent – the beginnings of something brand new was beginning to appear. The Rus were becoming Russian.

---

150 A document of the period refers to the 'language of the Varangians' as English.

Chapter 17

THE PULL OF BYZANTIUM

*"If a wolf comes among the sheep, he will take away the
whole flock unless he is killed"*

- Russian Primary Chronicle

In some ways it's surprising that the Rus held on to a
Viking identity as long as they did. The original Viking
raiders that had plied the waters of the Volga and the
Dneiper, had always been a minority population. The vast
area they conquered, from Novgorod, in the northwest,
to Kiev, the current capital of the Ukraine, was populated
by Slavs, while the Scandinavians were no more than a
privileged military caste. They took local wives, and although
a constant stream of immigrants from Sweden would have
slowed the process, gradually they began to merge identities
with the Slavic population.

The slow evolution is represented in the names of the
Princes of Kiev. Helgi was followed by Ingvar (sometimes
rendered as the slavic Oleg), who was followed by the purely
slavic Sviatoslav, and Vladimir. As the names began to
change, the dress and habits followed. A Byzantine chronicle
provides a physical description of Sviatoslav during a visit
with the emperor John Tzimiskes in 971. Sviatoslav is
described as more of a slavic Khan than a Viking sea-king.

He came rowing in a Viking boat, pulling the oars along with his men like a good Viking, but there the northern comparisons stopped. He was of only medium height, with light blue eyes obscured by bushy brows and a snub nose. His head was completely shaved except for a topknot on one side, which was braided as a sign of his noble status. He wore a simple white tunic, indistinguishable from those of his men except for its cleanliness, and wore no decorations other than a dangling gold earring in one ear.

This process was sped up by contact with Constantinople. A treaty in 945 had thrown open the gates of Constantinople to the Rus, exposing them to the great lure of Orthodox civilization, and it was their eventual adoption of Christianity which, more than anything else, marked the great transition from Rus to Russian. It needed time to take root, and was not fully embraced for several generations, but it locked the nascent Russian state to the Byzantine cultural orbit.

Ironically, it was the great Rus defeat by Greek fire in the 940's, that had indirectly paved the way for Christianity. Prince Ingvar had returned to Kiev badly weakened by the attempt to take Constantinople. Several of the surrounding tribes which had fallen under Rus domination took the opportunity to revolt, and Ingvar was forced to expend most of his energies putting them down.

The most troublesome of the client-states were the Drevlians, an eastern Slavic tribe that inhabited part of what is today the Ukraine. When news reached them of Ingvar's defeat, they took the provocative step of ceasing all tribute payments to Kiev. Ingvar couldn't immediately respond, pressed as he was by other concerns, so the Drevlian issue was left to fester.

When Ingvar had finally stabilized Kiev, he sent the Drevlians a demand for the backpay they owed, with threats of retribution if they should withhold even a small amount. The delay in addressing the problem, however, had given the Drevlians the impression that Ingvar was powerless, so their prince, Mal, responded with words to the effect that 'an equal does not pay tribute'.

The Prince of Kiev immediately set out with his army for the Drevlian capital of Iskorosten, now the modern Ukranian city of Korosten, and at the sight of the massed troops, Mal's bravado evaporated. Formally apologizing to Ingvar, he handed over the gold that was owed. A wiser ruler would have left it at that, but on the way back to Kiev, Ingvar decided that the Drevlians hadn't been punished enough. Defying his authority had to have a higher price. Ordering his men to continue on to the capital, he turned back with his bodyguards.

When prince Mal was informed of the demand for more gold, he stalled by claiming to need to inspect his treasury to see if the funds were available. When he asked his advisors what to do, one supposedly offered, "*If a wolf comes among the sheep, he will take away the whole flock unless he is killed.*" Mal heeded the words. At his sign, a group of Drevlians burst out of the gates, massacred Ingvar's guards, and captured the Prince of Kiev.

According to a Byzantine source, the grisly revenge Mal took was one the Vikings could appreciate. Ingvar was held down on the ground while two young birch trees were bent toward him. Each of his feet was secured to a tree, and then the saplings were released, ripping the unfortunate man in half.

Having a leader cut down in the prime of life, was a nightmare for any medieval society. It usually left a young successor and, if a regent didn't grab control firmly, all the attendant horrors of a civil war. This would indeed have been the fate of Kiev since Ingvar's only son was only an infant, if it had not been for his remarkable wife Olga. Not only did Olga have the loyalty of the nobility of Kiev but, according to the colorful account given in the Russian Primary Chronicle, she was also a more effective leader than her late husband.

The news of Ingvar's death was followed closely by a group of twenty ambassadors from Prince Mal with a proposal of marriage. The request was not quite as outlandish as it at first seemed. Royal widows were among the most eligible wives of the medieval world. They would frequently look to remarry quickly to avoid upheaval, and such a marriage offered the chance of a dramatic rise in political fortunes for ambitious suitors.

What was unseemly was the boldness of the ambassadors. Mal rationally assumed that a newly widowed Olga would be feeling vulnerable and open to suggestion, so instead of tactfully ignoring his part in her husband's murder, his emissaries openly admitted it. When they were shown into her quarters they told the grieving widow that Ingvar was 'like a ravening wolf' who deserved to be killed. Now, they continued, Olga had the chance to marry a real prince.

Surprisingly, she seemed open to the idea. Her husband would not rise from the grave, and how he died was not as important as the fact that he was dead. Olga said she needed a day to think about it, but strongly hinted that this was only a formality. Pleased with her pragmatic approach, the ambassadors withdrew to their camp, agreeing to visit her the next morning.

As soon as the Drevlians had gone, Olga ordered her men to dig a deep ditch just behind her citadel. By the morning it was finished, and when the ambassadors arrived – dressed in their finest clothes as a token of respect to the woman who was about to become their princess – Olga had them seized, dragged past her citadel and buried alive.

Even as her servants were leveling the earth of the mass grave, Olga sent a message to Mal. She would gladly marry him, she said, but only if he provided a grand enough escort. The twenty ambassadors he had already sent were an insufficient honor guard for a woman of her status. She would arrive in state with the most noble men of Iskorosten, or not at all.

Prince Mal, perhaps impressed by her sense of decorum, eagerly sent the leading men of the city with as sumptuous an honor guard as he could afford. When they arrived at Kiev, Olga was the model of civility, offering the use of her own private bathhouse to wash the dust from their long journey. When they were all safely inside, however, Olga had the door barricaded and then set fire to the building, ignoring the agonized screams.

As the embers flared, she calmly sent a final message to Mal requesting that she be allowed to conduct the customary funeral feast for her dead husband when she arrived at Iskorosten. The prince, still unaware that anything was amiss, hastily agreed. When he saw her approaching the city with a large group of retainers, he rode out to greet her, asking where his ambassadors were. She replied that she had been so excited to meet him that she had ridden ahead, and that the rest would soon join them. Satisfied, the prince escorted her into the city to a great feast had been prepared.

Olga gave every appearance of the joyful bride, but had carefully instructed her men not to touch a drop of alcohol – a proscription that neither Mal nor his soldiers noticed. When the Drevlians were deep into their cups, the lethal widow gave a signal and her guards drew their swords, butchering all of their bleary-eyed hosts.

Cutting their way out of the city, Olga and her retinue joined her army, which was hiding nearby, and reappeared before the walls of Iskorosten. The terrified inhabitants, now without their prince or leading men, begged for mercy, and to their immense relief, Olga agreed. Her terms were surprisingly modest. Instead of honey or furs – the usual stuff of tribute – she asked only for some birds; three pigeons and three sparrows from each household. Unfortunately for the Derevlians this was an old Viking trick. When she got the birds she had her men attach rags dipped in a flammable material to the feet of each bird. When they were lit, the panicked animals returned to their nests, lighting the houses on fire.

Before long, the wind had turned the scattered flames into a raging inferno. The panicked citizens came pouring out of the ruined gates into the waiting arms of Olga's army. They showed no mercy. Those who weren't slaughtered on the spot were rounded up and sold into slavery. Only in the morning, with Iskorosten a blackened, deserted ruin, was Olga finally sated.

Whether or not Olga was as cold-blooded as the legends make her out to be, she was certainly an effective ruler. The Russian Primary Chronicle notes with succinct admiration that "although she was a woman in body, she possessed a man's courage." Her shrewdness not only kept the throne safe for her son, but also increased its authority.

Regardless of the numbers of Drevlians left alive, the message that Kiev's new ruler was not to be trifled with quickly spread. To her credit, Olga chose not to govern with the sword. Although focused on revenge, she was not blinded by it, and was shrewd enough to realize that forcing Kiev's client tribes to pay a tribute each year built up murderous resentment. The gold usually came out of each chief's personal hoard, lessening his ability to reward his men, and thereby weakening his authority. This virtually ensured that the moment Kiev's grip slipped, there would be a rebellion.

To convert the chiefs from potential enemies to firm allies, she abolished the hated payment, replacing it with a simple tax on every household.[151] The local leaders, freed from the financial burden, were then allowed to handle all minor administrative or legal issues. No longer would Kiev rule by fiat. Olga had in effect, transformed rebellious allies into full members of her government. Her regency also saw the construction of numerous trading centers, as well as the first stone buildings in Kiev, Novgorod, and Pskov. The system she devised worked remarkably well, and provided a firm foundation for Kiev's continued growth.

Olga spent the rest of her son's minority successfully dodging marriage proposals and steadily building up Kiev's power. As successful as the regency was, however, Olga seems to have been aware of a lingering problem. No matter how politically integrated she made the various tribes, they still saw themselves as different from the inhabitants of Kiev. There was no underlying unity beyond a common ruler, no big identifying idea that could turn the people of individual cities into a unified state.

In an attempt to rectify this, Olga took the boldest move in a career full of them. She traveled to Constantinople around the year 955 – ostensibly to shore up trade relations – but in reality to officially adopt Christianity. The ceremony was carried out in the golden church of the Hagia Sophia,

---

151 Outside of the Byzantine Empire, this was the first legal tax system in Eastern Europe.

with the emperor Constantine VII standing in as her godfather.[152] As a token of respect, Olga took the Christian name of Helena after the emperor's wife.

Her personal conversion may have helped to seal an alliance and perhaps squeeze more trade privileges out of Constantinople, but Olga was quickly disabused of any notions that her people would follow suit. There was a small Christian community in Kiev, but the vast majority of her subjects were pagan, worshiping a variety of Viking, Turkic, and Slavic gods. The aristocracy in particular were vocal supporters of Thor, and instead of uniting them behind her, she risked undermining the stability that she had worked her entire regency to maintain.[153]

Olga did her best to spread the new faith, bringing Bibles, priests, icons, and vestments back with her. She ordered the construction of several churches in multiple cities, and publicly attended them, but all to no avail. The aristocrats, particularly the new arrivals from Sweden, violently resisted, as did most of her family. Her son, Sviatoslav refused to even consider it, informing his mother that the gentle virtues of patience, forgiveness, and mercy were hallmarks of a feeble religion that would see him mocked by his own men.

Olga may have failed to establish Christianity in her son's generation, but she did at least plant the seeds for it to take root in the next one. Sviatoslav, in a conscious rejection of his mother's conciliatory policy towards Byzantium, carried out the last major Rus attack on the empire. While he led the army overland – yet another sign that the old Viking ways were dying out – he left his mother in charge of Kiev,

---

152 He left a detailed account of the entire ceremony in a book he wrote to his son.

153 This includes the yearly influx of Vikings from Scandinavia.

as well as of the education of his three sons, Yarolpolk, Oleg and Vladimir.

She performed both tasks admirably, although the latter would take several years to manifest. The last glimpse we get of her, fittingly enough, is once again acting as a military commander. When a group of raiders invaded in 969, she organized a vigorous defense, which managed to drive them off. She died a few months later, having lived a life more suited to a Valkyrie (a Viking deity that rewarded bravery in battle) than a saint.[154]

Her reign marks the beginning of a great watershed in European history. By converting to Christianity, she had chosen to align Kiev with Europe instead of Asia, to look west instead of east. The Viking roots of the Rus were gradually supplanted by Byzantine ones, and Kiev would drink so deeply from Constantinople's cup, that the three modern states which claim descent from the House of Rurik – Ukraine, Belarus, and Russia – continue to see themselves as the heirs to ancient Greece and Rome.[155]

Olga may not have been responsible for all of this, and in fact may have died considering herself a failure, but the Orthodox faith she championed would one day give her people the common identity she envisioned, and make possible a vast empire.

---

154 She had certainly earned her saintly credentials, however, by her robust adoption of the faith. In 1547 the Orthodox Church proclaimed her a saint, giving her the title Isapóstolos 'Equal to the Apostles', an honor only four other women share.

155 Constantinople was called 'the second Rome' because of its function as the capital of the Eastern Roman Empire. When it fell in 1453, Orthodox Russian Christians dubbed Moscow 'the third Rome'.

Chapter 18

FROM RUS TO RUSSIAN

"Every king of Europe marries a princess of Kiev."
- Russian Primary Chronicle

As much as Sviatoslav admired his mother – he ordered that she should be buried according to Christian custom as a sign of respect – there appeared to be little danger that Odin or Thor would have to give way in Kiev. His immediate neighbors may have been falling like dominoes – Poland, Denmark, Norway, and Hungary all had or were about to accept Christianity, but Sviatoslav was aggressively pagan. Thor demanded victory, and only victory would keep his nobles loyal.

His first advance, while his mother still lived, had been against the Khazars, whom both Olga and Ingvar had tacitly acknowledged as their overlord. In a brutal, six year campaign, he annihilated their forces, culminating with a sack of Atil, their capital city. Clearly, he had inherited his mother's vindictive streak. The city was smashed beyond recognition. The tenth century Arab writer, Ibn Hawqal, who visited the ruins shortly after, remarked, "*No grape or raisin remained, not a leaf on a branch*".

The triumph inspired Sviatoslav to try to conquer in the west, and he savaged his way through the Balkans, adding present day Bulgaria to his domain. Within his first ten years on the throne, he had carved out the largest state in Europe, stretching from modern Romania to Kazakstan. It was a vindication of the old gods, dramatic evidence that the *Allfather* was more powerful than Christ.

A clash with Byzantium, the great bastion of the new faith, was inevitable, but unfortunately for Sviatoslav, Byzantium was, at that moment, in the midst of a revival. The scholar-emperor who had baptized Sviatoslav's mother had been replaced by the militant John I Tzimisces. In a series of sharp strikes, the new emperor drove the Rus back, pinning Sviatoslav inside an old Roman fort on the Danube. After more than two months of a siege the Prince of Kiev surrendered, humbly rowing across the river to meet with his counterpart.

The emperor John met him on top of his favorite white charger, dressed in golden armor with the heavy Byzantine crown on his head. He accepted the offer of peace on the condition that the Rus pull their forces out of the Balkans, and abandon the most recent of Sviatoslav's conquests.

Worse humiliation was to follow. On the return trip to Kiev, while attempting to negotiate one of the dangerous rapids along the Dneiper, a group of barbarians ambushed Sviatoslav. They had probably been bribed by the emperor John to do so, an indication of just how nervous the Rus made the emperor feel. Sviatoslav's head was cut off and made into a drinking cup as a warning to the Rus in any future dealings.[156]

---

156 Sviatoslav apparently impressed the barbarians with his last stand. Their leader allegedly drank a toast from the skull-cup and prayed that he would have a son as brave as the dead warlord.

Sviatoslav's death threw Kiev into chaos. It was made worse by his sons who began a slow-burning civil war that lasted for nearly a decade and forced the youngest brother Vladimir to flee.

Although the Rus were well on the way to becoming fully slavicized, they still had strong Viking contacts, and Vladimir chose Sweden as his place of exile. There he was greeted by relatives who helped him pick a Swedish princess for a wife, and agreed to raise an army to overthrow his brother.

With several hundred Swedish and Norwegian Vikings at his back, it didn't take long for Vladimir to seize most of the important Rus cities. He dispatched his brother and offered to share power with him. When Yaropolk arrived to discuss terms, his men were ambushed and he was cut down by Vladimir's soldiers.

Not content to simply take his brother's crown, Vladimir rode to the convent where Yaropolk's wife had taken refuge. The abbess tried to protect her by barring the gates, but Vladimir had his men hack through them with their axes, and sent them surging through the cloister to find her huddled in a room. After she had been violated by Vladimir, he forced her to marry him to lessen the resistance of his nobles to the new regime.

As a political ploy, the marriage worked, so Vladimir repeated it six more times, collecting along the way – if the Russian sources are to be believed – eight hundred concubines. He divided these among his major cities so that wherever he traveled he would have a range of female company.

His prodigious appetites were matched with even greater ambition. He expanded and secured his borders by crushing the tribes inhabiting present-day Slovakia, and forced both the Lithuanian and Bulgar tribes to recognize him as their overlord. The success both increased his prestige and made his neighbors nervous. King Boleslav of Poland hurried to sign an alliance with the Rus warlord to prevent him from moving toward the Polish border.

The most gratifying recognition of his power came in 988 when the emperor Basil II sent his request for six thousand Varangians, offering his sister's hand in marriage in return. The stipulation that he convert to Christianity first, probably didn't bother Vladimir too much. Paganism had its downsides for an aspiring autocrat since the crowded pantheon of Slavic and Nordic gods all too accurately reflected the political realities of Vladimir's territory where every prince had a fortified citadel and could declare themselves independent. Odin may have been the *All-father* but he was certainly not all powerful, and like the Prince of Kiev, could easily get drowned out by a hundred other petty gods.

Vladimir had already tried to address this by promoting Thor as the supreme deity, but this ploy had failed miserably. In Kiev he had built a huge temple to house both the Slavic and Viking gods, and had placed a wooden carving of Thor in the center. This was taken as a slight to the other gods, and in the uproar that followed, two men were killed.[157] Vladimir stubbornly kept to his worship of Thor, but it was a losing battle.

This unease with paganism is reflected in a curious story in an early Slavic chronicle with the wonderful name of *Tale of the Bygone Years*. Convinced that he needed a new religion, Vladimir sent envoys to find out about the world's major faiths – Christianity, Islam, and Judaism. Islam was rejected because of its taboo against alcohol, not to mention the less

---

157   According to one source they were Christians that Vladimir had killed as a human sacrifice to consecrate the temple.

than thrilling prospect of being circumcised as an adult.[158] Judaism was dismissed as well because the Jews lacked a homeland – a powerful argument to the medieval mind. That left only Christianity and the choice to follow either western Catholic doctrines or eastern Orthodox ones. That decision became an easy one once his diplomats returned from their missions. The western ones had gone to the Holy Roman Empire and found squat, dark Romanesque churches. Those in the east, however, had attended a full Divine liturgy in the Hagia Sophia. "*We didn't know*", they breathlessly reported to Vladimir, "*if we were in heaven or on earth. We only knew that God lived there.*"

The story may be apocryphal, but it captures something of Vladimir's decision. Kiev was already moving toward Byzantium, and away from the lure of the east.[159] Christianity, particularly the Orthodox version, was far more attractive than his native paganism. It had only one God, and an all-powerful one at that. Byzantine autocracy was modeled on this belief in divine authority. Just as there was only one God in heaven, there was only one emperor on earth. God didn't need permission from his angels or their cooperation. He spoke, and things happened. This was the model that Vladimir wanted to impose on Kiev.

There were also other reasons to draw closer to Byzantium. He was acutely aware of the limitations of his own power and the deep roots of the great empire to his south. However strong he might appear to be right now, the campaigns of his

---

158 Vladimir supposedly said "Vodka is the joy of the Russians and we can't do without it."

159 Generally speaking, the great religious dividing line in the east was along the forest / steppe border. The Vodka drinkers of the forests tended to embrace Christianity, while the hashish smokers of the steppes converted to Islam.

father had taught him an important lesson. The Rus couldn't sustain the type of warfare in the Balkans that the Byzantines could. They lacked the organization, the bureaucracy, and the hierarchy to really impose themselves. Without changing that, Kiev's power was ephemeral and it would suffer the fate of countless other kingdoms of the east – vast today and vanished tomorrow.

The conclusion to which Vladimir came – to convert to Christianity – was the realization that he could accomplish far more as an ally of Constantinople than as a Viking sea-king. With that step, he spiritually and culturally cut the ties with his Viking heritage.

A cynical observer, and there were many of them in Vladimir's time, would say that his conversion was purely a political move, but, strange as it may seem, he appears to have been genuinely changed. The man who had raped his own sister-in-law now organized daily food drives for the ill and destitute. He laid out his own table for the sick, and when told that some were too ailing to make it, he arranged for wagons of bread, fish, vegetables, and mead to be taken to them.

He dismissed his non-Byzantine wives and his small army of concubines, and ironically – considering the amount of blood that he had spilled – abolished the death penalty. Schools were founded in several cities, and a part of each year's tax revenue was set aside for alms.

Judging by Vladimir's children, the effort to increase literacy was a dramatic success. His amorous activities had resulted in quite a few daughters, which he proceeded to marry off to the various crowned heads of Europe. So many were exported that the ambitious men of Kiev grumbled – undoubtedly under their breath – that there was a shortage of eligible brides. '*Every king of Europe*', went the complaint, '*marries a princess of Kiev*'. Part of the attraction was their learning. Vladimir's daughter Anna married King Henry I of France and she was familiar enough with the court bureaucracy to act as regent for their son Philip. A document dating from early in her regency was well stocked with the customary crosses and marks of noble French witnesses that couldn't sign their own names. Only one signature graces the vellum – Anna the Queen – written in proud Cyrillic characters by her own hand.

Not all of the old Viking traits disappeared, however. Vladimir intended for Kiev to be a Christian city and would not tolerate dissent. His first action upon arriving in his capital was to burn down the temple he had made to the old gods. The carving of Thor was tied to a horse's tail and dragged down to the Dneiper river where it was symbolically beaten with clubs and then thrown into the water. The entire population of the city was then driven down to the river – at spear point – for a mass baptism.

On the ruins of his pagan temple, Vladimir built a great church in imitation of those in Constantinople. He named it St. Basil after the Christian name he had adopted, and spent the rest of his reign strengthening the clerical infrastructure of Kiev. By the time of his death, no less than seven bishops were needed to administer the spiritual life of the kingdom.

Perhaps the most profound effect of Vladimir's conversion was that it brought with it the Cyrillic alphabet.[160] Vladimir needed to use a written language, and Viking runes were unsuitable for long or complex texts. His adoption of Cyrillic opened the Rus up to the deep literary tradition of Constantinople, and further cemented cultural ties with the

---

160 This was designed by the missionary St. Cyril who discovered that the Slavs didn't have a written language. He based it on his native Greek alphabet.

empire. When Vladimir's son, Jaroslav, issued Kiev's first law code, he did so in Cyrillic, and based it on Byzantine and not Viking precedents.

Physically, the kingdom centered around Kiev even began to look like its southern neighbor. Byzantine craftsmen and artists flowed north, and the wooden halls of the Vikings were replaced by stone buildings. Under Vladimir's stewardship nearly every town got brick and marble gates in imitation of the imperial capital, and stone churches with onion domes to mimic the arched roofs to the south.[161]

Under Vladimir and his son, Russia's market towns swelled to real cities with populations over sixty thousand. The inhabitants were Slavs, who were no longer seen as targets to be raided, but as Christian subjects to be protected. Even the Viking way of life based on animal husbandry was abandoned in favor of agriculture, and cavalry replaced the shield wall.

A sentimental connection to the north remained – both Vladimir and his son hosted Viking sea-kings – but they had clearly begun to think of themselves as distinct.[162] They no longer used the Norse language or even Viking names and within a generation, they even began to view the Swedes as trading rivals instead of allies.[163]

Within a hundred years of Vladimir's death, the Viking imprint on the east had all but disappeared. Despite the role they played in founding the first centralized state, virtually all that's left of the Viking legacy in the east is the name 'Russia', and Vladimir's seal on the Ukrainian flag. The Viking roots

---

161 The best example is the St Sophia of Novgorod that Vladimir built.

162 At least three different kings of Norway - Olaf the Stout, Magnus Olafsson, and Harald Hardråda - were hosted at Kiev.

163 A few Scandinavian names did cling on until the fifteenth century, but only in a corrupted form. Ivarr became Igor, Olaf became Uleb, etc.

were scoured away by the cultural pull of the eastern Roman Empire, a process completed in 1472 when the niece of the last Byzantine emperor married Ivan the Great.

If the Rus became Slavic, however, they also changed the Slavs. They gave the Slavic world its first centralized state and its first lasting dynasty. They brought order to an unstable region, and provided a foundation for the Slavic empire that would come.

Perhaps it is to be expected that the Viking influence would quickly wane since the Scandinavians were always a tiny majority among a vast Slavic population. At least a part of the reason that it ended when it did, however, was because by Vladimir's time the Viking world itself was changing. The days of footloose adventurers and prowling sea-wolves were over. Scandinavia had become a land of kings.

THE HOMELANDS

Chapter 19

VIKING KINGS

"Our ravens croak to have their fill... the wolf howls from the distant hill"

- King Harald's Saga

The Viking Age is often judged by its impact on other cultures. It's remembered as a time of destruction – the brutal sacking of monasteries, the ruin of much of Anglo-Saxon England, Ireland, and the Frankish Empire – but there was creation too. Colonies were founded in Iceland and Greenland, a Duchy was created in Normandy, great trading cities like Dublin and York flourished, and Russia gained its first centralized state. All of this, however, is focused outwards, and neglects the effect the Viking Age had on the Norse homelands.

The most obvious impact can be seen from the mind-boggling amounts of loot – coins, silver, plate, and slaves. According to the various Frankish chronicles, in the ninth century alone, roughly forty-five thousand pounds of silver was handed over in payments to the Vikings, an amount representing perhaps a third of the total that was carried off.

The tenth century was even more lucrative. In Anglo-Saxon England, King Athelred the Unready paid a hundred and eighty thousand pounds of silver in bribes. This was something on the order of forty million English silver pennies, an amount that contributed greatly to the king's unpopularity.[164]

The flood of silver coming from England was increased by plunder from Ireland and the two Frankish kingdoms, as well as trade from markets ranging from Greenland to Byzantium. The availability of precious metals led to the development of a coin based economy instead of a barter system, and further integrated Scandinavia into the wider European marketplace. In the great Viking trading towns like Hedeby and Birka, the Vikings even began to mint their own coins based on Frankish, Byzantine, or Anglo-Saxon models.

Most of this wealth flooded into lands dominated by a warrior culture that prized individual prowess. Great figures built halls and gave generously to their followers. They were described as 'ring-givers' and passed out bracelets (or torcs) for the arms and neck, weapons and armor, and ingots of gold, silver, or iron. Plunder was used as personal ornamentation or buried in hoards to burnish reputations. The constant demand spurred the growth of luxury markets, which in turn drove the Vikings to exploit ever more extensive routes of trade.

This exploration sparked a second, more profound change. During the two and a half centuries of the Viking age, the Norse probably had contact with a wider variety of cultures than any other single people on earth. From Anglo-Saxon England and imperial Byzantium in particular, they picked up models of a centralized form of government, which they

---

164 Although it is notoriously difficult to calculate value across the centuries, one silver penny would probably have fetched several chickens or a dozen loaves of bread in the mid tenth century.

brought back to Scandinavia. Returning sea-kings found that their vast resources could be used not only for personal adornment, but to support armed companies of men. These slowly coalesced into royal armies which – supported by a Byzantine style administration – further centralized power. As their wealth increased, so did their ability to do kingly things, like constructing stone buildings, raising walls, and decorating their palaces.

By the close of the tenth century, this process was nearing completion. Strongmen were being transformed into petty kings who vied for control of the wealthy market towns of Scandinavia. The old Viking dream of the sea-kings – dominance at sea – was vanishing, replaced by men who wanted to gain territory on land.

Surprisingly, given the size of its coasts, the first to unify was Norway. Unlike the origin stories of most countries, Norway's founding myth is a love story. Around the year 860, Halfdan the Black, the petty king of an area in the southeast around modern Oslo died, leaving his kingdom to his ten-year old son, Harald Fairhair. According to the Heimskringla, an Icelandic account of the history of Norway, the boy fell in love with a nearby princess, but she refused to marry him until he was king over all of Norway. Harald took an oath not to cut or comb his hair until the job was done, and proceeded to slowly expand his territory.

A more likely scenario is that the ambitious Harald was simply continuing a process that had been going on for several decades. His particular genius was to use fleets to do so. Each petty sea-king that he conquered boosted the power of his own navy and made it harder to resist. The climactic battle occurred at Hafrsfjord, where the king crushed an alliance of petty kings and jarls and brought western Norway under his control. Although he probably only controlled the southern and western coasts, for the first time it is possible to talk about a kingdom of Norway.[165]

It was in Harald's best interests to suppress the old Viking traditions of sailing out for plunder in the summers, because this in turn created the very sea-kings that he had struggled so long to overcome. Any raiding that took place would have to be either by his authority or permission, a fact that must have rankled many grizzled sea-wolves. Many of them chose to leave Norway for freer lands in Iceland, the Orkneys or the Faeroes, forced out by Harald's uncompromising control.

If he had really won Norway for a woman's love, it was the highest dowry Harald ever paid. Over the course of his fifty years he allegedly collected two hundred wives and had more sons than he knew what to do with. Even three generations later, nearly every jarl in Norway could credibly claim to be related to the first king.

This tremendous fecundity, however, undid most of Harald Fairhair's hard work. He chose his favorite son Erik Bloodaxe to replace him and even ruled jointly with him for a few years. This might have proved effective if there had been fewer claimants to the throne, or if his heir had behaved with more restraint. Erik, however, did his best to thin the family ranks – a good amount of the blood on his axe belonged to half-brothers – and lopped off the heads of countless jarls who resisted him as well.[166] When a younger half-brother named Håkon the Good, who had been raised in England safely out of reach of Erik's hatchet, arrived with an English army at his

---

165 Having accomplished his goal, the dreadlocked king trimmed his mane, earning his surname 'Fairhair'.

166 According to later sagas Erik killed eighteen of his nineteen brothers.

back, Erik gave in without a fight. He was as tired of Norway as they were of him, and left for greener pastures in England.

Håkon was the baby of the family, and had been born when his father was already an old man. He proved to be a far more competent administrator than this brother, and an innovative general to boot. When the sons of Erik Bloodaxe invaded, he crushed them at a hill which was later named the 'Blood Heights' due to all the carnage. When Erik's nephews tried again two years later, he positioned his army around ten standards spread a massive distance apart along a ridge. This created the illusion that his force was much larger than it in fact was, and the unnerved invaders turned and ran.

In addition to his martial abilities, Håkon is also responsible for attempting to introduce Christianity to Norway, a religion which would thoroughly change Scandinavia, as it did other lands. The new faith, to which Håkon had probably converted in England, had much to recommend it. Not only did it provide a model of centralized power – as Vladimir had realized, God brooked no challengers to his authority in heaven – but it brought with it literacy as a free gift. A literate king, or at least one who employed literate men, could make his wishes known without face-to-face contact. The old system of personal charisma extended only as far as the king could physically go, but his writ could extend much farther. Literacy meant contracts, uniform laws, and official documents, the glue with which a kingdom was held together.

Unfortunately for Håkon, and subsequent Norwegian history, the population was firmly pagan and the king's attempt to impose Christianity only managed to alienate most of his subjects. Perhaps over time he would have had been successful, but in 961 the royal nephews invaded again, and although Håkon's army was victorious, he was mortally wounded in the struggle.

Erik's oldest son Harald Greycloak was chosen as the new king, but he had little real authority. While Norway had been plagued by infighting, powerful kings had risen to the south and united the kingdom of Denmark. It was to these rulers that the sons of Erik Bloodaxe had appealed, and when they invaded Norway it was at the head of a Danish army. Harald Greycloak had won his throne, but the price for Danish aid had been to accept the Danish king as an overlord. After less than a century of independence, Norway had slipped back into chaos.

Chapter 20

HARALD BLUETOOTH

*"...Harald who conquered for himself the whole of
Denmark and Norway and made the Danes Christian."*
- Inscription on the Jelling Stone

Medieval Denmark was considerably larger than its
modern incarnation. Extending across parts of
Germany, Sweden, and Norway, it had the densest
population and was by far the most powerful of the Scandinavian
kingdoms. Much of its strength was due to a remarkable tenth
century family that ruled from their stronghold of Jelling on the
eastern side of the Danish peninsula.

The family patriarch was Gorm the Old who started
life as a typical Viking sea-king but managed to kill off or
neutralize the surrounding petty rulers to unite most of the
Jutland peninsula under his control.[167] He was a Viking of
the old type, a raucous worshiper of Odin, Thor, and Frey
who claimed descent from Ragnar Lothbrok and spent each
summer raiding.

Gorm was generally suspicious of Christians, probably
because of the powerful German kingdom directly to his

---

167 He is also called Gorm the Sleepy, or Gorm the Worm. According to
tradition he was the son-in-law of Harald Klak, the petty king who had
converted to Christianity to enlist the support of the Franks.

south, and was said to go out of his way to be cruel to them. He had good reasons to be worried. Thanks to the missionary activity inspired by the Frankish emperor, Louis the Pious, a century before, there was a small Christian community in the Jutland peninsula, and they would make a splendid pretext for the German king Henry the Fowler to intervene in Danish affairs.

Whether Henry used that excuse or another one is unclear, but early in Gorm's reign a German army was sent over the Danevirke and Gorm was forced to recognize his southern neighbor as an overlord. This hardly checked the king's raiding activities, although he does seem to have generally avoided German lands. His companion in most of these raids was his oldest son Canute, who was as vigorous a plunderer as he, and the two of them ransacked the coasts of northern France and the British Isles. Gorm's younger son, Harald Bluetooth, stayed with his mother Thyra, a formidable woman who had led the Danish army against the invading Germans.[168] She had a better reputation among Christians than her husband, and although pagan, may have exposed her son to at least a form of the new faith.

The last years of Gorm's life were not happy ones. His wife died before he did, and the grieving king raised a great stone in her honor, with deeply carved runes that called her 'the ornament of Denmark'.[169] His own end was clouded by treason. As he aged, Gorm began to fear for his favorite son's life. He vowed to kill anyone who threatened Canute's life – or even informed the king of his death. When word reached the court that Canute had actually been killed while

---

168 Harald's nickname is thought to be due to a conspicuous rotten tooth.

169 This is the first mention of 'Denmark' as a nation and has therefore been called the country's "birth certificate".

attempting to take Dublin, there was an understandable reluctance to go tell the king. Finally, Thyra thought of an ingenious solution.[170] While Gorm was away, she had the throne room hung in black for mourning. When the king returned, he realized immediately what had happened and cried out '*My son is dead!*' Since he had blurted it out himself, there were no executions, but death was still given its due. Two days later Gorm was dead of a broken heart.

That at least is the legend, but there are some hints that foul play may have been involved. Canute had been shot in the back by an arrow while he was watching some games, hardly a likely death for a Viking. The two brothers had been together when it happened, and there were many who whispered that Canute's blood stained Harald's hands.

Tenth century Scandinavia was a violent place, however, and such unpleasantries could easily be forgiven if the new king provided effective leadership. The first thing that needed to be done was to take care of Gorm's corpse. Harald gave it a magnificent funeral, raising a huge mound of rough stones over his father's body. In the center was an ornate wooden chamber filled with the valuables of Denmark's first true king. He then raised a second rune stone with an inscription informing posterity that he had made it to honor his parents.

Having taken care of his predecessor's remains, Harald Bluetooth could now turn to the business of stamping his own authority over the kingdom. He did so in a way that thoroughly eclipsed his father. If Gorm the Old created the kingdom of Denmark, it was his son, Harald Bluetooth, that created the Danish nation. He joined together the disparate tribes of the Jutland peninsula into a single

---

170 Obviously the chronology is confused since Thyra was already dead by this point.

people, joining them temporarily with parts of southern Norway and Sweden.

Harald Bluetooth needed a unifying idea to tie his people together, something larger than just a shared king or common laws. He found it in Christianity, and in 965 he officially converted. Much deliberation seems to have gone into his decision – the contemporary Saxon historian Widikund describes Bluetooth as a man who was 'eager to listen but late to speak.'

The chronicler goes on to describe the colorful argument that led to Harald Bluetooth's conversion. As expected, the abandonment of the old gods was hotly debated, culminating in a furious exchange between several members of the court and a German missionary named Poppo. The Danish nobility was willing to admit that Christ was a god, but held that he was not nearly as powerful as Thor or Odin. Poppo retorted that the latter two were in fact nothing but trolls and that Christ was the only God. Throughout the exchange Harald Bluetooth had remained quiet, but now as swords were being drawn, he broke in, wondering aloud if Poppo was willing to back up his claims with a test.

The cleric unhesitatingly agreed. A bar of iron was heated in a fire until it was glowing red, and the king commanded the monk to grab it with his bare hand. Poppo, declaring his faith in the power of his God, reached into the coals and seized it, holding it up before the assembled court until Harald begged him to put it down. He did so calmly, showing the various notables his undamaged hand. The impressed king converted on the spot.

Another compelling reason for baptism was just south of Harald Bluetooth's borders. Henry the Fowler's son,

Otto I, had traveled to Rome and been crowned emperor of a new 'Roman Empire'. In addition to his German lands he owned northern Italy, the Low Countries, parts of France, and much of central Europe. He was still relatively young, and was well on the way to earning his epithet 'the Great'.[171] Such a man would always be looking to expand his territory, and there was every reason to believe that Denmark would be the next course on the imperial plate. Bringing the gospel to the heathen Danes was precisely what a conscientious emperor should be doing.

By accepting baptism, Harald Bluetooth deftly took away the major pretext for invasion. Christian monarchs did not go to war with each other – at least not with the blessing of the pope – and Harald made sure that everyone knew that he and his dynasty were Christian. At his capital of Jelling, where the great pagan burial mounds were, he built a wooden church and exhumed his father's body. Gorm's bones were carefully wrapped in a rich cloth woven with threads of gold and transferred to the crypt of the new church.

On the stone he raised to commemorate his father, he carved a figure of Christ emerging from the twisting thorns and the snake's coils of the pagan religion.[172] The image encapsulates Harald Bluetooth's vision for his reign. This was to be a new era for Denmark, liberated from the clutter of the past, led by the faith of the future and a glorious new dynasty.

Top down conversions are never really quick; the old religion lingered on for decades, but Harald's adoption of

---

171 He was fifty-three when Harald Bluetooth converted. He lasted another eleven years on the throne.

172 This is believed to be the earliest depiction of Christ in northern Europe. A representation of Harald's Jelling Stone is on the modern Danish passport.

Christianity marked a turning point for Denmark and all of Scandinavia.[173] Unlike Håkon the Good in Norway, Harald Bluetooth's conversion stuck, and he succeeded in overcoming much of the pagan resistance.

Perhaps he was able to do this because of his frequent demonstrations of raw power. The rest of his reign was spent churning out massive public works that overawed potential usurpers. The ancient Hævejen – *'army road'* – which followed the watershed of the Jutland peninsula and led down to the markets of Hamburg was bisected by the Vejle Fjord, roughly six miles south of Jelling. To allow his armies to cross, Harald Bluetooth built a great bridge over the river and marshy ground. Its scale was mind-boggling. Over half a mile long, and more than twenty feet wide, it could support a weight of nearly six tons. More than a thousand huge posts – for which whole oak forests had to be cut down to provide the timber – were driven into the ground to provide support

Just attempting such a structure was a statement of raw power. Even the densest woods would rot quickly in the marshy ground, and the entire thing would need to be rebuilt. This was not made to last the ages or be a permanent legacy. It was a message of strength for the here and now. No one else in Denmark – in the past or in Harald's time – could have made such a thing, or done it so lightly.

Harald Bluetooth's rise was noticed by the surrounding states. When Rollo's grandson, Duke Richard the Fearless

---

173 This can best be seen in Viking graves. Danes began to be buried oriented east to west – so they would face the returning Christ – but they still were outfitted with representations of Thor's hammer and other goods which would come in handy in Valhalla. The tradition of ship burials was also continued, although by this time usually with simple iron nails arranged in the outline of a ship.

was temporarily driven from Normandy in the middle of the tenth century, he appealed to Harald for help. Harald not only helped him recover his territory, but repeated his aid two decades later when one of Richard's neighbors invaded Normandy.

The most profitable request for aid, however, came from Norway. Years before, Bluetooth had married off his sister to Erik Bloodaxe, and when the latter had been overthrown, his son Harald Greycloak had come to Denmark to request aid. Bluetooth cannily gave his nephew some troops in exchange for an oath of loyalty. In 961, after the hard work of usurpation had been accomplished, he traveled to Norway and forced the reluctant Greycloak to recognize him as a superior.

His nephew turned out to be a more effective king than Harald Bluetooth had realized or wanted. By seizing control of the eastern coastal trade routes, Greycloak extended his power into modern Finland and Russia, lessening his dependence on his uncle. Such a situation could obviously not be tolerated, so in 970, Harald Bluetooth had his ambitious nephew assassinated, and took control of western Norway, appointing a more pliant vassal to manage things while he was in Denmark.

Harald Bluetooth's triumph in the north was the high water mark of his reign. There were rumblings of danger from the south, where the aging Otto the Great had noticed the growing threat, but he died in 973 and the threat passed. Unfortunately, it was Harald Bluetooth himself who undermined his own reign. For years he had carefully appeased his southern neighbor by sending tribute to Germany, but the combination of Otto's death and the victory in Norway seem to have gone to his head. When ambassadors from the youthful Otto II arrived asking for the customary payment, he refused outright.

Harald Bluetooth had badly misjudged his man. The German emperor had resources far beyond Harald's young kingdom, and a more disciplined and cohesive army. Although the first battles went well for the Vikings, the imperial army pushed them back to the Danevirke and Bluetooth was forced to sue for peace.

The loss should not have been particularly crushing since Harald had kept the empire out of Denmark, but he had demonstrated the cardinal sin of the Viking world – weakness. The Norwegian king, a fervent supporter of Thor who resented both Harald's religion and political control, rebelled, and Norway slipped out of Danish control.

Everything seemed to crumble at once. Harald managed to keep his hold on Denmark, but just as he was preparing to push south against the Germans, his oldest son, Svein Forkbeard, who had been chafing under his father's authority, rebelled. Caught by surprise, the king fled to his stronghold at Jomsborg on the southern coast of the Baltic Sea.

He could not have chosen a better sanctuary. The Jomsvikings were Scandinavia's most famous company of warriors. They were a fiercely loyal group between the ages of eighteen and fifty, handpicked for their bravery.[174] They took strong oaths to live by a unique code of honor, and although staunchly pagan, would faithfully serve whoever paid them. Their fortress, situated on a harbor with easy access to the sea, was virtually impregnable.

---

174 The lone exception to this was a twelve-year old boy who defeated a Jomsviking in single combat and was rewarded with membership.

Harald Bluetooth was safe behind Jomsborg's walls, but he didn't get the chance to use it as a rallying point. In a skirmish outside the gates he was wounded, and died a few days later. The body was taken back to Jelling and interred in his church. He had written his own epitaph long before when he had raised the great Jelling stone during his years of triumph. Like many things he did, the carving – ostensibly to show filial devotion – was in reality a canvas to proclaim his own greatness. "*This stone*", he wrote, "*was raised by the Harald who conquered for himself the whole of Denmark and Norway and made the Danes Christian.*"

Both claims are highly dubious. Norway was only partially held – and rather tenuously at that – and the old gods had hardly loosened their grip on Danish hearts, but it shows how Harald Bluetooth wanted to be remembered. Conquest and conversion, the two ways he built the nation of Denmark were copied by his contemporaries in Sweden and Norway. As Harald Bluetooth lay dying, a Swedish minor king named Eric the Victorious was already consolidating the land around what is present day Stockholm. He and his son and successor, Olof Skötkonung, were accepted by the various sub-rulers as the first Swedish kings, and they duplicated the Danish model by converting to Christianity and using it to unite the main tribes.[175]

Ironically, the success of Harald Bluetooth and people like him was evidence that the Viking Age was beginning

---

175   Fittingly, Harald's name today is ubiquitous as a technology that unites disparate devices. Begun in 1994 by the Swedish company Ericsson, Bluetooth passes information wirelessly between phones and computers regardless of operating system or manufacturer. Just as the tenth century Viking king united fierce rivals, a Samsung phone will now communicate with an Apple computer. The two runes that make up the modern symbol for Bluetooth technology are the king's initials.

to wane. The days of untethered sea-wolves roaming the waves were gone, and much of the old energy in Scandinavia was dissipating as well. The summers were just as likely to see royal tax collectors arriving as footloose young men slipping their longboats into the fjords. The three Viking kingdoms were joining the rest of Europe, slowly congealing into centralized monarchies. There were still wild parts – Norway in particular had not accepted either Christianity or the concept of autocratic kings – but the sun was nevertheless setting.

Chapter 21

THE LURE OF ENGLISH SILVER

"Whim rules the child, the weather, and the field."
- Edda of Sæmund the Wise

Harald Bluetooth had been hurried to his grave by his son, and now that the old man was safely out of the way, Svein Forkbeard was crowned. The new king was ostensibly Christian like his father, but already had a reputation as a redoubtable warrior, largely acquired by his frequent summer raids into neighboring Christian kingdoms.

There was more to this than continuing long-standing Viking traditions. The physical achievements of Harald Bluetooth – the fortifying of the Danevirke, building fortresses and bridges, and handing out vast sums of money to his lieutenants – were made possible by the enormous amounts of silver that had been pouring into the Danish peninsula. By the tenth century, Vikings had become connoisseurs of the metal, being able to compare examples from the Islamic, Byzantine, and western worlds. The highest quality, both in amount and purity were Arabic dirhams. The millions of these coins flooding into the Jutland peninsula enabled first Gorm and then Harald

Bluetooth to establish themselves as gift-givers on a royal scale. In many ways, the kingdom of Denmark was built on Arab silver.

In the mid tenth century, however, the Arab supply began to dry up. Even worse, what little came from the eastern routes became seriously degraded in quality. When the Vikings first started trading with the Arabs, dirhams were roughly ninety percent silver; by the eleventh century that had plummeted to five percent. If Svein wanted to continue to act as his father and grandfather had, a new source of silver had to be found. Fortunately for the Danish king, there was a ready supply in a very familiar place.

England's recovery from the ravages of the Great Heathen Army, had been nothing short of remarkable. Alfred the Great had been followed by a brilliant son and grandson who built up the kingdom and briefly forced even the Scots to acknowledge them as overlords. In the process, they transformed themselves from kings of Wessex to kings of England. Their success in creating a stable, prosperous state is illuminated by the nicknames the English gave them. Edmund the Just was followed by Eadwig the Fair, who was followed in turn by Edgar the Peaceful.

England was among the most prosperous kingdoms of western Europe, far surpassing the crumbling remains of the Carolingian Empire.[176] Four generations of rule by Alfred's family had given it a rare sense of security, and had overseen the golden age of Anglo-Saxon England. Unfortunately, this stability started to collapse just as the Viking kingdoms were looking to exploit new revenue streams.

---

176 By the tenth century Charlemagne's old empire had split into three parts - Western Francia ruled by Charles the Simple, Eastern Francia ruled by Louis the Child, and a central kingdom ruled by Louis the Blind.

The trouble started when Edgar the Peaceful died, leaving two young sons behind. The older of the pair, the thirteen-year old Edward the Martyr, was crowned, but since he may have been illegitimate, he wasn't accepted by large parts of the north. After a short but turbulent reign he was assassinated under cloudy circumstances, and his ten-year old half-brother Athelred the Unready became king.[177]

There were suspicions from the start that Athelred's men were involved – although seemingly without his consent – and the slain king's body was unceremoniously dumped in a grave 'without royal honors'. What is clear, is that neither brother had control of government, but was surrounded – as all kings generally are – by grasping, ambitious courtiers acting in their name. Direction of the government began to founder, and power began to devolve to the nobility.

Athelred the Unready has one of the more unfortunate nicknames in English history. The Anglo-Saxon word '*ræd*' means 'counsel' or 'advice', and so the king's name 'Athelred' would translate as 'noble-counsel'. 'Unræd' or 'Unready', therefore, would mean 'without-counsel', probably referring to the low quality of advice the king got, not his state of preparation. It's also a pun on the king's name: "Noble-counsel un-counseled." Ironically, this may have been because he was showing signs of actually becoming a strong king. In the first decade of his reign, he managed to break the power of the great magnates and centralize power in his own hands. The king wanted to keep his own counsel.

Unfortunately for Athelred, however, just as he was getting to grips with the machinery of government, the Vikings returned. The second great wave of Viking attacks was, like the first, launched by Norwegians. In 991, a fleet

---

177 He was stabbed to death while visiting a royal hall in Dorset.

of more than ninety ships arrived, led by the adventurer Olaf Tryggvasson.[178] The local forces proved hopelessly inadequate to stop them, and the Vikings plundered Essex at will. Finally, in August an Anglo-Saxon army under the command of a seasoned veteran named Byrhtnoth, stood up to them. The English commander gallantly, but rather foolishly, allowed the Vikings to cross from the island they were on to the mainland, but fell early in the fighting. Those who stayed and fought were slaughtered to a man, the rest fled in a panic.

The disaster convinced Athelred that his army wasn't dependable, so he elected instead to buy the Norwegians off as a short-term solution. This led to a hemorrhaging of silver which illustrates both the wealth of England and the ineffectiveness of the strategy. Athelred paid the Vikings ten thousand pounds of silver, but after collecting it, Olaf Tryggvasson continued to raid, this time with the newly crowned Svein Forkbeard and his Danes along for the ride.

The two plundered the south, taking all major towns except for London where they were bloodily repulsed. Despite this little victory, Athelred again turned to the Danegeld, paying the two Vikings sixteen thousand more pounds of silver to leave. This time, the king attached the usual condition of baptism. When it was awkwardly discovered that both were already baptized Christians, the ceremony was switched to confirmation, with Athelred standing in as a sponsor for Olaf.

Both Vikings were satisfied, and each returned home to their respective countries soon after. In Olaf's case, this had less to do with the ceremony than it did with the thousands of pounds of silver that came with it. Olaf

---

178 One of the many great-grandsons of Harald Fairhair, the first king of
     Norway.

intended to make himself king of Norway, and now he had the resources to do it.

Svein Forkbeard watched these developments with interest. Olaf Tryggvasson was slightly older, and the two were close allies, but he probably watched his colleague's career with mounting tension. In 997 Olaf successfully seized the throne from Svein, and set about founding a new capital at Trondheim. One of his first building projects was a church – Norway's first – which he used as a propaganda tool in his goal of forcibly converting the Norwegians to Christianity.

The new king, known for his prodigious strength, must have been an imposing figure. Not only did he compel his reluctant jarls into the new faith, but he also imposed it on Norway's far-flung territories with the result that the Faeroes, the Orkneys, and Iceland had all accepted Christianity by 1000. Even Greenland was well on the way to do the same. That same year a converted Leif Erikson left Olaf's court on his voyage of discovery.

Although deeply resented by many of his subjects, it wasn't Olaf Tryggvasson's religion that proved his undoing. A few years before, Svein Forkbeard had married off his sister to a Baltic chieftain. The union had proved unhappy, and against Svein's wishes, the woman had fled to Norway where she was not only given shelter by Olaf Tryggvasson, but taken as his wife. This ill-timed act convinced the Danish king that Olaf was his enemy.

Forkbeard had been wary of his old colleague for some time. Much of Olaf's success at converting people was due to his massive flagship *The Long Serpent*, which cruised up and down the fjords, imposing the king's authority.[179] It was well known that Olaf wanted to expand his territory. He had already tried to marry the widowed queen of Sweden, and there were was a belief that he was now attempting to set himself up as king over all of Scandinavia by insinuating himself into the Danish royal family.

The fears resulted in a Danish-Swedish alliance, and a combined fleet of seventy ships that managed to ambush Olaf as he was sailed between Denmark and Norway. The Norwegian fleet of eleven ships was quickly overwhelmed, with only *The Long Serpent* successfully resisting. When it was clear to Olaf that even his great flagship was lost, he leapt overboard, clutching his weapons to speed his descent.

The triumphal Svein Forkbeard divided Norway up with his allies, taking most of the south for himself. He was now the most powerful Scandinavian king, having restored most of his father's territorial holdings. It was at this moment, with Forkbeard at the height of his career, that Athelred the Unready, made the worst mistake of his reign.

While the Scandinavian kings had been occupied, Athelred had been trying vainly to stem the increasing Viking tide. Buying off Olaf and Svein had only demonstrated that extortion worked, and in the immediate years after, the English king had handed out another 108,000 pounds of silver in increasing installments.[180] In his frustration, Athelred came to believe that his northern subjects in the Danelaw were either harboring or encouraging the raids.

---

179 It was a hundred and forty eight feet long, and powered by a crew of sixty-eight rowers.

180 To put this into context, six times as many Anglo-Saxon coins have been found in Scandinavia as in England. The largest single collection was found in Stockholm.

The paranoia made it easy to believe that there was a Danish plot on his life, so on the 13th November, 1002, he ordered the liquidation of every Dane in the kingdom.

The slaughter, remembered as St. Brice's Day Massacre for the feast day on which it took place, was among the more foolish things Athelred ever did. The population of the Danelaw may have had some vestigial Scandinavian traditions, but they had repeatedly demonstrated loyalty to the English crown since the days of Athelred's grandfather. One of the thousands who died in the bloodbath was Svein Forkbeard's sister Gunnhild, who had settled in England with her Danish husband.[181] Not only did Athelred alienate his own citizens, but he also earned the animosity of a Danish king at the peak of his powers.

Svein wasted no time. The next year he was in England harrying the west, but was driven off by a combination of unexpectedly stiff local resistance, and a famine which made it difficult to live off the land. As he gathered additional troops, other independent Vikings kept up the pressure. The Jomsvikings, led by their leader Thorkell the Tall, conducted a profitable raid in Canterbury that netted forty-eight thousand pounds of silver from Athelred's government. It should have been more, since they captured the archbishop of Canterbury, the same man who had presided over the ceremony welcoming Olaf into the faith. But the stubborn cleric had refused to allow his parish to pay a penny for him, and the annoyed Vikings beat him to death.[182]

---

181 In 2008, remains of some of the victims of the massacre were found where they had been thrown into a ditch in Oxford.

182 They did so during a feast that got out of hand, supposedly carrying out the deed with the dinner bones. Thorkell the Tall was so disgusted that he promptly switched sides and fought for Athelred.

By 1013, Svein Forkbeard was ready, and he invaded England in force, not to punish Athelred, but to overthrow him. The hapless English king, who had seen his reign begin with such promise, was deserted by most of his subjects. The great-grandson of Alfred shamefully fled to Normandy, leaving England to the Vikings. London surrendered in December and Svein Forkbeard was crowned on Christmas Day of 1013.

Svein had accomplished what even the ferocious Ivar the Boneless had failed to do, but he didn't enjoy his new crown for long. Within a few weeks he fell ill, and by February he was dead. The body was washed, embalmed, and attended to by Svein's teenaged son Cnut, and then sent back to Denmark for burial. The great Viking dream of conquering England seemed over just as it had begun.

Ironically, it was only now, with the Viking spirit half-tamed and the days of the sea-wolves vanishing, that the most successful – and least appreciated – of the sea-kings arrived.

Chapter 22

THE EMPEROR OF THE NORTH

"Moribus inclutus facet hic rex nomine Cnutus"

(Here lies king Cnut, illustrious for his conduct)

- The original epitaph of Cnut

Svein Forkbeard may have had two crowns, but they weren't of equal importance to him. His beloved eldest son Harald II was crowned king of Denmark, while young Cnut was given the unenviable task of governing the half-conquered England. The young man at least looked the part. The earliest description of him describes his 'exceptional height, prodigious strength, thick head of fair hair, and clear and penetrating eyes'. The only flaw in this ruddy complexion was his nose, which was 'thin and rather hooked'.

Unfortunately for the new king, his subjects had soured on Danish rule. The citizens of the Danelaw confirmed his elevation, but the rest of the country didn't follow suit. They may have feared the father, but they saw no reason to pay homage to the son. As a mark of their determination to oust the invader, they sent a delegation to recall Athelred the Unready.

The disgraced Anglo-Saxon king who had spent three and a half decades ruining his reputation, now saw it rehabilitated within a few months. He had been living in Normandy with his wife Emma and their two sons at the court of his Norman brother-in-law, Duke Richard the Good. The English, however, didn't exactly welcome him with open arms. Before allowing his return, he was made to swear that he would not punish anyone who had supported Swein Forkbeard, and that he would enact certain reforms that his nobles suggested.[183]

Athelred agreed, and crossed the Channel leading an army composed of both Norman and English recruits. Cnut had taken the sensible step of acquiring hostages from the leading nobles to ensure their loyalty, but his army was caught unprepared and they defected anyway. Realizing that his position was hopeless, he fled to his fleet at Sandwich, on the southern coast, pausing only long enough to mutilate his hostages and leave them bleeding on the beach for his disloyal former subjects to take care of.

For Athelred, regaining his kingdom without a single battle must have been an exhilarating moment, a soothing balm for the long years of humiliation. Sadly, it didn't last. Within a year his son Edmund Ironside revolted, establishing himself in the Danelaw, and defying every attempt by his father to bring him under control.

Even more serious, was the fact that Cnut hadn't given up. The exiled king sailed directly to his brother's court where Harald II received him warmly, aiding in the recruitment of an army to reclaim England. This was probably motivated

---

183 This was the first recorded agreement between an English king and his subjects - a grandfather of the Magna Carta and subsequent constitutional history.

less by fraternal loyalty than a desire to see a potential competitor out of his kingdom, but either way it proved effective. Within two years Cnut had a fleet of two hundred ships to carry his army of ten thousand Vikings.

The invasion, so soon after Athelred's triumph, broke something in the aging, and now sick king. He took no part in the defense of the kingdom, delegating those responsibilities to his son, Edmund Ironside, and his brother-in-law, Eadric "the Grasper" Streona. With Edmund, England was at least in capable hands. His vigorous defense of London won him the admiration of his father's subjects, and when Athelred finally expired a few months later, Edmund was unanimously elected as king of what was left of the kingdom.

Athelred had lived long enough for one final humiliation. His brother-in-law, Eadric Streona, had issued a vote of no confidence by publicly deserting to Cnut, winning lasting infamy as the most notorious traitor in English history. The combined Danish and English army pursued Edmund into Wessex where two inconclusive battles were fought.[184]

Cnut withdrew into Mercia, and Edmund Ironside surprisingly went after him, forcing him to retreat further. The small victory convinced the waffling Eadric Streona to rejoin the English side, where he was welcomed largely for the men he brought with him. Edmund needed to raise additional fresh troops, so he set off through Essex. As he was marching through open country, however, Cnut managed to surprise him. The battle was hard fought and

---

184　During the second battle, Edmund's forces were winning until Eadric Streona found a man who looked very much like the English king. Cutting off his head, Streona brandished the bloody item and shouted that Ironside was dead. The English soldiers fell back in confusion, and would have been routed but for a heroic stand by the very much alive Edmund.

bloody, and at the climactic moment Eadric Streona once again deserted his countrymen and handed the victory to the Danes.

Edmund Ironside was wounded in the fighting, and most of his nobles were killed. He fled with what was left of his army to an island in Gloucestershire, and there came to an agreement with Cnut. England north of the Thames would be Danish, while he would retain the south. Furthermore, the lands of the king who died first would be given to the survivor, whose children would be heirs to the entire kingdom.

The treaty amounted to an unconditional surrender. Both sides could see that the stricken Edmund Ironside wouldn't live much longer, while Cnut was in the bloom of life. It was little more than a tactful agreement – perhaps as a nod to Edmund's heroic defense of his kingdom – to spare the English sovereign the humiliation of exile.

In any case, Cnut didn't have long to wait to claim his prize. Edmund only clung to life for a few weeks before succumbing to his wounds. On January 6, 1017, Cnut was crowned, becoming the first Viking king of England. Little more than a century after Alfred had defeated the Vikings, his descendants had ceded it all to the Danes.

If history had taught Cnut anything, it was that English crowns did not sit easily on Viking heads. He had already lived through one coronation that had failed because the English preferred even the most unpopular native monarch to a foreign one. Under no illusion that anything had changed, he set about firming up his control.

Potential threats were ruthlessly crushed. Edmund Ironside's younger brother was executed, as were many native earls who had supported the late English king. Displaying a good sense that had escaped his two predecessors, Cnut also had Eadric Streona killed, exposing his head on London Bridge.[185] Not all those who had remained loyal to Edmund were punished, however. One noble in particular, a half-Danish man named Godwin had been unwaveringly faithful to the English king, and was therefore greeted with skepticism when he then pledged himself to Cnut. The king asked him why he should trust a man who had until recently been his implacable enemy, and Godwin responded with the argument that his constancy was proof against suspicion. The king, he continued, should instead be wary of those who switched sides during the war. He, on the other hand, had proved his loyalty even when his side was obviously doomed. Could Cnut's English allies claim the same thing? Charmed, Cnut made Godwin the first Earl of Wessex, and even allowed him to marry his sister-in-law. The formerly obscure noble became the most powerful native earl in England.

To strengthen his legitimacy Cnut married into the native royal family. Athelred the Unready's Norman widow Emma was both eligible and relatively young, and more than happy to abandon her two sons to regain royal power. The fact that Cnut was already married to an Englishwoman – Aelfgifu of Northampton – was tactfully overlooked. Aelfgifu faded quietly to the background, and Emma took up residence with Cnut. The new marriage proved successful, and in a short time Emma presented her husband with a boy that they named Harthacnut. Since Cnut already had two sons

---

185 One English source entertainingly claims that the execution was the result of a chess game. Eadric checkmated the king and despite veiled warnings, uncharacteristically stuck to his decision and refused to change the results.

– Swein and Harald Harefoot – by his first wife, the succession was now secure.

Cnut had crushed all opposition to his rule, so he disbanded his army, keeping only forty ships and their crews as a standing army. To pay off his veterans, he needed to raise the enormous sum of seventy-two thousand pounds of silver, roughly half of what Athelred the Unready paid out during his entire reign. It is a measure of Cnut's control – and England's financial stability – that he was able to do it. Ironically, he used the system that his predecessor had put in place to bribe the Vikings. The usual officials were sent out, and a final Danegeld payment was collected from the English to pay off the army that had conquered them. No sooner had Cnut released his forces, however, than his elder brother, Harald II, king of Denmark, died.

Cnut only had his small English army available, but he picked up some Viking recruits and sailed for Denmark to press his claims for the crown. There was considerable irony in this latest campaign. After more than two centuries of abuse, the tables had finally turned. Now an English army was setting out to conquer Denmark. Accompanied by Earl Godwin and other English nobles, Cnut plundered his way to the Danish capital of Jelling, sweeping all resistance aside.[186] The campaign inaugurated a remarkable decade of conquests, unparalleled in Viking history. Within a year he had been accepted as king of Denmark, and was recognized as the dominant figure of Scandinavia.

The Swedes and Norwegians resisted his growing power, but they were both entering periods of weakness. At the

---

186 Earl Godwin distinguished himself during the campaign by leading a daring night raid on one of Cnut's enemies.

battle of the Helgeå in 1026, Cnut's longships defeated the combined navies of his enemies and he was recognized as king of Norway and parts of Sweden.

Cnut returned to England where he received the submission of three Scottish kings – including Shakespeare's Macbeth – and possibly a representative of Viking Dublin. The Irish battle of Clontarf had been fought in 1014, the year Cnut had prepared his invasion of England. The shattering of Irish Viking power had left a vacuum that allowed Cnut to dominate the western colonies and their important trading contacts.

Cnut had ascended to heights beyond even the wildest imaginations of those first raiders who had poured out of Scandinavia in the eighth century. He ruled a vast northern Empire, stretching from the Baltic to the Irish Seas, from Scandinavia to the Orkneys, the Shetlands, and the Isle of Man. He had become the greatest of the sea-kings, ruler of the only North Sea Empire in history.

Cnut intended to be more than a simple conqueror, however. His vision was to unite his disparate holdings into a single state. English style coins were minted in Scandinavia, so that merchants hawking their wares in Copenhagen or London were paid with similar coins. He also brought his system of weights and measures into line with those used in Constantinople, hoping to integrate his lands into the broader European marketplace.[187]

By 1027, Cnut's status as one of the premier monarchs of Europe was confirmed when the Pope personally invited him to watch the coronation of the new Roman Emperor Conrad II. Although Cnut traveled leisurely to

---

187　He essentially created a Viking version of the Euro and the Common Market

Rome as a pilgrim, the trip was a public relations triumph. The Emperor was a similar age, and the two hit it off immediately. They walked side by side in the processions, and were seated next to each other in public. The German territory of Schleswig, the land bridge between the German empire and Denmark, had been a source of conflict between the two kingdoms for generations. As a measure of his affection for his new-found brother monarch, Conrad donated it to Cnut, and the Dane pledged his daughter Gunnhild to Conrad's son.

The coronation itself left a lasting imprint on Cnut. As soon as he returned to England he commissioned a replica of the imperial crown, and assiduously cultivated the image, if not the title, of imperial rule. He ruled England for nearly two decades, on the whole wisely and well. When he died in 1035, he was genuinely mourned. The body was taken to Winchester and interred in a crypt in the cathedral.

He should be remembered as one of England's greatest monarchs, but instead he remains curiously distant. One reason is surely that most of what he built collapsed shortly after his death. Within a decade all of his children were dead and his empire had crumbled to dust. England returned once more to its native dynasty, and a Norwegian king conquered Denmark.

Cnut was a man caught between two worlds. He was too Christian to be immortalized by the pagan skalds, and too pagan to serve as a Christian hero. In many ways, the greatest of the Viking sea-kings wasn't really a Viking at all. He took great pains to cast himself as a just and orderly ruler, made two pilgrimages to Rome, and used his influence to exempt his subjects from Roman tolls. In stark contrast to his ancestors who had targeted churches and earned the nickname 'sea-wolves' for their predatory activities, Cnut endowed numerous religious houses and donated countless precious chalices, crosses, and illuminated manuscripts to churches across his extensive lands.

The most famous vignette from his life is not prowess in battle or generosity with spoils, it is of him sitting in a chair and commanding the waves to retreat. Far from a delusion of grandeur, this was his lesson to his flattering courtiers – that even the power of the greatest of kings was ultimately empty. Only the divine should be worshiped.

But despite all of the king's pious activities, the offerings, tax exemptions, and church building, he could never quite shake the Viking reputation for paganism.[188] When he donated some gifts to a French cathedral, its bishop expressed surprise, writing that he had heard Cnut was 'a heathen prince'. The bloody battles and cloudy marital situation contributed to the unease, and there were few glowing accounts written of his life. As much as he was appreciated by his English subjects, he was never fully accepted as one of them.

Cnut's ambiguous place in English history was mirrored by the Vikings themselves, whose world was rapidly changing. The restless days of adventuring young men, plundering monasteries, exploring the oceans, and returning as sea-kings were over. Although Christ had not yet completely vanquished Odin, the pirates had largely turned to merchants, and the skalds to priests. The Viking

---

188 Cnut's tradition was to build a church or chapel on the site of his
     important battles to commemorate those who died there.

skill at shipbuilding had been turned to the construction of magnificent wooden churches, and missionaries were active throughout the north.[189]

Almost as profound was the political change. Once, the Vikings prided themselves on their independence. Now, the same people who had proudly informed a French ambassador that they recognized no king, faithfully paid taxes to a monarch and served in his army. As the kings consolidated their power, the old spirit of exploration began to wane. Vinland was abandoned, contact with Greenland lapsed, and Scandinavia began to lose its dominance at sea.[190] Only in the half-tamed west of Norway did a flicker of the old Viking spirit remain.

189 The prominent cross, displayed on every Scandinavian flag, is evidence of the thoroughness of the eventual conversion.

190 In addition to the waning impetus for travel, the Scandinavians didn't have the population to maintain their naval supremacy. By the fourteenth century German ships of the Hanseatic League had sacked Copenhagen and maintained a trade monopoly within most of Scandinavia.

Chapter 23

THE END OF AN AGE

"Mighty Harald is fallen, And we are all imperiled..."
                                                    - King Harald's Saga

No family better symbolized the changing world than the pair of half-brothers Olaf the Stout and Harald Hardråda. They were the sons of a remarkable woman named Åsta Gudbrandsdatter who married, in quick succession, two petty kings in the southeast of Norway.

Olaf was a product of the more distinguished marriage, and could claim descent on his father's side from Harald Fairhair, the first Norwegian king. Harald Hardråda, on the other hand, was the youngest son of Åsta's second marriage to a mild, non-entity named Sigurd the Sow. Harald was rebellious and ambitious – qualities he inherited from his mother – but looked up to his older brother.[191]

At age thirteen, Olaf left home to go raiding in the Baltic, proving himself to be a gifted soldier. In 1014 he

---

191 Later he would claim that his father was also descended from Harald Fairhair. While certainly possible, this is most likely an invention to strengthen his dynastic ambitions.

led an attack on London, helping to destabilize Cnut's early reign and force his precipitous flight.[192] The young Viking crossed the Chanel and wintered at the court of Duke Richard the Good of Normandy where he accepted Christianity and was baptized at Rouen with the Duke serving as his godfather.

The newly Christian Olaf returned home with a vision of uniting Norway under the new faith much as his ancestor Harald Fairhair had done politically. At first all went well. Olaf crushed a collection of his enemies and within a year had established himself over a larger area than any previous Norwegian king. He brought the Orkneys firmly under his control, drove the Danish nobles out of Norway, and married one of the Swedish king's illegitimate daughters. At the same time he established a competent administrative network that made it possible to govern the entire country.

King Olaf, however, was not especially popular. Although a highly intelligent man who was an accomplished poet and a gifted strategist, he was fiercely protective of his authority and at times bordered on arrogant. His relationship with his nobles, who were unused to a king that actually ruled, was never good, and his attempts to Christianize his peasants led to a smoldering discontent. On one occasion he cut out the tongue of a man who refused to convert, and on another blinded a noble who proved intractable. There was a vague suspicion that it was more than piety that drove him. As the Saga of Olaf Haraldsson put it, Olaf was 'of little speech... but greedy of money.' All that was needed was a spark to turn dissent into rebellion.

192 In the attack, Olaf allegedly had his men attach ropes to London Bridge and row upstream, pulling the entire structure down. Although it's highly unlikely, this episode has been suggested as the origin of the nursery rhyme.

It was provided by Cnut, who had been annoyed by Olaf's success at reducing Danish influence in Norway. In 1028, the English king's money fanned the growing hostility into an insurrection that toppled Olaf from his throne.

The exiled king fled to the court of his brother-in-law, the Grand Duke of Kiev, Jaroslav the Wise. He spent a year gathering mercenaries, and in 1030 he attempted to regain his throne. Leading a motley group of Danish, Swedish, and some Norwegian Vikings, he crossed into Sweden where he was met by his fifteen-year old half-brother Harald Hardråda with six hundred more men.

If Olaf expected to be welcomed back by his former subjects – or at least to overawe them with his military strength – he was disappointed. On July 29, a collection of Norwegian farmers and nobles met his army as he attempted to enter the country near a northern farm called Stiklestad, and barred his way.

The most famous battle in Norwegian history was fought – at least according to Snorri's red-blooded account – in the darkness of a solar eclipse. The king's army gave a good account of itself, but was probably heavily outnumbered. Olaf, leading from the center of his line where the fighting was heaviest, was wounded in the knee and as he stumbled back, suffered a ghastly wound in the neck. He slumped over a stone and was felled by a third and fatal blow to the stomach.

With the king's death, his army disintegrated, scrambling to escape the carnage. The victorious nobles pursued, halting only when the setting sun made killing difficult. Olaf's body was quietly buried in the bank of a nearby river, and those members of his army that escaped discreetly returned to other occupations.

The defeated Olaf's influence, however, had only just begun with his death. As the country languished under foreign domination, the Norwegians began to rehabilitate their native king. Within a year his body was exhumed and found to be miraculously preserved. His death, fought auspiciously under darkness similar to that of Calvary, served as proof of his sanctity and that year he was canonized with the blessing of the Pope.[193] A magnificent cathedral was built over the site of his burial, with its high altar enclosing the stone he had died against.

In death Olaf was much more potent than he had been in life. He became the champion of the poor and oppressed, the great defender of merchants and sailors, a lion of the faith. The inconvenient details – that the army he commanded at Stiklestad was made up largely of foreign pagans, that the Norwegians themselves had killed him, and that he was at times a divisive, grasping ruler *"slightly addicted to concubines"* – were quietly dropped. The rejected monarch became *rex perpetuus Norvegiae*, the eternal king of Norway, patron saint and national icon.

Olaf's half-brother Harald Hardråda, cuts an altogether different figure. A giant of a man – supposedly seven and a half feet tall – he had a personality that was as large as his frame. From his mother he had absorbed a precocious ambition as well as a cunning mind, both traits that were already on display at the battle of Stiklestad. The fifteen year-old Harald had fought bravely, but had been seriously wounded, surviving only by hiding under some corpses under a ditch until darkness made escape possible.

---

193 At the time, canonization was usually a local matter. Olaf's championing of Christianity in one of the more benighted corners of Scandinavia won him the admiration of Rome.

He fled to a remote part of eastern Norway where he managed to hide in a farm until his wounds had healed enough to travel. Rumors of his survival had undoubtedly begun to be whispered, so as soon as he was able he headed east to the welcoming court of Jaroslav the Wise. It was a dangerous journey, and the chances of restoring his position in Norway were slim, but Harald's confidence characteristically didn't slip. As he traveled, the teenager composed a poem, glorifying both his past and future. *"My wounds were bleeding as I rode; From wood to wood I crept along; And down below the (nobles) strode, killing the wounded with the sword. Who knows, I thought, a day may come when they follow their rightful lord. My name will yet be great at home."*

Harald spent several years in Kiev, providing valuable service to the Grand Prince. Jaroslav who was in need of an experienced commander – as well as the five hundred Vikings Harald had brought with him – and the Norwegian became a respected captain, leading several assaults on the neighboring Poles and various steppe nomads. Wanting to elevate his position further, Harald asked Jaroslav's permission to marry his daughter, but was coldly rebuffed. He may have scored some victories against Kiev's enemies, but he had hardly won enough renown to court the Grand Prince's daughter.

If Harald wanted a reputation to match his ambitions, there was only one place large enough to win it. So, after three years among the Rus, Harald and his men braved the rapids of the Dneiper and headed for Constantinople.

The Vikings called it 'the great city', and in 1034 when Harald arrived, it fully justified its lofty reputation. The city had just witnessed the coronation of a new emperor,

Michael IV, with all of the attending pomp and public ceremonies. The rumor in every corner of the city was that a fresh military campaign was being planned, and the addition of five hundred Viking warriors to the celebrated Varangian Guard was an unexpected boost.

If the two men ever saw each other face to face, Harald would not likely have been impressed by the emperor. Michael IV was the son of a peasant from the southern coast of the Black Sea, and before being crowned had made a tidy career as a money-changer, and – some said – as a particularly talented forger. He owed his elevation completely to his looks and his older brother, a powerful eunuch who had introduced him to the recently widowed Empress Zoë. She had fallen madly in love with Michael, and despite being more than three decades older, had married and raised him to the throne. As thanks, Michael had immediately confined her to the women's quarters of the palace, completely excluding her from any share in power.

He may have been an ungrateful boor, but Michael proved to be a competent administrator who guided the empire to a minor economic boom. Unfortunately, he also suffered from epilepsy and his incapacitating fits made it impossible for him to lead his armies in battle. This was a serious concern because the empire was hard pressed on every side. In the Balkans, the Serbs broke free from imperial control and northern Greece was raided, and in Asia Minor marauding Arabs sacked several important cities. Michael desperately needed competent military men to staunch the bleeding, so the arrival of Harald must have seemed like a godsend.

Harald's days in Constantinople would prove among the most fruitful of his life. He had found an employer with both the need for his services and seemingly unlimited funds. There was the small matter of his noble status since the Byzantines were reluctant to allow Scandinavian royalty to join the Guard, but it was fairly easy to conceal, and in any case, Michael was hardly in a position to be picky.

Fittingly for the man who is considered the last of the Vikings, Harald first saw action at sea. The Byzantine navy was tasked with clearing the eastern Mediterranean of Arab pirates, and Harald led many of the assaults from his longship. He was then sent into Asia Minor to push the Arabs out of Byzantine territory.

In these campaigns, Harald's bravery won him the loyalty of most of the Varangian Guard, and he was soon appointed as its commander. His standard, a raven banner that he had named 'Land-Waster', fluttered at the center of the imperial line, a rallying point where the fighting was thickest.

Imperial service took Harald to the far ends of the medieval earth. The Land-Waster flew in every corner of the empire, and in some cases a good deal beyond. In five short years, he fought from Syria to the Caucuses, crushed a Bulgarian uprising, raided in North Africa and the Cyclades, and even took part in a delegation to Jerusalem where he bathed in the Jordan River.[194] In one remarkable series of raids, he supposedly captured eighty Arab strongholds, only stopping when he reached the Euphrates.

Triumphs like these were noticed by the emperor, who rewarded the commander of his guard by raising him to a noble rank and minting a coin in his honor. That same year, Michael IV launched his most ambitious campaign, an invasion of Sicily, which would hopefully oust the Arabs and return the island to imperial control. The Byzantine

---

194 His harsh treatment of the rebels earned him the nickname 'the Bulgar-burner'.

general appointed to oversee the operation, a giant of a man named George Maniaces, was taking no chances.[195] In addition to the Varangian Guards, he collected a huge army of mercenaries, including a contingent of Normans led by William Iron-Arm.[196]

Even among the large army, Harald Hardråda soon distinguished himself. Maniaces used the Varangians as the tip of the spear, sending them crashing into the center of the enemy lines. He also sent them on repeated raids, hoping to break the will of the Sicilian Arabs. This allowed Harald to personally capture several cities, both by force and trickery. On one occasion, after surrounding a particularly well-defended town, he realized that his soldiers were unlikely to be able to storm their way inside. He had noticed, however, that several species of birds were using the thatched roofs to construct their nests. Each morning they would fly out into the surrounding countryside to forage, and return in the evening. He decided to copy Olga's trick and instructed his men to capture as many of them as they could, treating the townspeople to the unusual – and presumably amusing – sight of hundreds of Vikings scurrying around trying to trap birds.

Their laughter, however, was soon muted by horror. Harald attached shavings of wood smeared with wax to the backs of the birds and lit them on fire. When the

195 Physically, Maniaces was a man that the Viking Harald could respect far more than the diminutive emperor. One Greek chronicler claimed that the general's appearance was "neither gentle nor pleasing, but put one in mind of a tempest… his hands seemed made for tearing down walls or for smashing doors of bronze."

196 William would win lasting fame – and his nickname – by defeating the emir of Syracuse in single combat. One of his brothers, Robert Guiscard, would lead an attack on Constantinople, another, Roger, would conquer Sicily and found a powerful Norman Kingdom.

panicked animals were released they flew straight to their nests, starting a blaze in nearly every building in the town.

Although he covered himself in glory, the Sicilian campaign was not a success. After alienating his Norman mercenaries in a petty argument about a campsite, the volatile Maniaces struck one of his inept commanders – a man who happened to be the emperor's brother-in-law – in the face. Maniaces was recalled in disgrace and the entire campaign collapsed.

Harald Hardråda escaped any blame for the fiasco, but his career abruptly stalled as well. Michael IV's epilepsy was growing worse, and by the time Harald returned from Sicily it was apparent to everyone that the emperor was dying. Swollen from dropsy, he exhausted himself searching for both divine and secular cures until December of 1041 when he finally expired. He had characteristically refused his wife's repeated requests to see him, forcing her to remain in her gilded prison, and bullied her into adopting his nephew Michael V as her heir.

The new emperor proved a more reluctant patron for Harald, whose own appetites had begun to get him into trouble. He was arrested at least twice, although both accounts of his punishments are somewhat fanciful. The first time, on the emperor's command, he was *"exposed to a lion for debauching a woman of quality"*. As befitted a Viking hero, Harald responded by strangling the beast, and was released by his astonished guards. The second arrest, was more serious. He was accused of keeping a larger share of booty than he was entitled too, a serious

– and quite believable – charge.[197]

Fortunately for Harald, the weak Michael V only lasted four months before being overthrown in a bloody coup. In the confusion, Harald managed to escape his prison, and join in the fighting, supposedly personally blinding the emperor as revenge for his incarceration.

By this time Harald Hardråda had had enough of Byzantium, and, with burnished reputation in tow, he returned to Kiev to claim his bride.[198] Waiting for him was a decade worth of accumulated loot that he had been sending back to Jaroslav for safekeeping. The fact that the Grand Prince handed over his daughter without further protest was a dramatic confirmation of Harald's elevated status. Jaroslav's other daughters were married to the kings of France and Hungary, and his son was married to the Byzantine Emperor's daughter.

Part of this newfound acceptance was wealth. His time in the east had netted Harald so much plunder that when he loaded it into his longship *Dragon*, it nearly sank. According to the Vikings themselves, his riches were almost as legendary as his martial skills. "*Nobody*", they claimed, "*had ever seen anything like it in the possession of a*

---

197 A later Norse Saga claims that the real reason was that the Empress Zoë - now in her mid sixties - had fallen in love with him. When he spurned her advances, she threw him in prison.

198 According to the Vikings, he bypassed the great chain guarding the imperial harbor by positioning his crew at the back of his boat. When the front of the vessel had cleared the chain, he rushed everyone to the front, tipping it over the barrier.

single man.[199] But the marriage was also recognition of his abilities as a commander and a reputation that had spread throughout the north. He was now an equal to the most elevated monarchs of his day; all he needed was a crown.

To correct that final omission, Harald sailed with his new wife to Norway, where his nephew Magnus had been crowned king. In typical fashion, he reintroduced himself to his kinsman by demanding half of the king's treasury and land. When Magnus refused, Harald cheerfully unfurled the Land-Waster and set about imposing his authority.[200]

The desperate Magnus tried everything he could think of to stop his uncle, including sending assassins to kill him in his sleep. Harald dodged this by keeping a log in his bed while he slept on the floor, easily dispatching the confused assassins who hacked uselessly at the blankets. The civil war was mercifully ended after only two years when Magnus abruptly died without an heir, charitably naming Harald as his successor.[201]

---

199 Harald's wealth clearly impressed the Danish king, Svein Estridsson. In particular, one of the coins Harald brought back – the (now quite rare) gold Byzantine nomisma of Michael IV – provided the model for the Danish king's money. He released a silver penny that was an exact copy of the Byzantine coin.

200 One account claims that the banner itself was the cause of the civil war. When asked by the Danish king, Svein Estridsson, what his most prized possession was, Harald responded that it was the Land-Waster because he had never lost a battle while holding it. This failed to convince the skeptical Svein, who casually remarked that he would only believe it if Harald attacked a real enemy like Magnus and won three times in a row to show it wasn't a fluke.

201 Magnus, known as 'the Good', wrote down the laws of Norway on a parchment which - due to its color - is called the Grey Goose. It is a surprisingly enlightened collection of edicts ranging from weights and measures to succor for the sick and the poor. It was transmitted to the rest of Europe through the Hanseatic League and became the basis for much of modern European sea law.

It was this nineteen-year reign that won Harald the name '*Hardråda*' or 'Hard Ruler' by which he is known to posterity. He had gained more than wealth during his time in the south – Byzantium had shown him what pure autocratic rule looked like, and he intended to copy it in the north. His half-brother, Olaf, had lost the throne to rebellious nobles, but Hardråda would show them no mercy. Quite a few of the stubborn jarls were forced "to kiss the thin-lipped axe", as the dreaded Land-Waster lived up to its name. Those who defied him, or moved too slowly obeying him had their lands harried and destroyed. The important trading center of Hedeby was sacked, and frightened merchants began calling him the "Thunderbolt of the North."

Hardråda may have been a pitiless king, but there was more to his reign than destruction. Byzantium had given him a taste for autocracy, but it had also made him appreciate the influence of royal patronage, and of grand gestures. When Iceland suffered a terrible famine, Harald sent several ships loaded with food for its relief, securing both a short-term surge in popularity and the lasting admiration of the skalds. Charity, however, was not to be confused with softness. The same year he aided Iceland, a revolt in the uplands of Norway was brutally suppressed, and in 1050, as a symbol of his power, he built a new city at the head of the Oslo fjord to intimidate the south.[202]

Most of Harald's private activity, however, was ironically, the construction of churches. Although his own grasp of Christianity might have been tenuous, his wife was thoroughly Orthodox, and she brought priests and missionaries with her. Harald supported these efforts,

---

202 In time, Oslo would become the national capital.

and the man who had made much of his money looting religious houses, became a patron of the church.

The one thing that Harald never outgrew was his love for adventure. Usually this was in the form of battle, but occasionally he combined it with trips of exploration. Over the course of two decades he brought the Orkneys, Hebrides, and the Shetlands under his control, and attempted at least one expedition to the far west. Years after his death, Icelandic skalds sang how he had "*explored the expanse of the Northern Ocean and... seen at length the darksome bounds of a failing world...*"

When exactly Harald Hardråda found the time for a northern cruise isn't clear, since there was hardly a year where he wasn't fighting. After overcoming his nephew Magnus, he tried to add Denmark to his kingdom, spending the better part of fifteen years warring with its king, Svein Estridsson.

By 1064, even Harald Hardråda was tired of the struggle. Svein had turned out to be a remarkably slippery opponent, and had worn down the Norwegians by refusing to commit to a pitched battle. The yearly raids had neither eroded Danish support for their king nor been particularly rewarding for Hardråda's men. Since the Norwegian king was bored, and Svein wasn't going to spontaneously quit, the two reached a peace settlement where they agreed to recognize the other's dominions and to refrain from attacking each other.

Perhaps one reason why Harald was willing to make peace, was that his attention was already shifting across the North Sea to England, where King Edward the Confessor was clearly dying. The Anglo-Saxon monarch had no heir, and Harald Hardråda had what he considered to be a reasonable claim to the throne. There was no greater prize to an old Viking than England, and this seemed a tantalizing opportunity.

Official justification for an invasion was usually not even an afterthought for the Vikings, but in this case, Harald Hardråda actually had one – a possibility that must have acutely whetted his appetite.

In Norwegian eyes, Edward should never have been king in the first place. Two decades earlier, Cnut's childless son Harthacnut had named Magnus of Norway as his successor, stipulating that Magnus *and his heirs* would inherit the English crown. Before Magnus could claim his prize, however, Edward – with the help of the powerful Earl Godwin – had seized the throne instead. Magnus had never been in a position to correct this oversight, but this hardly invalidated the claim. Since Hardråda had in turn succeeded Magnus, he was therefore owed the throne of England as well.

Of course, the English had no intention of handing over the country to the Vikings – especially not to one with Hardråda's reputation – so when Edward died on the fifth of January, 1066, they crowned Earl Godwin's son Harold king instead.

The news was probably brought to Hardråda by the new king's brother Tostig, who had been exiled from England and was trying to recruit an army to return and overthrow his sibling. In the spring of 1066, Tostig visited the Norwegian court and convinced Harald Hardråda to press his claim, most likely with exaggerated promises of native support.

After raising a massive fleet of two hundred and forty ships containing around nine thousand men, the Vikings crossed the North Sea and raided Scotland before putting back to sea and continuing down the Northumbrian coast. They landed on English soil nine miles from the city of York, and were met by a hastily mustered Anglo-Saxon army commanded by two teenaged earls.

The battle was a short and bloody one, and although both earls survived, the English army was routed. Hardråda entered York unopposed, carrying the Land-Waster ahead of him. Probably on Tostig's advice, the Vikings didn't loot the city. Before his exile, Tostig had been the earl of Northumbria, and he wanted to be restored to an intact earldom. So Hardråda only asked to meet with the chief representatives of the city to discuss terms.

After a short conference, the city fathers agreed to hand over hostages, asking for a few days to gather the requisite tribute. They agreed to deliver both to the nearby site of Stamford Bridge, a convenient crossing of the Derwent river. Satisfied, Hardråda returned to his ships to collect supplies and rest.

When the assigned day to collect the captives arrived, Harald decided to split his forces, leaving part of them to guard the ships while the rest marched the several miles to Stamford Bridge. Since it was a hot day, most of his men left their mail shirts and the bulk of their weapons behind on board the longships.

When the Viking army reached Stamford Bridge, they caught sight of a cloud of dust rising from the direction of York. Tostig somewhat naïvely assured Hardråda that it was the people of his former earldom come to surrender, but as they got closer, the Norwegians could see the sun glinting off of metal. The deluded earl weakly proposed that they were bearing tribute, but instead it proved to be an Anglo-Saxon army led by the English king.

Harold Godwinson's march from London to Stamford Bridge remains one of the most impressive military feats of the early medieval period. The king had been in London when word of the invasion had reached him, and he had immediately bolted north, covering the nearly two hundred miles in just four days. He had then taken the precaution of posting guards on the main roads to stop any news of his arrival from reaching the Vikings. When he suddenly appeared therefore, he took them completely by surprise.

Hardråda was now in a nightmarish position. Cut off from his ships and only half-armed, his men were scattered and disorganized. Fortunately, as he hurriedly rallied his men around the Land-Waster, a group of Englishmen rode forward and asked for a parley. At its head was Harold Godwinson, the diminutive – by Hardråda's standard – king of the English. He begged his brother, Tostig, to withdraw, offering up to half the kingdom if he would leave in peace. When Tostig asked what the king would give Hardråda, he is said to have responded *"Six feet of English soil – or, since he's a tall man, a little more."*

This was, as it turned out, the culminating battle in more than two and a half centuries of English and Viking battles, and fittingly no quarter was asked or given. Hardråda sent three runners to fetch the men guarding the ships – a round trip of more than sixteen miles – and went roaring into the attack, swinging a massive battle-axe with each hand.

Even only half-armed, the Vikings at first seemed indestructible. The English came crashing into their shields, but were thrown back with terrible slaughter. In the momentary pause Hardråda led a tactical retreat across the bridge, reforming his shield wall on the other side.[203] For a brief moment it looked as if Viking courage would trump Anglo-Saxon numbers. Harald Hardråda rushed forward, a lone wolf turning on the pursuing hounds. But as he raised his twin axes an English arrow struck him in the throat, stopping him in his tracks. As the 'thunderbolt of the North' fell, the English tide swallowed the Land-Waster, breaking what remained of the Viking army.[204] The carnage was terrible. A lucky few managed to reach the ships, but most fell at Stamford Bridge, or were drowned while trying to swim to safety. Only a tenth of the ships that had landed a week before were needed to take the survivors back to Norway.

It was, in a way, a fitting end to the Viking Age. After three pitiless centuries of the Norse winter, Ragnarok had come, leaving the old gods dead on a blood-soaked field. The Valkyries had summoned their heroes surely Harald Hardråda despite his nominal Christianity would have fit right in – and the former order had been swept away.

There was no better representative of the vanishing epoch than the grizzled king. Harald Hardråda had traveled the length and breadth of the Viking world, from the wide Dnieper where it passed by Kiev to the mighty rapids that led to gleaming Constantinople. He had seen the legendary throne room of the emperors, dripping in gold and bristling with hidden passageways. He had

---

203 Supposedly the bridge was blocked by a single giant Norseman who held the entire Anglo-Saxon army at bay, building a defensive wall with the corpses of the forty men that he had dispatched. He was finally killed by an enterprising Englishman who floated underneath the bridge and stabbed the giant from below, mortally wounding him.

204 Two raven banners are depicted in the Bayeux Tapestry.

walked in the orange groves of Sicily, washed in the marble fountains of Palestine, and seen the fog-shrouded islands of the north Atlantic.

He had known the Viking world as few others had, in all the waning splendor of its twilight. He had worn the nicknames of 'Hard-Ruler', 'Jerusalem-Farer', 'Troop-Leader', and 'Poet', accolades any Viking would have been proud to bear. And when he was buried in his capital of Trondheim, the sun finally set of the Viking Age.

THE VIKING LEGACY

*"No man lives till eve, Whom the
fates doom at dawning."*

- Edda of Sæmund the Wise

The world the Vikings left behind was fundamentally changed from the one that they had come crashing into nearly three centuries before. The part they are usually given in this transformation is one of destruction. Even now, almost a millennium after Hardråda died at Stamford Bridge, the enduring image of them is of wild barbarians, leaping from their dragon ships, axes hungry for gore.

But although they were violent – and they waged war with a ferocity that their victims couldn't equal – the destruction they brought was ultimately creative. As one historian put it, the burning of the tares makes for richer soil at the next planting. They altered the political and economic landscape wherever they went, and played a critical role in building the foundations of western Europe from Ireland to Russia.

It was the Vikings who exposed the sprawling empire of Charlemagne, revealing fundamental flaws in the organization of that would-be-Roman Empire. As it broke apart under the hammer blows of the Vikings, the survivors were forced to create smaller, more efficient states. Out of the ashes of the Viking assault rose the four great medieval powers of Western Europe: France, England, The Holy Roman Empire, and the kingdom of Sicily.

All four of these were direct products of the Viking age, and three of them were founded or consolidated by Viking descendants. Before the Norse arrived, England was politically divided and loosely organized. By wiping out all but one native kingdom, the Vikings ensured that it would be unified by the house of Wessex into a single nation.

Scotland too, benefited in the long run from Viking depredations. The native Picts, Strathclyde Britons, and Northumbrians who dominated it were all destroyed, leaving the unlikely Scots – Gaelic-speaking Irish immigrants – to unify the northern third of Britain.

In France, the Vikings founded a state, the Duchy of Normandy, that would redraw the map of Europe. Just two days after Harald Hardråda fell, William the Conqueror, great-great-great-grandson of the Viking Rollo, landed on English soil. He defeated Harold Godwinson at Hastings and was crowned king of England, integrating the island into the broader orbit of western Europe. His successors invaded Ireland, whose brilliant monastic culture had been shattered by the Viking attacks, and added Scotland and the surrounding islands to the western European political orbit.

Other Normans headed south and west, campaigning in Spain and northern Italy. They crossed to Sicily and founded the west's wealthiest medieval kingdom there, a rival to mighty Constantinople. At the same time, Viking traders in the east were establishing the market towns and trade routes with Byzantium that would bring Roman institutions far beyond the borders of the ancient Roman empire. The centralized states that they founded would eventually develop into what is today the Ukraine, Belarus, and Russia.

There was more than brute force to these sea wolves. They were makers of law – the term itself comes from an old Norse word – and they introduced a novel form of trial by jury to England. A century of innovation in shipbuilding climaxed in the great dragon ships, vessels which could cross oceans or sail up fjords and rivers. This technological achievement, one of the brightest of the age, allowed them to establish a sophisticated trading network stretching from Baghdad to the coast of North America.

But perhaps the greatest Viking trait was not their martial or navigational skills, but their remarkable adaptability. They had a genius for absorbing whatever local traditions they encountered, combining them into new, and dynamic forms. In France, these 'filthiest of God's creatures' created the model chivalric state, in Iceland they set up a Republic based on individual rights, and in Russia they became autocratic defenders of Orthodoxy.

Where there were no native foundations to build on, the Vikings showed a willingness to experiment, combined with a stubborn practicality. They claimed that Odin himself had advised that "*No better burden can a man carry on the road than a store of common sense.*" In Iceland in particular, there were plenty of opportunities to put this belief into practice. When changing ecological conditions made it apparent that they would have to abandon some of their rights, they held a vote, deciding to willingly place themselves under the Norwegian crown. In the same gathering they agreed to adopt Christianity – although the majority were still pagan – in order to avoid a religious war. The Christian Icelanders, in turn, preserved their pagan past, faithfully recording both Norse mythology and the exploits of their heathen ancestors.

This Viking pragmatism flowed back to Scandinavia as well. Cnut introduced Anglo-Saxon style coins to the Viking homelands, and distributed them by means of a government that was based in part on a Byzantine model. The knowledge of southern agriculture and social institutions that returning Vikings brought back with them transformed Scandinavia even more than the wealth that accompanied it. But the most far-reaching change was a result of Christianity, imported from continental sources as far apart as Rome and Russia. What was true of physical distance also spanned the spiritual spectrum of the new faith. Saint Olaf had kinsmen across Europe; he was baptized in Catholic Rouen and took shelter in Orthodox Novgorod.

The very alien-ness of the Vikings to the modern world is, in a way, a testament to their adaptability. The Norse homelands today are model social democracies, known for their stability, order, and unflappable citizens. Their flags all proudly display a cross, and instead of raiding, they hand out peace prizes. They could hardly be more different than the brutal, and bloodthirsty pagan warriors who overturned the medieval world.

And yet, there is something bewitching about that vanished age, with its blend of exotic beauty and violence, its cunning raiders and wild, untamed adventurers. The pull they still exert can be seen all around us from cruise ships to NASA probes named *Viking*, from common nautical terms to town names that end with -bec in France or -by in England.[205] Three of the days of the week are named after Viking gods, and a Viking king's name graces Bluetooth, the ubiquitous wireless technology that connects our phones and computers.[206]

Perhaps it is a longing for, as a nameless exile once mused in the Anglo-Saxon poem, The Wanderer, a time that *"has grown dark under cover of night, as if it had never been."* Or perhaps it is a resonance with individuals who pitted themselves against the world and – for two and a half centuries – carried all before them. Either way, one suspects that the Vikings themselves would be pleased with their enduring reputation. *"All men are mortal"*, they were fond of saying, *"only a noble name can live forever."*

---

205 "Bekk" in Old Norse means stream, "by" comes from the word for farmstead.

206 Wednesday for Odin, Thursday for Thor, and Friday for Frey.

BIBLIOGRAPHY

Primary Sources

Adam, and Francis Joseph Tschan. History of the Archbishops of Hamburg-Bremen. New York: Columbia UP, 1959. Print.

Airt, Seán Mac, and Gearóid Mac Niocaill. *The Annals of Ulster (to A.D. 1131)*. Dublin: Dublin Institute for Advanced Studies, 1983. Print.

Attwood, Katrina C., George Clark, Ruth C. Ellison, Terry Gunnell, Keneva Kunz, Anthony Maxwell, Martin S. Regal, Bernard Scudder, and Andrew Wawn, trans. *The Sagas of Icelanders: A Selection*. New York: Penguin, 2000. Print.

Flodoard, Bernard S. Bachrach, and Steven Fanning. *The Annals of Flodoard of Reims, 919-966*. Peterborough, Ont.: Broadview, 2004. Print.

Rimbert, Hans Olrik, and Frederik Nielsen. *Ansgars Levned*. Kjøbenhavn: Wroblewsky, 1885. Print.

Savage, Anne, ed. *The Anglo-Saxon Chronicles*. Trans. Anne Savage. Wayne: BHB International Inc, 1997. Print.

Sturlason, Snorre. *Heimskringla or The Lives of the Norse Kings*. Trans. A. H. Smith. New York: Dover Publications Inc., 1990. Print.

Secondary Sources

Barker, Adele Marie, and Bruce Grant. The Russia Reader: History, Culture, Politics. Durham, NC: Duke UP, 2010. Print.

Baker, Alan. *The Viking*. Hoboken, NJ: J. Wiley, 2004. Print.

Byock, Jesse L. *Viking Age Iceland*. London: Penguin, 2001. Print.

Foote, Peter, and David M. Wilson. The Viking Achievement; a Survey of the Society and Culture of Early Medieval Scandinavia. New York: Praeger, 1970. Print.

Kendrick, T. D. A History of the Vikings, by T.D. Kendrick .. New York: C. Scribner's Sons, 1930. Print.

Peddie, John. *Alfred: Warrior King*. Thrupp, Stroud, Gloucestershire: Sutton, 1999. Print.

Stenton, F. M. *Anglo-Saxon England*. Oxford: Clarendon, 1971. Print.

Wolf, Kirsten. Viking Age: Everyday Life during the Extraordinary Era of the Norsemen. New York: Sterling, 2013. Print.

Also by Lars Brownworth

The Normans
From Raiders to Kings

"Lars Brownworth's 'The Normans' is like a gallop through the Middle Ages on a fast warhorse. It is rare to find an author who takes on a subject so broad and so complex, while delivering a book that is both fast-paced and readable."
    Bill Yenne, author of *Julius Caesar: Lessons in Leadership from the Great Conqueror*

There is much more to the Norman story than the Battle of Hastings. These descendants of the Vikings who settled in France, England, and Italy – but were not strictly French, English, or Italian – played a large role in creating the modern world. They were the success story of the Middle Ages; a footloose band of individual adventurers who transformed the face of medieval Europe. During the course of two centuries they launched a series of extraordinary conquests, carving out kingdoms from the North Sea to the North African coast.

In *The Normans*, author Lars Brownworth follows their story, from the first shock of a Viking raid on an Irish monastery to the exile of the last Norman Prince of Antioch. In the process he brings to vivid life the Norman tapestry's rich cast of characters: figures like Rollo the Walker, William Iron-Arm, Tancred the Monkey King, and Robert Guiscard. It presents a fascinating glimpse of a time when a group of restless adventurers had the world at their fingertips.

Also from

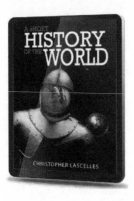

A Short History of the World
Christopher Lascelles

'A clearly written, remarkably comprehensive guide to the greatest story on Earth - man's journey from the earliest times to the modern day. Highly recommended.'

Dan Jones, author of
The Plantagenets: The Kings Who Made England

There is an increasing realisation that our knowledge of world history – and how it all fits together – is far from perfect. We might all know about the odd event, but there is a good chance that if we had to talk about what was happening in the world before or after, or even at the same time, we would not be quite as knowledgeable.

A Short History of the World aims to fill the big gaps in our historical knowledge with a book that is easy to read and assumes little prior knowledge of past events. The book does not aim to come up with groundbreaking new theories on why things occurred, but rather gives a broad overview of the generally accepted version of events so that non-historians will feel less ignorant when discussing the past.

To help readers put events, places and empires into context, the book includes 36 original maps to accompany the text. The result is a book that is reassuringly epic in scope but refreshingly short in length. An excellent place to start to bring your historical knowledge up to scratch!

38880927R00179

Made in the USA
Middletown, DE
30 December 2016